MORTGAGING
THE AMERICAN
DREAM

WHAT WERE WE THINKING?

MORTGAGING
THE AMERICAN
DREAM

WHAT WERE WE THINKING?

R. MICHAEL CONLEY

BEAVER'S
POND
PRESS

ISBN 13: 978-1-64343-884-9

Library of Congress Catalog Number: 2020908509

Printed in the United States of America

First Printing: 2020

24   23   22   21   20   5   4   3   2   1

Cover and interior design by James Monroe Design, LLC.

Beaver's Pond Press, Inc.
939 Seventh Street West
Saint Paul, Minnesota 55102
(952) 829-8818
www.BeaversPondPress.com

To order, visit www.ItascaBooks.com
or call (800) 901-3480. Reseller discounts available.

To my two precious grandchildren, Keri and Sam,
with hopes that the American Dream will be
as open to you as it was for me.

—Your loving grandpa

Acknowledgments

Writing a book is not for the faint of heart. It can be a long journey filled with high hopes and noble aspirations that inevitably clash with practical realities and dead-end streets. One day up, the next day down, you just keep plugging away as the sentences turn into paragraphs and paragraphs into chapters until that wonderful day of completion—but all one word at a time.

The challenge is made easier, however, when you are blessed with a supportive family, associates, friends, and a publisher with a cadre of professionals ready to help you turn a raw manuscript into a finished product that is worthy of reading. I was fortunate to have such a team and would like to acknowledge their support with my heartfelt gratitude and appreciation.

To my family: My best friend and wife of fifty-two years, Sharon; my daughter Kristen, her husband Todd, and their kids, Keri and Sam, and my daughter, Heather, and husband, Matt. Thanks, gang, for your love and support as I was out doing research, interviews, and countless rewrites of my manuscript. And special thanks to Keri and Sam, for inspiring and motivating me to write this book. Your generation will bear the brunt of our intergenerational malpractice, and I hope this book will, in some small way, help to keep the doors of the American Dream open for you.

To my classmates: I call this a multidisciplinary textbook with a personality and relied heavily on you to fulfill the personality part by so graciously sharing your stories on how the American Dream played out for you. Alphabetically, many thanks to Mike Bernick, Charlie Darth, Karen Holtmeier, Andrea Hricko Hjelm, Art Jentsch, Curt Lange, Bud Schaitberger, and Brad St. Mane. Sadly, Bud and Brad passed away before this book was finished, but I hope, in a small way, it memorializes what they meant to so many people. A day seldom goes by that I don't think of them.

To Bob Wieman, a World War II pilot, special friend, and member of the Greatest Generation, for sharing your experiences and so patiently putting up with my endless questions, and to your lovely wife, Barbara. You so reflect the values of your can-do generation and are truly the best of the best.

To my publisher, Beaver's Pond Press, and your terrific team of inside professionals and outside contractors for once again helping me turn my second book with you into a finished product. To my account manager, Alicia Ester, for so tactfully guiding me through the process as you assembled all the moving parts, and to your most able assistant, Becca Hart, for coordinating the labyrinth of details.

To my editor, Kellie Hultgren, KMH Editing, for once again accepting the challenge of working with me on this project. You were tough, but you kept me focused on the integrity of the book, and I simply couldn't have done it without you. Like the first book you mentored me through, *Lethal Trajectories*, you were a wonderful guide, and it was for good reason that I specifically requested your help on this book.

To Jay Monroe, James Monroe Design, LLC, I loved your work on my *Lethal Trajectories* book so much that I couldn't imagine doing this one without you. Your ability to capture the persona of the book in your design work, and your creativity and craftsmanship are, in my estimation, beyond compare.

To Rachel Anderson, RMA Publicity, my long-term publicist, thank you so much for embarking on still another journey with me to take the message to others. We make a good team.

As the researcher and writer of this book, so laden with charts, graphs, and statistics, I made a best faith effort to check and cross-check my facts, but I accept full responsibility for any errors of omission or commission.

Last, and most important, I give all thanks, praise, and glory to the Good Lord for allowing me to use whatever talents I've been given for writing this book.

Sincerely,
R. Michael Conley
May 2020

Contents

PART III

Weathering the Storm | 265

Author Notes:
What were we thinking?

Indeed, what were we thinking when we mortgaged the American Dream?

Get used to it. It's a haunting question that future generations will ask, and we won't have a good answer.

In truth, we don't have a clue; we don't even know where to start. Perplexed and struggling with disconnects between our expectations and reality, we watch the chasm widening.

With one foot in an old way of life we have always known and the other in a complex world we don't understand, we are caught in a twilight zone of uncertainty. In these uncharted waters, we are confronted with two separate—but highly interconnected—megachallenges:

First, we are on a collision course with a perfect storm we don't see coming, though we can feel the early tremors now. Second, we are borrowing heavily on the future to keep an unsustainable Ponzi scheme going and saddling future generations with our IOUs to do it, mortgaging, in effect, their access to the American Dream. Our pleasure, their pain.

This was never our intent. We didn't even know we were doing it. But like a chronic disease, it crept up on us and insidiously grew until it became too noticeable to hide. The warning signs were there, but they went ignored or unnoticed. Gradual at first, the forces of change are now morphing into existential threats.

It is a complex story with troubling implications, and my search for answers has taken me on an unending journey of discovery. My search was painfully slow earlier on; it was the metaphorical equivalent of matching random pieces of a giant jigsaw puzzle scattered across a table without a picture or even straight-edged borders to frame its dimensions.

The pieces remained disconnected until I recognized the *totality* of the challenge and the need to develop a broad framework for connecting the dots. With frightening clarity, the picture of a perfect storm began to emerge, a threat of epic proportions. As I began to appreciate its destructive power, my thoughts turned to my grandkids and the unsustainable future we were leaving them. It was a story that needed to be told.

There are many moving parts in this story, and I found it a challenge to organize and tell it in a way that would connect at a gut level. My goals were to keep the story moving, avoid entrapments in the weeds of a data overload, and personalize it to any extent I could. I met the first two goals through careful editing and endnotes provided for readers with more than a casual interest in the topics.

I have addressed the human part of the story through my reflections and those of my high school classmates of 1961. Our anecdotal stories—often related to the American Dream—appear in vignettes called "Reflections and Profiles" that provide a human barometer of the times from those who were there.

Believing the best way to learn about something is to teach it, write about it, or experience it, I did all three. In my process of discovery, I began to see the connections between the perfect storm, the American Dream, and the time bombs we were leaving others in taking out an indiscriminate mortgage on their dream. Our proclivity to waste, overconsume, and overspend in search of instant gratification has fostered an addiction to debt and the "play now, pay later" culture that goes with it.

It is not just an American problem; it is a global problem. Hopefully, we will awaken to find we cannot indefinitely draw down on the future to pay for the present, nor can we borrow our way into prosperity.

It is fair to ask by what authority I write this book, and my response might surprise you. As a former senior executive of a Fortune 500 company, my orientation was toward issues of the bottom line, quarterly earnings, and market share. However, my research and a cacophony of global events changed all that, and I began to see a higher bottom line—one transcending the parochialism of business. Call it the bottom line for humankind and the need to address the perfect storm while there is still time.

Paradoxically, though I write about climate change, I'm not a climatologist. Nor am I a social scientist writing about our unwarranted expectations and behaviors and the threat they pose to the American Dream. I'm not a geologist, though I tell of our festering fossil-fuel crises—and opportunities. I'm not an economist, though I forecast the shockwaves of an economic tsunami of unimaginable proportions, and my warnings of a new cold war with an explosion of new asymmetric threats are shaped by years of research, international travel, writing, and publishing more articles on geopolitical topics than I care to mention.

In a peculiar way, this lack of specific credentials is a strength. It has allowed me to approach and challenge the data in an unbiased, multidisciplinary manner. Devoid of preconceived notions and ideologies, I was free to pursue the truth wherever it took me. As a generalist, I was able to focus on the *totality* of our challenge in search of optimal solutions—unbeholden to any one discipline, mindset, or cause.

Prior to writing this book, I borrowed an idea from Ayn Rand and George Orwell and used fiction to deliver a message. My novel, *Lethal Trajectories,* graphically described how a perfect storm could be triggered and its catastrophic impact on the world. It included thirty-five pages of endnotes and a bibliography demonstrating the facts that drove the story.

My novel led to the formation of my company, Weathering the Storm, LLC, with a mission to "Awaken, engage and help people weather the storm." At WeatheringtheStorm.net, I have published and archived a series of articles on topics pertaining to this perfect storm. I have also taught a college-level Osher Lifelong Learning Institute (OLLI) course entitled "The Perfect Storm" through the University of Minnesota, and I have taken my show on the road, with presentations to concerned audiences.

In many respects, this book expresses the collective concerns of these audiences, namely, What is happening? How did it happen? And what can we do about it? It will be a troubling read for some, but that's okay. If you are troubled, you're getting it.

My book may displease ideologues and interest groups that see the world through a narrower—often self-serving—prism. The search for optimal solutions requires a longer view of the threats we face and the need to factor in the intergenerational consequences of the quick-fix solutions we so often apply in this day and age.

This is not a book for the faint of heart, and I make no attempt to sugarcoat the threats. It is late in the game, but we can still take measures to mitigate the sharper edges of the perfect storm if we awaken and respond to it accordingly. Our challenge could even be turned into a new catalyst for reenergizing the American Dream and creating opportunities never before imagined. It *is* possible—if we are willing to learn from the past and resiliently apply our experiences toward creating a better future, if not for us then for the loved ones who follow us. The consequences of doing nothing are unimaginable.

I can't promise you will like or agree with everything in this book, but I can promise it will be a game-changer for those who read it.

—R. Michael Conley

Introduction

t is all but impossible to appreciate exponentially growing threats in linear terms, but that is precisely what we attempt to do; we are hardwired to think that way. We may get by with it on the lesser issues, but the dynamic changes when the threats are of a global and systemic—and often existential—nature. This book speaks to the threat of the perfect storm and how the mortgage we are taking on our inheritance, the American Dream, will complicate our future and deal a crushing blow to those following us. These colliding forces will ultimately reach a point of critical mass and, if triggered, produce a chain reaction of disastrous consequences. I present this complex story in three parts:

Part I: The Perfect Storm Primer: The first six chapters describe the structural forces of the perfect storm, its key operating dynamics, the aspirational role of the American Dream in this saga, the deleterious impact of our mortgage on that dream on all generations—particularly those following us—and the consequences we might reasonably expect. Summaries at the end of each chapter highlight the elements that contribute most heavily to these developing forces.

Part II: Pathway to the Perfect Storm: Chapters 7–14 provide a panoramic view of the growth and development of the perfect storm from World War II to the present. We track the milestones and watch the storm insidiously grow into the threat it poses today.

Further, we will begin to see how the systematic erosion of the American Dream is a product—but also a shaper—of the trajectory of the perfect storm.

Each chapter covers a single decade and starts with a brief statement of the relative position of the class of '61 at its beginning and end. Linking historic events with the changing patterns in our lives, the "Reflections and Profiles" sidebars put a face on those milestones and describe how the American Dream played out for one group of people over the timeframes covered.

Each chapter closes with a summary highlighting the milestones that contributed most to the storm, their effects on the American Dream, and a "Snapshot" that provides measurable and comparable metrics from one decade to the next.

Part III: Weathering the Storm: This section, comprising chapters 15–18, projects what it might be like to live through the perfect storm, based on extrapolations from trends since World War II. It offers a comprehensive plan, "Reenergizing the American Dream," for mitigating the sharper edges of the storm and building a sustainable new economy and way of life. It closes with a few personal observations and lessons learned from writing the book.

By the final chapter, you will have a good understanding of

- what the perfect storm is and how the insidious forces causing it have evolved,

- why this storm is the greatest challenge we will ever face,

- how the mortgage we are taking on the American Dream will torpedo future generations and stifle our chances to weather the storm,

- where the perfect storm could take us if we fail to act while there is still time, and

- what the future could look like if we turn this challenge into a catalyst for reenergizing the American Dream.

PART I

The Perfect Storm Primer

A journey of a thousand miles begins with a single step.
—Chinese proverb

– 1 –

Setting the Stage

In our quest to sustain the unsustainable,
we are mortgaging the American Dream.

—R. Michael Conley

We were the "tweeners." Born in the middle of World War II, we bridged the generational gap between the Greatest Generation battling the war and baby boomers following the war. Known officially as the Silent Generation, we were part of the fifty million or so Americans born between 1928 and 1945. My high school class of 1961—the newborns of 1943—represented the tail end of this transitional cohort. Though we escaped the Great Depression, our early years were shaped by its ripple effects.

We were there at the birth of the Nuclear, Space, Computer, and Digital Ages; the building of the Interstate Highway System; jet travel; and a globalized economy. We lived through the entire Cold War and watched America emerge as the preeminent global superpower. We came of draft age when John F. Kennedy became the first president to be born in the twentieth century, and many of us were in uniform during the earlier years of the Vietnam War or anti-war activists in the great social revolution of the 1960s. We were first-time voters *before* the enactment of Medicare and the Civil Rights Act that so changed the face of America, and we were thrilled to watch Neil Armstrong set foot on the moon to beat the Soviet Union in perhaps the greatest technological race of all time.

Though caught in the maelstrom of these times, most of us were more concerned with the mundane tasks of finishing high school, choosing the military service we would join (or be drafted into), getting through college, and embarking on a career in a 1960s job market ripe for the picking. We got married, purchased houses—maybe in the suburbs—and started families, our offspring to be later dubbed Gen Xers and Millennials. Indeed, we were living the American Dream of unlimited opportunities, upward mobility, and a gut-level belief and expectation that we would all live better than our parents had.

But something happened along the way. We got sidetracked by new habits and behaviors that were at odds with what we had learned from our Depression-era parents. As postwar living conditions improved, our rising expectations were reinforced and ravenously fed by a vast new expansion of credit. The quest for instant gratification, aided and abetted by this easy access to credit, spread. We became increasingly self-absorbed in an intoxicating new "play now, pay later" culture that we subsequently passed on to our kids. They, in turn, refined it into an art form.

As a nation, we went on a spending spree, buying things we didn't make with money we didn't have while committing to entitlement promises we could never keep. We squandered resources and voraciously borrowed more and more to keep the good times rolling, accumulating in the process a mountain of debt that could never be repaid. Systemic problems were either ignored or temporarily resolved with quick-fix, pain-free solutions pegged to the panacea du jour; kicking the can down the road became an integral part of our new political DNA.

Our insatiable appetite for bigger, better, and faster was turbocharged by a growing population with rising expectations. This multiplier effect went unnoticed as we blithely consumed an ever-larger slice of the world's finite resources. To keep it all going, we mortgaged the American Dream. Bit by bit, that mortgage reached alarming proportions, to the degree that it may soon overwhelm the generations following us, cutting deeply into their access to the American Dream we so enjoyed.

These developments were contagious. While Americans were leading proponents of unbridled consumption, it has now become a global condition that is exacerbated by newer threats, such as climate change, ecological destruction and shortages, modern asymmetric warfare, and the like.

Let's pause here for a look at the bigger picture—the underlying rationale, if you will, for this book.

The Big Picture

Our story revolves around four separate but interconnected themes that need to be understood if this story is to make sense: the perfect storm, the American Dream, the mortgage taken on that dream, and the consequences of our actions.

For purposes of our story, the perfect storm[1] describes not only our current, shifting paradigm—the world we live in today—but also the devastating consequences that loom ahead if we stay on our current course. The speed and intensity of this growing storm have accelerated over the decades. While multisystemic in nature, and at different stages of development, the storm forces are approaching a critical point. Taken separately, each set of forces might be manageable, but in combination, the chain reaction could erupt with a fury that will change human history.

The second element, the American Dream, is aspirational in nature. It plays a crucial role in shaping—and is shaped by—the broader forces of the perfect storm. With roots dating back to the proclamation in the Declaration of Independence that "all men are created equal" and that the "right to life, liberty and the pursuit of happiness" should be available to all, the dream was popularized in 1931 by historian James Truslow Adams in his book *The Epic of America*. It became the national ethos of the American people and other citizens of the world. While its vision and meaning vary from person to person and nation to nation, we will define the American Dream in this book as the unlimited opportunity for success, prosperity, and upward mobility through hard work and personal effort—without systemic barriers or artificial constraints that prevent it from happening for any sectors of society.

The American Dream was built around dream enablers such as cheap energy, abundant natural resources, new technologies, unlimited opportunities, and, at least in the earlier years, an unshakable belief that each generation would live better than the generation it followed. This optimism was contagious and has spread to represent the rising expectations of people and nations everywhere.

The American Dream is viable as long as the relationship between the dream enablers and the populations that draw on them is consistent. Some of the enablers, such as food, are renewable, but others, including fossil fuels, minerals, and water, are finite. So long as the rate of depletion is within the range of replenishment rates and/or finite resources are moderately withdrawn or replaced with substitutes, equilibrium is maintained. When the scale is tipped, however, through overconsumption, wasteful practices, a failure to conserve, and a wanton disregard for others, we trigger a set of feedback loops that skew the imbalance even more. This is the mortgage on the American Dream.

Climate change, for example, has affected everything from crop production and air quality to Earth's fundamental organic life-support systems. Our injudicious use of fresh water is draining aquifers at a rate far exceeding any hope of replenishment. Like our untenable drawdowns of natural resources, our national debt and the interest paid on it have eaten into the funds that future generations will need to support their economies. Something has to give: we are living beyond our means and borrowing heavily on the future to support an unsustainable way of life. As our dream enablers are gradually depleted, leaving fewer resources for others, the opportunities for future generations to achieve the same access we enjoyed to the American Dream will decline dramatically.

Finally, as a consequence of the widening gap between our rising expectations and the finite resources needed to sustain them, the world will become a more dangerous and difficult place in which to live. We already experience these consequences every day. The Millennials were the first generation to feel the backlash as they watched the dream enablers slip away before their very eyes. They are, in fact, the first modern generation to not expect to live as well as their parents. Decades of a throwaway culture, escalating carbon footprints, and misuse of natural resources have taken a toll. Now, with more than ten thousand baby boomers retiring daily, the crushing cost of funding the entitlement promises of yesteryear will shift more to them. Few expect the same benefits to be available when they retire.

Though we never set out to mortgage the American Dream, through benign neglect and indifference it insidiously became part of our new norm. To be sure, the warning signs were there: economic stagnation, rising energy prices, runaway debt, the devalued dollar and erosion of its purchasing power, unfunded entitlement programs, global destabilization, a planet sickened by climate change, rainforest destruction, the wasteful consumption of resources, and the list goes on . . .

The warning lights are flashing, and even Mother Nature seems to be conspiring against us as ferocious storms, droughts, floods, forest fires, rising temperatures, and famines pound us with an unparalleled frequency and severity. Some slough it off as cyclical phenomena, while others dub it a hoax. I call it apathy, ignorance, and denial.

Self-absorbed, it is easier to ignore these existential threats and hope for technological panaceas that will never come. It might have worked that way in the past, but not anymore. The perpetuity of the American Dream is not a given, not by a long shot.

As intoxicating as it was on the way up, the fallout will be devastating on the way down as the IOUs we've taken on our future come due. Operating in uncharted waters, we now find ourselves floundering in a twilight zone we don't understand with a perfect storm approaching. The storm forces are building, feedback loops are in play, and tipping points draw nearer. Time is running out.

Summary: Setting the Stage

Our situation has changed dramatically over the past several decades, and our days of borrowing heavily on the future—in effect, mortgaging the American Dream—are limited. The following concepts and ideas are key in understanding the big picture:

1. **The perfect storm represents the shifting paradigms of today and tomorrow.**

    •   It reflects our paradigms—the world we live in now—and the directions we are taking.

    •   It represents the entire systemic structure within which our efforts must be directed.

    •   It suggests a dire outcome should the massing forces collide.

2. **The American Dream is a critical component of our shifting paradigms.**

    •   It represents our traditional aspirational visions of opportunity and upward mobility.

    •   It transcends America and is now a part of the world's growing expectations.

    •   It has been weakened as the availability of dream enablers erodes through misuse.

    •   It now shows disturbing and growing gaps between expectations and reality.

3. **The mortgage taken on the American Dream is compromising our future.**

    - We are drawing heavily on the future to support our current paradigms.

    - We saddle others with our IOUs by reducing their access to the American Dream.

    - Our actions will intensify and accelerate the pace of the perfect storm.

    - We are weakening our ability to mitigate the sharper edges of the perfect storm.

4. **The consequences of an erupting perfect storm will be a catastrophe for humankind.**

    - We are on an unsustainable path and running out of time.

    - We are actively moving toward this new paradigm now.

    - We will feel the growing ripples of the perfect storm as we draw closer to its epicenter.

-2-

The Gathering Storm

Face reality as it is, not as it was or as you wish it to be.

—Jack Welch

Every generation has its own unique set of problems, a reflection of the times that contributes to the "brand" of that generation. The American Revolution, Civil War, World Wars, and Great Depression are but a few examples. They shaped the future in ways that can never be minimized.

None will compare, however, to the coming perfect storm and the profound changes it will make in our world once ignited. It is fair to ask why. The answers aren't simple, but four distinct features differentiate the perfect storm from major threats we have previously faced. First, it is an all-pervasive global threat that knows no geographic boundaries; it will touch everyone, leaving no safe havens. Second, it is multigenerational in nature, with no specific start or end dates; it was created by and will contaminate all generations. Third, its explosive potential exceeds the sum of its parts.

Fourth, it is unique; we are operating in uncharted waters, oblivious to the monstrous threat ahead.

Had we possessed a map, we might have recognized certain patterns: how, for instance, seemingly random events were interconnected. With a template, we could have appreciated the systemic nature of these events. Instead, we have acted like an inept meteorologist, treating temperatures, precipitation, and barometric readings as isolated events rather than as interrelated parts of a complex storm system.

The good news is that the perfect storm model provides a framework for identifying the storm's parts and the forces that drive them. The model helps the end user identify and weigh the importance of each part, connect the dots in a meaningful way, and plot out future trajectories. In addition to the model, we will use the following four guiding principles throughout this book:

1. We conceptualize the perfect storm in its totality, as one huge systemic force and not an isolated set of random events.

2. We appreciate the storm's dynamic nature, the cause-and-effect relationship of its moving parts, and the counterforces each part is likely to produce if tweaked.

3. We factor in the impact of the propellant forces and how they can change the tone and direction of the storm.

4. We use the cumulative data to forecast future trajectories and cross-check results wherever possible.

Let me share how the process of discovery played out for me:

Mike Conley

As I immersed myself in what I would later refer to as the "perfect storm," I was confused and overwhelmed. There were so many moving parts, with varying degrees of importance, that I just couldn't seem to get my arms around it. Though I knew the parts were interconnected, I lacked a framework for connecting them in any meaningful way.

It was like dumping a bag of puzzle pieces out on a table and attempting to assemble them as is, with some pieces faceup and others facedown, and with no picture of what the finished puzzle should look like. With little sense of size, scope, or structure, I couldn't see the connections. Groping in the dark, I realized the need for a working model and methodology for identifying, weighing, and connecting the pieces in an organized fashion.

First and foremost, I needed a systematic approach that framed the threat in its totality. It required a wide-reaching model and a template for connecting multiple systems in a cohesive manner. Through trial and error, I wrestled with ways to organize the data into the fewest possible categories and settled on what I call the 4-E Forces: (1) Economic and Geopolitical, (2) Energy and Technological, (3) Environmental and Ecological, and (4) Expectations and Behavioral forces. As I sorted the data into these cells, I could better understand the forces that were operating and interreacting within each. I started to see the possibilities when one E-Cell collided with another. Some cells, like energy and the environment—fossil fuels and climate change—had a synergistic capacity to exponentially intensify the magnitude of the risk.

While there was nothing all that sophisticated about my system, it helped me plot out the major forces in play and view them in their systemic totality. From this angle, I found it easier to consider policy and cost trade-offs when contrasted against a bigger picture. For instance, if we tried solving our global energy problems by using more coal, what would that do to the environment? By contrast, if we shot for a zero-emission energy environment in ten years, what would that do to our energy mix and costs, and did we even have capacity to do so? The E-Cells helped me visualize the problem in a broader context.

The model also helped me to better understand the inter-relationships of the moving parts and even capacity issues. For example, it was easier to conceptualize the dynamic interplay of fresh water, a growing global population, and changing dietary habits that favored more water-intensive meats and crops and then weigh these factors against Earth's capacity to provide fresh water on the scale needed to sustain our growing demand.

There's more to the model than just the schematic, and I developed a seven-point process to use with it. It serves as a constant reminder that seeking solutions for the perfect storm, we will need to consider a vast panorama of possibilities. A tweak in one direction could easily spark major consequences in other areas. It is a tool that has helped me keep this bigger picture in mind.

Developing the Perfect Storm Model

The perfect storm model provides a visual framework for identifying and mapping the storm's DNA, with a heavy focus on the *totality* of the storm—not just its respective parts. To create it, I sorted "DNA" data into the four distinct E-Cells and applied a seven-point process, illustrated here with the example of energy.

1. **Define the major storm cells::** The descriptive heading of the storm cell is "Energy and Technological Forces" Our focus in this example will be on energy.

2. **Aggregate the data:** Data aggregated under "energy" could include energy systems, raw fuels, grids and infrastructures,

resource availability, supply-and-demand dynamics, and so forth.

3. **Develop intracell metrics:** Metrics are determined by what we wish to measure. Energy could be measured in miles per gallon for the family automobile or "quads" of energy used nationwide. Whatever the measurement, metrics must be a part of any plan.

4. **Develop intercell metrics:** These metrics can identify cause-and-effect impacts of converging E-Cells. For example, a gallon of gasoline produces about twenty pounds of carbon dioxide. With metrics like this, we can measure some of the carbon trade-offs in energy policies, gross domestic product (GDP), and a variety of carbon footprint scenarios.

5. **Identify trends and make projections:** With aggregated data, the number of tracking and trending possibilities is unlimited. The complexity of tracking and extrapolating trend lines will vary, but the added forecasting capabilities will enhance strategic planning. For example, a future ban on the production of gasoline- and diesel-powered cars will greatly impact future energy requirements.

6. **Identify priorities and trade-offs:** With a common set of metrics and a better sense of the comparative impacts of our decisions, we can better weigh the trade-offs in search of optimal solutions. By doing so in a systemic manner, we can reduce many of the unintended consequences tied to myopic thinking. A robust renewable energy program will, for example, reduce our carbon footprint dramatically.

7. **Develop an action framework:** The Perfect Storm Model (chart 2.1) provides a diagnostic tool for inputting data that

is germane to the challenge—in this case, energy. Like a CT scan providing a radiologist with a big-picture look at the key problem areas, the model provides a similar framework with which to capture key data and develop a plan. The economic cell might include the cost of energy in relationship to the GDP; the environmental cell, a look at the carbon footprint from each energy source; and the behavioral cell, data on our attitudes toward the use of fossil fuels. Taken collectively, the model ensures that key inputs are factored into the big picture for weighing trade-offs and developing optimal solutions for complex problems. Using the framework, the end user can input the data they feel most relevant to the problem they are addressing.

The Perfect Storm Model

The model I developed as I accumulated data and repeated the seven-point process resulted in the perfect storm model (chart 2.1). The chart reproduced here is in no way all-inclusive; rather, its bullet points illustrate the manner in which some of the storm's forces can be categorized and connected. The brief outline of each E-Cell includes a few of its more contentious challenges. The propellant drivers represent the dynamic power of exponential growth, aggressive feedback loops, and anthropogenic (human-made) forces that shape the direction and velocity of the looming storm. As these forces collide and feed off each other, we can begin to appreciate the storm's synergistic power. We will use this model throughout the book to frame the perfect storm, and the next few chapters will take an in-depth look at each E-Cell.

**Chart 2.1: The Perfect Storm Model
Examples of Driving Forces**

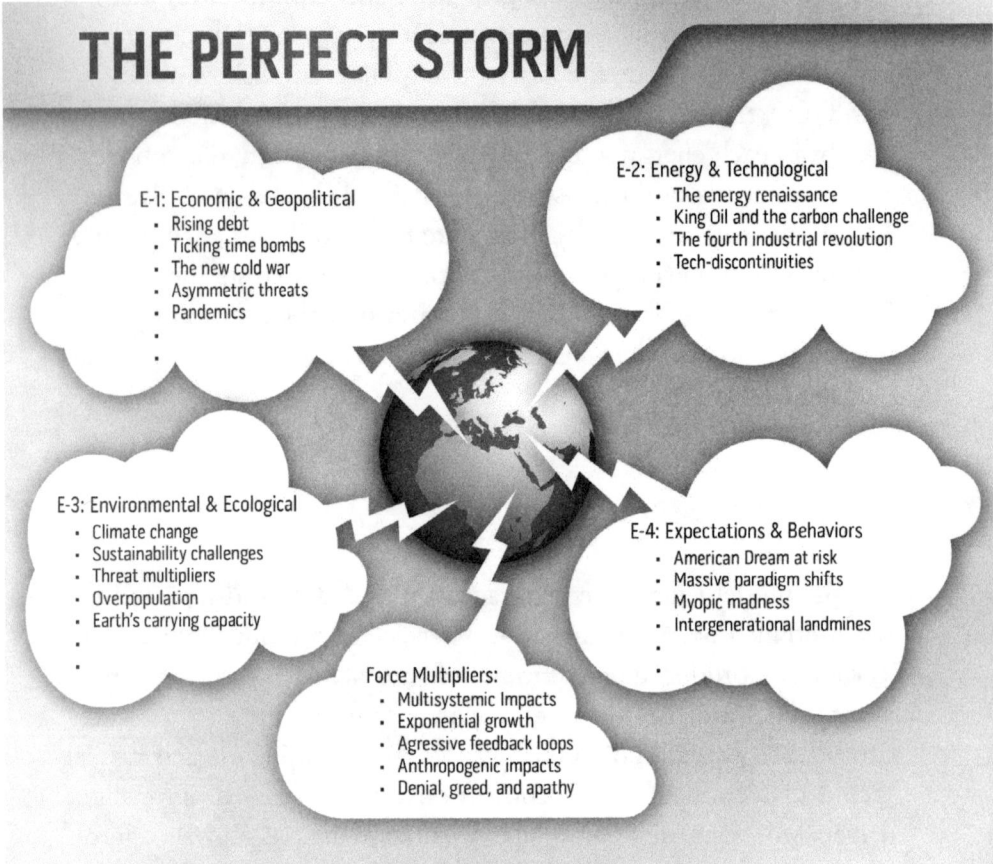

THE PERFECT STORM

E-1: Economic & Geopolitical
- Rising debt
- Ticking time bombs
- The new cold war
- Asymmetric threats
- Pandemics

E-2: Energy & Technological
- The energy renaissance
- King Oil and the carbon challenge
- The fourth industrial revolution
- Tech-discontinuities

E-3: Environmental & Ecological
- Climate change
- Sustainability challenges
- Threat multipliers
- Overpopulation
- Earth's carrying capacity

E-4: Expectations & Behaviors
- American Dream at risk
- Massive paradigm shifts
- Myopic madness
- Intergenerational landmines

Force Multipliers:
- Multisystemic Impacts
- Exponential growth
- Aggressive feedback loops
- Anthropogenic impacts
- Denial, greed, and apathy

Build Your Own Model

1. Use or discard illustrated e-cell forces
2. Input forces as desired
3. Weigh the impacts of the converging forces as illustrated
4. Develop strategies around the framework provided

E-1: Economic and Geopolitical

Coming off the 2008 global economic meltdown, the greatest since the Great Depression, the global economy has only cosmetically recovered. Systemic problems have not been fixed, and many of the egregious practices that caused it are now being repeated. Worldwide, central banks have pumped enormous amounts of money into their monetary systems to stimulate recovery, with disproportionately poor results. Sovereign debt defaults, credit bubbles, and currency wars are building below the surface and could erupt at any time.

In the United States, we continue to spend money we don't have for things we don't make using devalued dollars that are propped up by our world reserve currency status and the petrodollar system (discussed later). Monetary and fiscal policies on steroids have fostered our spending addiction. Unfunded entitlement liabilities and a growing mountain of debt are exploding just as baby boomers are retiring in droves, leaving fewer active workers to pay for an expanding base of retirees. The federal government continues to spend more than it takes in by borrowing money or "printing" it (now accomplished through electronic transfers to Fed banks), or, to put it more politely, monetizing debt at prodigious rates. How long can this Ponzi scheme go on?

The global balance of power is shifting as China's superpower status grows. A new cold war will be fought over the control of finite resources and markets, not ideology. Russia and China are flexing their muscles, and new global alliances are being formed. The Middle East is embroiled in a second Arab Spring, and Shia/Sunni conflicts rage. Terrorism is still a threat, and nuclear proliferation and the growth of asymmetric threats such as cyberwarfare are escalating. It is a more dangerous world.

E-2: Energy and Technology

Energy makes the world go around, and high up on the energy chain is oil. As the primo energy source fueling around 90 percent of all transportation and distribution systems, it is, indeed, the mother's milk of economic growth. Wars are fought over it, and currencies are built around it. The mere suggestion of a shortage or glut roils the markets and destabilizes economies. As future access to *affordable* oil diminishes, the economic ripples will worsen.

Fortunately, a new energy renaissance in the making offers real hope for the future. Taking that renaissance to scale, however, and building infrastructures to support it—without economic disruptions—will be a long, difficult, and expensive transition. Our power plants, grids, and infrastructures are dated, and our renewable energy systems still produce only a fraction of the energy we need—though the share is rapidly growing. Snarled in political gridlock, vested interests, and denial, we still resist change.

As we enter what is becoming known as the fourth industrial revolution, the rapid growth of bioscience, artificial intelligence, robotics, digital, and other "smart" technologies will continue to outpace our ability to assimilate them into mainstream culture and daily operations. In some instances—including cyberwarfare—they could become lethal.

E-3: Environment and Ecology

The ravages of climate change are increasingly visible, and our response has been sluggish, clouded in denial and glossed over by overriding political and economic interests. The *visible* manifestations of climate change—well documented by the National Aeronautics and Space Administration (NASA), the National Oceanic and Atmospheric Administration (NOAA), and the International Panel on Climate Change (IPCC)—are everywhere: in rising greenhouse gas levels and record high temperatures; melting glacial and sea ice in the Arctic, Antarctica, and Greenland; rising sea levels with elevated acidification rates that threaten life-giving coral reef systems; costly storms and weather patterns with widespread droughts, floods, forest fires, and famine-threatening crop failures, all turbocharged by changing climatic conditions. Intelligence and military planners view climate change as a threat multiplier that will exacerbate geopolitical issues almost everywhere.

The ecological time bombs inherent in our wasteful and indiscriminate use of finite natural resources—combined with a population explosion and an aging demographic—are straining our capacity to meet future demand. In drawing down aquifers, destroying coral reefs, overfishing oceans, contaminating fresh water supplies, polluting the oceans and atmosphere, abusing our topsoil, and squandering ores and precious metals at alarming rates, we are borrowing heavily on accounts we cannot rebuild. Despite dire warnings, these time bombs keep ticking away, and tipping points draw closer. And our wasteful practices and unsustainable lifestyles are mortgaging the future of those who follow us.

E-4: Expectations and Behaviors

The American Dream helped shape our expectations and behaviors, but many of those dream enablers are disappearing. Still, we expect to be able to buy what we want, when we want it, assuming that easy credit and a seemingly unlimited market will always be available to us. As we move away from this dream, we will enter a new paradigm of fewer choices and a reduced ability to take advantage of them. The train has left the station, but we haven't even packed our bags. As our confusion mounts, don't look for our political leaders to be on the bleeding edge of change; kicking the can down the road is part of our current norm. The disconnects between our expectations and reality are widening, the rules are changing, and our comfort zones are disappearing. Is it any wonder we are uneasy and even fearful?

The Propellant Forces

In addition to the energy generated within these storm cells, there is an even greater energy fueling the growth of the storm forces. These propellant forces are whoppers. Insidious and exponentially expanding, they are, like a powerful ocean current, driving us toward a chain reaction that will ignite the perfect storm.

The list of propellant forces is long, but we will focus on the three most powerful and prevalent among them: exponential growth, feedback loops and tipping points, and anthropogenic forces. A deeper look into each one is revealing.

Exponential Growth

We are myopically hardwired to look at threats in a linear and not an exponential sense. Where we assume a linear progression of 1-2-3-4 and project an outcome of 5, the perfect storm is growing exponentially in a 1-2-4-8 progression with an outcome of 16. Linear thinking will almost always cause us to underestimate threats and apply mere bandages when major surgery is required.

We may understand the concept of an exponential threat at an intellectual level, but it gets garbled in what I call the longest journey in the world: the path from the brain to the heart that transmutes a random thought into a conviction that will energize us into some form of action. The connection more often than not short-circuits and dies of inaction, ignorance, or denial.

Suppose you were asked this question: "What would you rather have: three million dollars today or one penny doubled daily for thirty-one days?" Take your pick and then look at chart 2.2 for the answer.

Chart 2.2: Exponential Growth

At End of Day	Total ($)	At End of Day	Total ($)
1	.01	16	327.68
2	.02	17	655.36
3	.04	18	1,310.72
4	.08	19	2,621.44
5	.16	20	5,242.88
6	.32	21	10,485.76
7	.64	22	20,971.52
8	1.28	23	41,943.04
9	2.56	24	83,886.08
10	5.12	25	167,772.16
11	10.24	26	335,544.32
12	20.48	27	671,088.64
13	40.96	28	1,342,177.28
14	81.92	29	2,684,354.56
15	163.84	30	5,368,709.12
		31	10,737,418.24

In linear terms, it's a no-brainer; who wouldn't opt for millions of dollars up front versus a few pennies over a longer time frame? Our answer changes, however, when we understand the explosive power of exponential growth. As the chart points out, those selecting the second option would more than triple their return by opting for the penny-a-day approach.

Bottom line—we are doomed to failure whenever we apply linear solutions to the exponential threats of the perfect storm. Underestimating the threat makes it easy to ignore any sense of urgency in addressing it. Denying the threat or pushing responsibility off onto others is not the answer, and yet that is exactly what we do. Far easier, it seems, to let the time bombs tick than try to defuse them.

Feedback Loops and Tipping Points

A feedback loop is a self-reinforcing mechanism that accelerates the growth or decline of a given condition. A number of feedback loops are already hastening the growth of the perfect storm and rapidly changing the equation. Over time, they will overwhelm the system. When this occurs, we will have reached a tipping point: the point at which the condition cannot be reversed. It will be the start of a new and more dangerous paradigm.

Feedback loops are complex, well disguised, and often beyond the scope of our radar screens until they are too developed to ignore. The following well-known feedback loops demonstrate the size, scope, and diversity of some of the loops now in play.

1. The albedo feedback loop relates to climate change and works like this: A buildup of greenhouse gas emissions trap more heat. The trapped heat melts large ice sheets, leaving less of a white surface (albedo) to reflect back the sun's heat into space. More of the sun's energy, in turn, is absorbed into the newly opened waters. The warmer waters and temperatures cause more ice to melt over time, reinforcing the feedback loop and accelerating the pace and intensity of this climate-change cycle.

2. The feedback loop of debt and fiscal/monetary policy looks like this: Our national government borrows twenty to thirty cents or more on every dollar it spends. The deficits are made good by borrowing or printing money, which adds to a national debt that already exceeds our GDP. The debt-servicing charges (interest paid on the debt) grow with the debt, and the charges consume a progressively larger share of the annual budget—requiring more borrowing for other items. As conditions worsen, interest rates will rise to attract new money, increasing, in the process, the amount of money needed to finance the debt-carrying charges.

3. A feedback loop featuring a trifecta of forces accelerates the percentage of healthcare costs to GDP as a growing influx of new baby boomers swells the Medicare ranks: New technologies emerge, and the unit costs of medical and pharmaceutical care increase. People live longer due to better medical care, thereby lengthening the timeframe in which they will receive medical benefits. As more retirees live longer and consume costlier care over a longer period of time, a disproportionately higher burden of costs will be borne by a disproportionately smaller workforce to subsidize an expanded base of recipients.

4. A "moral hazard" feedback loop describes an undue risk that institutions and people take on when they don't bear the consequences of their actions. Though most frequently applied to banks that are "too big to fail," the concept applies at almost all levels in our "play now, pay later" culture. An egregious example is the Tax Cuts and Jobs Act of 2017. It was passed by Congress even though the Congressional Budget Office said it would add almost two trillion dollars to the national debt over ten years. In the short term, it primed the economy, while in the long term, the added financing charges on the debt would be passed on to future generations. Many in Congress would be long gone before the full consequences of their actions were felt.

These are only a few examples of the feedback loops in play and the exponential power they generate. As threat multipliers feeding the perfect storm, they can erupt with a speed and intensity that exceeds our level of comprehension. Left unchecked, they will overwhelm the system and propel us beyond new tipping points. For example, the ability of the eroding Amazon rainforests to function as a carbon sink is approaching a tipping point at which its capacity to absorb carbon will no longer be sustainable at the levels needed to stabilize the atmosphere and thwart the rate of greenhouse gas buildups.

Anthropogenic Forces

Human activities are significant contributors to climate change, ecological destruction, and the carrying capacity of our planet. The combination of a growing world population with greater per-capita consumption, wasteful practices, and damaging usages of resources contributes heavily to the toxic strains on our planet and environment. Half-hearted efforts and an overdependence on technology without major behavioral modifications will do little to change the results.

The fresh water supply challenge, for instance, has strong anthropogenic overtones. Case in point, in its transition from an agrarian to an industrialized economy, China experienced a massive rural migration to urban areas. In this urbanized setting, citizens moved toward a more meat-intensive diet. A pound of beef requires about 1,800 gallons of water to produce, versus about 132 gallons for a pound of wheat or 449 gallons for a bushel of rice. While China's per-capita meat consumption is far below that of the United States, with its more 1.3 billion people, even a slight uptick changes any aggregated equation. Drought conditions are increasing worldwide.

To support our thirsts, we draw heavily on our aquifers—the fresh water savings accounts we rely on. Because it can take a lifetime or more to replenish a depleted aquifer, however, they are effectively a nonrenewable asset. Sadly, our Gravity Recovery and Climate Experiment (GRACE) satellites[1] now confirm major aquifer depletions throughout the world.

The list of anthropogenic effects is horrifyingly long, and many examples will be provided in future chapters. For now, this short list of anthropogenic threats demonstrates the scope of the problem.

Ten Anthropogenic Threats

1. Deforestation, eliminating rainforests and the carbon sinks they provide.

2. Destruction of topsoil, coral reefs, croplands, and other food-producing resources.

3. Depletion of finite resources, such as fossil fuels, minerals, and physical commodities.

4. Degradation of ecosystems and resources with a diminished capacity to self-heal.

5. Deterioration of climate, with increasing frequency of droughts, floods, and severe weather patterns.

6. Destabilization of global power structures and escalating sources of conflict.

7. Devaluation of currencies, purchasing power, and monetary resources.

8. Demand discontinuities caused by overconsumption, waste, and personal behaviors.

9. Debilitating tendencies to apply quick fixes and accept practices that do long-term harm.

10. Detractive behaviors that divide and polarize people, issues, and institutions.

The ten "De-" threats represent a slow form of genocide. Most are correctible, but the political will and economic self-interests that now prevail seem to outweigh the dangers of doing nothing.

Summary: The Gathering Storm

The perfect storm is one of the greatest threats to humankind. The operating model, process, and framework described here will be used throughout this book to connect the dots in a meaningful way. Key concepts and ideas covered in this chapter include the following:

1. **The perfect storm model provides a framework for identifying the storm's DNA.**

    - It breaks the major storm forces down into four categories called E-Cells.

    - Each E-Cell is a force unto itself and is further amplified when colliding with other E-Cells.

    - Upon reaching critical mass, the collective E-Cell forces could erupt in a perfect storm.

2. **The seven-point process provides a methodology for using the perfect storm model.**

    - It is designed to accommodate and leverage the use of the perfect storm model.

    - It provides guidance for exploiting data sets for useful research and policy purposes.

    - It has the built-in flexibility to fit the needs of any particular user.

3. **Three propellant forces contribute heavily to the perfect storm's rapid growth.**

    - Exponential growth is a heavy contributor to the gathering storm.

- Aggressive feedback loops are or will soon be driving us toward tipping points beyond which we cannot recover.

- Anthropogenic forces are accelerating the storm's buildup.

4. **The systemic structure of the perfect storm is a focal point throughout the book.**

    - Effective research and policy efforts require a systemic look at the issues addressed.

    - The dynamic structure of the storm requires system-level solutions.

    - The interrelated nature of the moving parts precludes isolated approaches.

-3-

Economic and Geopolitical Forces

If goods don't cross borders, armies will.

—Frederic Bastiat

The perfect storm is a complex mechanism with an infinite variety of moving parts. Constantly in motion, the storm cells are always moving, evolving, and shaping and reshaping the footprint of the coming storm. Like any living organism, it has a unique DNA, which we will now examine in detail, starting with the first of the four E-Cells, economic and geopolitical forces.

E-1.1: Economic Forces

The macro- and microeconomic forces shaping the storm are too large and diverse to cover in full detail. Here we focus on four bedrock forces: the world's reserve currency and petrodollar systems, the Federal Reserve and the global role of central banks, fiscal and monetary policies and the economic implications of each, and the time bombs lurking out of sight.

The Reserve Currency and Petrodollar Systems

International currencies come and go. The Greek drachma, Roman denarius, Dutch guilder, and the British pound sterling are among the many currencies that have ruled supreme in their limited historical shelf lives. The US dollar has been the dominant reserve currency since the end of World War II, but other currencies, such as China's yuan, are now making serious inroads.

A currency is a medium of exchange used to purchase goods and services—everyday money. A *reserve* currency is a common currency held and used by countries for global transactions. For example, at the beginning of this century, the three most heavily used reserve currencies for all global transactions were the US dollar, with over 70 percent of the transaction market share; the euro, with 18.8 percent; and the Japanese yen, with 6.3 percent. By 2014 the dollar had lost ground, with roughly a 63 percent currency share, and the euro had climbed to over 22 percent.

The Chinese yuan was designated a reserve currency on November 15, 2015, and thereafter included as part of the International Monetary Fund's[1] basket of currencies, a hybrid currency form issuing what are called special drawing rights (SDRs).[2] Some feel the US dollar will eventually lose its powerful reserve currency status to an SDR currency. That is doubtful for now, but the dollar has certainly lost some of its former luster.

The reserve currency designation is of tremendous advantage to nations holding that status in that they can often purchase, sell, and borrow across borders without having to exchange their currencies, which non–reserve currency countries must do. The central banks of the world also hold large amounts of their currencies in reserve for international transactions, which increases the value of and demand for their respective currencies. Historically, there are three benchmark dates leading to the currency situation:

1944–1945: Leaders from several war-torn countries met in 1944 to establish an international monetary order for the postwar world. The United Nations Monetary and Financial Conference, known as the Bretton Woods Conference, established, among other things, the US dollar as the anchor currency for international trade, and the value of foreign currencies were thereafter pegged to the dollar. In turn, the United States agreed to let nations holding our dollars redeem them for gold at a rate of thirty-five dollars per ounce. Through this mechanism, the world currencies were tied into a modified gold-backed currency system.

1971: Over time, the United States got a little sloppy with its fiscal and monetary policies. As the dollar began to lose its luster, countries began cashing in their dollars for gold, creating a bank run that was rapidly depleting the US gold reserve.

Seeking to stem the gold drain, President Richard M. Nixon shocked the world markets on August 15, 1971, by taking the United States off the gold standard. He decreed that the dollar would henceforth become a fiat-based paper currency backed by the full faith and credit of the United States government—but not gold. The implications were enormous: among them, the United States could now print money without the limit of having an equal reserve of gold on hand. Nixon's move created a disequilibrium in the global currency markets as currencies were "floated" against each other to establish a transactional value.

1972–1973: OPEC[3] nations, in particular, were at a loss as to how to price their oil in dozens of different currencies with floating values. The Nixon administration worked out a quid-pro-quo arrangement with the Saudi government in which the Saudis agreed to transact oil sales only in dollars in return for American military protection. This system became known as the petrodollar system. As Saudi Arabia was the dominant OPEC player, the other OPEC nations soon followed.

Thereafter, all OPEC oil was sold and transacted in American dollars. For instance, if Germany wanted to purchase oil, it had to convert its marks—and later euros—into dollars to make the transaction. In turn, the central banks had to hold huge reserves of American dollars for future oil purchases, which all but guaranteed a steady demand for the American dollar—now backed by the "black gold" of oil. Over time, even non-oil commodities were heavily transacted in dollars.

Despite growing chinks in the armor, the financial bonanza of the petrodollar arrangement is still enjoyed by the United States today:

1. As a dominant fiat currency, the United States can print and borrow money with ease. With a steady demand for our dollars and as a recognized safe haven where countries can park their money, the United States has become a virtual cash-flow machine.

2. Through the process of petrodollar recycling, OPEC nations moved a good chunk of their dollar surpluses back into US treasuries or other US investments. In this manner, the United States gets a piece of the action both coming and going.

3. The US government and businesses have, as a result, access to cheap capital and other advantages by virtue of our world reserve currency and petrodollar status.

4. With few restraints, this has enabled the United States to engage in what some regard as fiscal and monetary policies on steroids. Unlike Greece, for example, the US has been able to print or borrow its way out of potential debt default situations. Our profligate spending, enormous deficits, debt, devalued dollars, and other transgressions have a direct impact on other nations, and it is deeply resented by many.

History has shown that no currency retains its dominant position forever, and the dollar's primo position is being chipped away daily in various ways. While we are unlikely to abruptly lose our coveted currency status, its relative strength will diminish. In a doomsday scenario, if OPEC suddenly decided to replace the petrodollar system with some other type of transactional currency system, like a basket of currencies, the need for central banks to hold large dollar reserves would diminish. They would quickly dump their large holdings and flood the market with unneeded dollars. The dollar would crash in a catastrophe of epic proportions for the United States and others. We would be wise to consider this as we deal with Saudi Arabia, overuse sanctions, or bully the world using the dollar and the supportive transactional mechanisms we hold as leverage. What goes around, comes around.

The Federal Reserve System

The Federal Reserve, the central bank of the United States, was signed into law in 1913. Established initially to regulate banks, oversee money supply, and provide a menu of institutionally related financial services, it has become one of the most powerful—and least understood—institutions in our country. The mere hint of a change in its discount rates or monetary policy—often through its forward guidance statements that hint at future monetary directions—can roil the international markets and send Wall Street into a tizzy. Working closely with equivalent central banks in other countries, its collective economic power is enormous.

In 1977, the Federal Reserve was additionally charged with promoting maximum employment and stabilizing prices and long-term interest rates. The additional function, known as the dual mandate, has, on occasions, put the Fed at odds with its original mission, a topic we will cover later.

The Fed is a quasi-public entity governed and controlled by an interesting mix of public and private officials. The presidentially appointed Board of Governors constitutes the Federal Reserve Board, but the real power resides in the twelve-member Federal Open Market Committee. Seven of its members are presidentially appointed, four are chosen on a rotating basis from one of the twelve regional Federal Reserve Banks, and the New York Fed president is a permanent member. The latter five positions represent the private sector through the federally charted commercial banks in their region.

The Fed's ability to redirect the economy through its control of the money supply cannot be overstated. For example, in a time of runaway inflation (described by some as too many dollars chasing after too few goods) in the late 1970s, Chairman Paul Volcker and the Fed raised the discount rate, tightened reserve requirements, and took aggressive actions to contract the nation's money supply. His draconian steps—widely criticized at the time—corrected the problem and attested to the Fed's awesome power.

By contrast, Chairman Ben Bernanke unleashed the power of the Fed in the Great Recession of 2008 to inject liquidity into the economy and stave off the collapse of megabanks deemed "too big to fail." Discount rates and reserve requirements were cut to the bone, and a number of complex new mechanisms were deployed to save the day. Most noteworthy were three different iterations of what has become known as quantitative easing, or QE[4] for short. With this policy, the Fed buys up government bonds and other assets to pump liquidity into the system. Using three separate QE initiatives, the Fed puffed up its balance sheet and electronically increased money supply by injecting several trillion dollars of new money into the economy. While not technically a case of "printing" money, it sure looked and felt like it. By monetizing debt (converting debt into legal tender) in this manner, the Fed accomplished its liquidity goals—after a fashion.

Both examples point to Fed strategies for stabilizing the economy. Though the challenges were different in nature and required different approaches, Volcker's actions were painful in the short run but helpful over a longer term, while Bernanke's had more of a "play now, pay later" flavor. The multiple QE injections had less of a marginal impact in their later stages. Many feel the artificially low-interest environment has created equity and debt bubbles that will eventually burst. Clearly, Wall Street and world markets seemed more focused on Fed policies than the underlying fundamentals of the economy or business.

Globally, Fed policies are carefully watched for their effect on interest rates, the value of the dollar, and global liquidity. Fed policies that devalue the dollar are harmful to foreign investors and purchasers of commodities. When the dollar loses value—meaning it takes more dollars to purchase a barrel of oil—the price of oil increases for them as a result of the petrodollar system. In effect, the United States ends up exporting inflation. Conversely, when the value of the dollar increases, the carrying charges to debtor nations climb because it takes more of their currency to pay back debt negotiated in dollars.

Collectively, the Fed and its worldwide central bank counterparts have an enormous impact on the global economy. In recent years, nations have devalued their currencies to improve trade balances and prop up their economies, but not without a price. With weakened balance sheets and massive long-term debt on the books, their ability to stave off the next economic meltdown may be severely compromised.

The Monetary-Fiscal-Economic Trifecta

Fiscal and monetary policies are intricately linked to the general economy in a cycle that ebbs and flows, though policies are seldom as completely linked as they should be. A quick review of their interrelationships reveals a number of startling disconnects.

Monetary policy deals primarily with money supply and interest rates. The Fed oversees this function and can rev up or slow down the economy by controlling the liquidity—money supply—in the system through its interest rate policies and other mechanisms. Interest rate policies heavily determine the cost of capital for expansion as well as balance of trade positions through the value of the dollar. For example, if the Fed rates are high, the long-term rates on housing will also be higher and perhaps even dampen the housing market.

Fiscal policy focuses on taxes and spending and is developed by Congress and the White House. The stimulative economic impact of lower taxes and/or greater government spending is powerful. (A hot economy is often grounds for the Fed to raise interest rates; a stagnant economy is grounds to lower them.) There are two categories of government spending at our federal level: nondiscretionary spending, which includes entitlements and the interest paid on our debt, and discretionary spending, which includes defense and all other forms of nonmandated spending. With nondiscretionary and defense spending accounting for about 70 percent of the federal budget, there is little wiggle room to reduce the federal budget without cutting into defense and/or entitlement programs—both politically unpopular moves. Instead, we lavishly spend, borrow, and print money to make up the difference, passing on still more IOUs to those following us.

Some of the key measures used to measure the economic outcomes of these policies include the GDP growth rate, unemployment levels, Wall Street market results, and consumer confidence indexes. In that about 70 percent of America's economy is consumer based, consumer spending is of more than casual importance. While fiscal and monetary policies can be doctored to quickly produce short-term results, the long-term fallout from overly aggressive policies is almost always harmful.

The three most problematic components in our national budget are deficits, defined as the annual budgetary shortfall in which spending exceeds revenues; debt, defined as the accumulation of all past deficits and further defined as public debt (monies owed to all creditors holding government securities) and gross debt (which includes both public and intragovernmental debt—the internal debt owed to the government trust funds for money "borrowed" from the trust funds and transferred to the general operating budget); and debt-servicing charges, the interest paid on our debt—a matter of growing concern.

As a barometer, in rounded numbers, the gross federal debt in 2018 of $21.4 trillion exceeded our GDP of $20.2 trillion by $1.2 trillion. The net interest of over $324 billion paid to service the debt in 2018 is expected to more than double by 2023. With even a slight uptick in interest rates, the debt-carrying charge will explode in future years, dramatically increasing the entire federal debt. Worse, these numbers do not reflect deficits accruing from the unfunded entitlement obligations coming due for future payment. With more than ten thousand baby boomers now retiring daily, the true estimated entitlement obligations are somewhere north of $100 trillion dollars—over five times our current GDP.

The bottom line: The United States is hemorrhaging red ink, with little in the till to fund future entitlement obligations. Those wonderful political promises of yesteryear will become a giant millstone around the necks of future generations. Political leaders know that quick fixes usually exacerbate the long-term problem, but they fear enacting fiscal policies that will hit voters in the pocketbook or spark a temporary setback to the economy. Easier, it seems, to pass the buck to others.

The Ticking Time Bombs: The United States, like other countries, has its own unique set of problems. In a consumer-based economy, there is always a danger when fewer discretionary dollars are available for consumer purchases. This periodically happens in a recessionary economy when the GDP contracts, consumer confidence plummets, and unemployment rates rise. There are several ticking time bombs of longer duration, and they are trending in the wrong direction:

- Rising debt, debt-servicing charges, and unfunded entitlement liabilities are an increasing drag on our economy.

- Healthcare costs, now accounting for almost 18 percent of our GDP, are rising. As our aging population grows, lives longer, and consumes more health benefits, the troublesome trajectory will continue.

- Student-loan debt—with rising default rates—is now the second-largest debt category in the country. It will continue to limit Millennials and others and constrain the future housing market and other consumer purchases.

- The continued erosion of the dollar's purchasing power will be a drag on people with fixed incomes; more discretionary dollars will be redeployed to purchase the basics, with fewer dollars left for nonessential consumer purchases.

- Rising energy prices will eventually create a de facto tariff on foreign goods shipped long distances to US markets, and vice versa.

- Looming trade wars and barriers will stifle the global economy.

- All Ponzi schemes come to an end: at some point, we will have to pay the proverbial fiddler, and it could get ugly. Higher taxes and budgetary cutbacks are the likeliest solutions, as we can only borrow our way into sustainable prosperity for so long.

Chart 3.1: Tip of the Iceberg illustrates our fixation on short-term metrics at the tip of the iceberg and inattention to the game-changing forces churning below the waterline. Our mass myopia is a prescription for disaster.

Chart 3.1: Tip of the Iceberg

The challenge: Redirect fixation on the tip of the iceberg issues and focus more on the churning forces below the waterline

Tip of the Iceberg Issues:
- The next election
- Quarterly earnings
- Wall Street impacts
- The latest events

Tip

Below the Waterline Forces:
- Climate change repurcussions
- Population & resources
- Exponential growth calculus
- Agressive feedback loops
- The Perfect Storm juggernaut

- Uncontrolled debt
- Unfunded entitlement liabilities
- Trade wars & broken treaties
- Currency warfare—petrodollar threats
- 4th Industrial Revolution blitzkrieg
- Asymmetric warfare, nuclear proliferation
- Fresh water & depletion of scarce resources
- Black Swan events e.g. pandemics
- Ignorance, apathy, denial, and hubris

E-1.2: Geopolitical Forces

The United States was clearly in the global driver's seat at the end of World War II. The Axis powers were thoroughly defeated, and our allies were in a sad state, with broken economies and damaged infrastructure—often dependent on the United States for massive aid a la the Marshall Plan[5] to rebuild Europe. Militarily, the United States was the sole possessor of the atomic bomb for a few years following the war.

The USSR was an active adversary, gobbling up many of the Eastern European nations—once occupied by Nazi Germany—as a buffer zone against the West. The *Iron Curtain* was more than an empty phrase coined by Winston Churchill to describe the captive countries under the wing of the Soviet leader, Joseph Stalin. The Cold War between the Soviet Union and the United States and their respective allies was the dominant geopolitical reality for the next forty-six years.

The takeover of China in 1949 under Mao Tse-tung reinforced the communist position, and the Korean War that soon followed was a "hot" manifestation of the Cold War. The Vietnam War that followed in the 1960s and later the Afghan War in the 1980s—pitting the Russian Army against Afghan fighters supplied with American weapons—further exemplified the global impact of the conflict.

With the fall of the Soviet Union in 1991, the Cold War ended. The power vacuum that followed was, in itself, destabilizing. As bad as it was, there was a tacit understanding between the two superpowers that nuclear war was unacceptable and that it was up to each power to "police" its own client states within their respective spheres of influence. In effect, each power acted as a super cop while vying for power, influence, and markets.

In the meantime, the Middle East had emerged as a quagmire of regional wars, with Israel often a lightning rod. During the oil shortages of the 1970s, the oil-rich OPEC nations became a significant force. Religious radicalism exacerbated Middle Eastern conflicts, and new forms of asymmetric warfare started to appear, most noteworthy, terrorist attacks. Over time, asymmetric warfare has escalated and become more sophisticated, particularly in the areas of cyberwarfare.

In 1991, the Gulf War to oust Saddam Hussein from Kuwait led to the deployment of hundreds of thousands of boots-on-ground troops, and the US Fifth Fleet became a semi-permanent fixture in the Middle East. Our military presence, detested by some and welcomed by others, was used again in the second Gulf War in 2003 and in Afghanistan—in what has now become the longest war in American history. Amid this turbulence, a number of global power shifts emerged that will shape global power structures for decades to come.

First, within a brief span of about twenty years, China transformed itself into the world's newest superpower. Its economic outreach is felt everywhere, and it has become a military force to be reckoned with, particularly in the China Seas and with its neighbors. The European Union has also become a major economic powerhouse, competing with the United States and China. India is a booming new economic force—with nuclear weapons—and Russia has reemerged as a contentious world player. Signs of a great Eurasian coalition to counter Western powers are now visible.

Second, we are entering into a strange new war; call it Cold War II. Unlike the first, which was fought over ideology as much as anything else, the new one will be focused on control of markets, technological supremacy, resources, currencies, and sea-lanes. With the advent of asymmetric warfare, smaller powers will play an increasingly important role.

Third, global power is based on a combination of alliances and military, economic, diplomatic, financial, and physical resources. In this equation, the United States is still a superpower, but the playing field is changing. Our relative economic power—and balance sheet—is not as dominant as it once was, and our recent disengagement from treaties and alliances has been highly destabilizing. The paradigm is shifting, but, through a combination of hubris, denial, and self-pride, we may not be facing reality. Time will tell.

Chart 3.2: Global Challenges and Hot Spots illustrates the multiple forces in play in the geopolitical arena. In this dynamic environment, a miscalculation could easily trigger unintended consequences. A move in one direction almost always invites multiple responses in other areas. The geopolitical changes and ramifications will be covered in more depth in later chapters. The key takeaway for now is that we live in a changing environment and must adjust our tactics and strategies accordingly. It takes time, but our time may be running out as geopolitical forces push us ever closer to the perfect storm.

This is only one of the four E-Cell threats embedded in the greater perfect storm construct. When factored in alongside growing energy challenges, the existential threat of climate change and dramatic ecological destruction, and a global population with growing expectations that greatly exceed reality, all of the afore-mentioned economic and geopolitical challenges will intensify by a wide margin.

**Chart 3.2: The Gathering Storm
Global Challenges and Hot Spots**

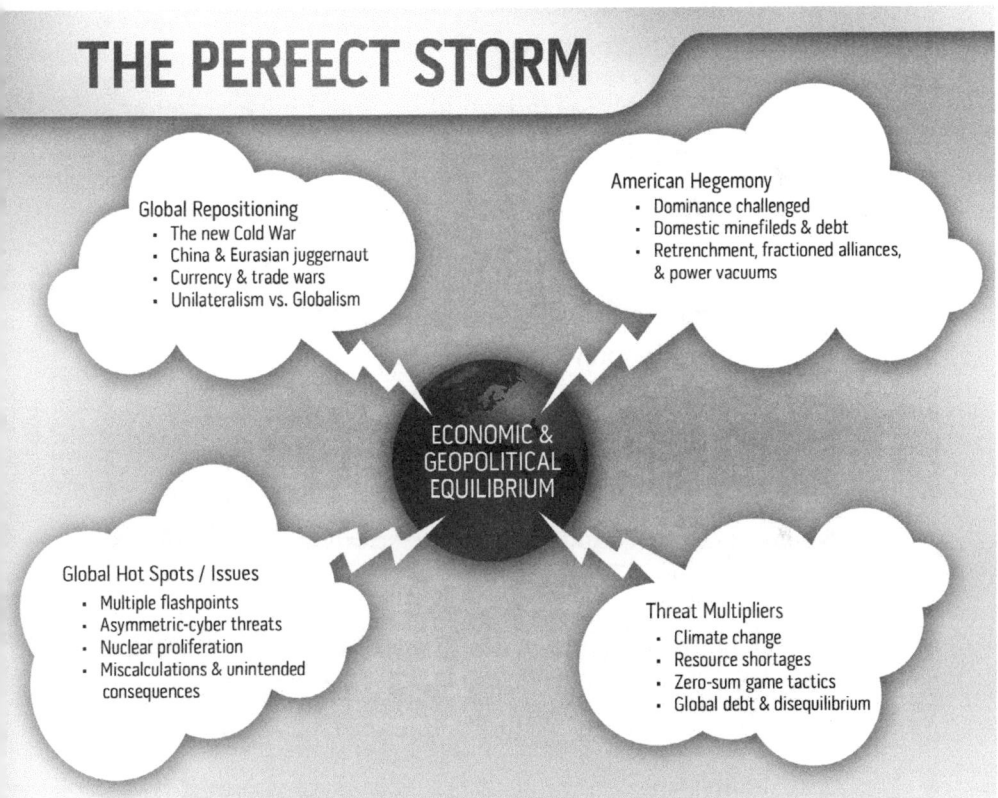

THE PERFECT STORM

Global Repositioning
- The new Cold War
- China & Eurasian juggernaut
- Currency & trade wars
- Unilateralism vs. Globalism

American Hegemony
- Dominance challenged
- Domestic minefileds & debt
- Retrenchment, fractioned alliances, & power vacuums

ECONOMIC & GEOPOLITICAL EQUILIBRIUM

Global Hot Spots / Issues
- Multiple flashpoints
- Asymmetric-cyber threats
- Nuclear proliferation
- Miscalculations & unintended consequences

Threat Multipliers
- Climate change
- Resource shortages
- Zero-sum game tactics
- Global debt & disequilibrium

Within the context of the perfect storm, several economic and geopolitical substorms are now in play.

Summary: Economic and Geopolitical Forces

The first of the perfect storm's four E-Cells, Economic and Geopolitical Forces, shapes the world we live in today. Traditional economic bedrock is weakening, and an emerging cold war will destabilize global power structures for decades to come. Key E-Cell drivers fueling the perfect storm are as follows:

1. **Key economic structures, once heavily favoring the United States, are gradually changing.**

   - The dollar's cherished reserve currency status will be increasingly challenged.

   - The petrodollar transactional system, an American bonanza, is at long-term risk.

   - The Federal Reserve—and world banks—now exert enormous economic power.

   - Aggressive fiscal and monetary policies present a number of long-term challenges.

   - Efforts to stave off the next economic meltdown are compromised by previous policies.

2. **The geopolitical arena is shifting significantly, and American hegemony is challenged.**

   - A new cold war is underway, and a strong Eurasian counterweight is in the making.

   - China, a new superpower, and Russian reemergence pose new threats.

   - The Middle East will be a tinderbox, and the Pacific Rim hotly contested.

   - US retrenchment has destabilized traditional power structures.

- New asymmetric threats, including cyberwarfare, will complicate the equation.

3. **The ticking time bombs in our path have different risk and volatility levels.**

   - Debt is a growing global problem: we cannot borrow our way into prosperity.

   - New power structures are destabilizing and can take unpredictable turns.

   - Giant bubbles—of a Ponzi-like nature—will pose an ongoing set of global threats.

   - An exclusive focus on the tip of the iceberg is concealing below-the-waterline risks.

   - Global hot spots are proliferating, and regional conflicts more likely.

   - Trade wars and nationalism could take ugly turns going forward.

   - Black Swan events, like pandemics, are possible.

4. **The economic and geopolitical threats are only one part of the E-Cell equation.**

   - Energy and technological challenges will expand the threat arena.

   - Climate change and ecological destruction will pose direct and indirect threats.

   - The resilience of humankind will be tested as never before.

-4-

Energy and Technological Forces

It has become appallingly obvious that our technology has exceeded our humanity.

—Albert Einstein

There's no energy crisis, only a crisis of ignorance.

—R. Buckminster Fuller

It would be difficult to imagine two forces with a greater impact on society than the energy and technological advances of the past several decades. They paved the way for the American Dream, connected the world, revolutionized agriculture, globalized travel, explored outer space, reinvented the workplace, and changed the way we live, communicate with each other, absorb information, and enjoy leisure. This chapter focuses on the Energy and Technological E-Cell forces, starting with energy.

E-2.1: Energy Forces

Energy is the master resource. It provides the capacity for doing work, growing food, running machines, transporting goods, and supporting virtually all facets of life. Four common elements are required to make the energy life cycle work: a raw fuel source (e.g., oil, coal, wind, and solar); a power source to digest and convert raw fuel into finished energy (e.g., power stations, refineries, furnaces, turbines, solar panels); a distribution system to carry the "finished" energy to the end user (e.g., the grid system, rail networks, fuel trucks, service stations, pipelines); and devices that convert the finished energy into a specific end user product or purpose (e.g., cars, planes, power tools, appliances, heating and air systems).

Humans have always sought the easiest and most practical way to complete this energy cycle using the most optimal fuel sources and technologies available. Availability of, access to, and affordability of fuels and fuel systems used are of paramount importance. As new energy discoveries and technologies evolved, our insatiable appetite for growth, speed, utility, and consumption also grew.

Over time, the coal-water-steam trifecta that powered the Industrial Age began to change. Electrical power—generated from a variety of fuels and fuel systems—spurred on the second industrial revolution. The internal combustion engine, jet power, and nuclear propulsion continued to advance, along with their respective infrastructures, and we are now entering a new energy renaissance led by nature's own renewable energy sources.

The post–World War II energy surge unleashed remarkable economic and industrial growth. Our per-capita consumption of energy also increased to accommodate our growing appetites for mobility and power-based conveniences. By the late 1970s, nuclear-powered electrical generation had come into its own, and global oil exploration efforts leapfrogged to support a thirsty world's love affair with the automobile and overseas jet travel. Globalization and the increasing needs of underdeveloped, energy-starved nations added to the demand. With the exception of two significant oil crises in the 1970s, a near-nuclear meltdown at Three Mile Island, and later, the Chernobyl disaster, the global energy juggernaut continued unimpeded into the new millennium.

Fuel systems are usually mission specific; different fuels serve different purposes. For example, the coal-heat-water-steam progression powered trains and ships and heated buildings for decades. Fossil fuels—mainly coal and natural gas—and nuclear energy produced the electricity (the conveyor of energy produced from these baseload fuels) that lit up our buildings, streets, and homes and electrified trams and trains. Natural gas heated over a half of the homes in America, and King Oil still fuels almost 90 percent of our transportation systems, though these percentages are dropping.

The metrics of energy and the net power produced by each energy source are confusing: how do a barrel of oil, kilowatt of electricity, ton of coal, cubic foot of gas, and a megawatt of nuclear power compare? In the British thermal unit (Btu)—which measures the amount of heat required to raise the temperature of one pound of water by one degree Fahrenheit—we have a common metric for all fuels. We know, for example, that the Btu value of a barrel of oil is equal to 3,412 kilowatts of electrical power or 1,031 cubic feet of natural gas. With common metrics, we can establish equivalent energy values for policy design purposes, such as comparing the amount of renewable energy it would take to replace one barrel of oil or a ton of coal.

The unit of energy most common to world and national energy budgets is a quad. To give a sense of magnitude, a quad of energy is equivalent to the power in over 8 billion gallons of gasoline. As a point of reference, the United States used about 97.5 quads of world's 575 quads of energy in 2015—roughly 17 percent. The percentages are changing, however, as China, India, and other underdeveloped countries continue to rapidly grow and use more energy.

King Oil: In Transition

Despite the current shale oil euphoria, it is not a panacea that will solve our long-term energy problems. Simply put, the supply of any type of oil—conventional crude, deep-water or unconventional shale and tar sands—will always remain a finite resource facing an ever-growing demand, and therein lies the problem. Our economies are built around King Oil, and without a full-court press to rapidly develop alternatives, demand is likely to exceed the global supply of accessible and affordable oil in the coming years. It can take decades to replace a mainstream energy system, and it will be challenging to make the necessary transition in an orderly manner, without significant economic disruptions, before time runs out.

New technologies and the marketplace are hastening the shift toward a greater mix of electrical, hybrid, and natural gas–driven by cars and trucks—but the transitional challenges are daunting. The enormity of the task and the time, capital, and political will required are mind-boggling. Among other things, oil has several distinctive features that make it difficult to replicate:

- High-density energy: It takes an equivalent of 1,700 kilowatts of electricity to equal the energy in just one barrel of oil.

- Portability: Oil energy can be transported and used almost anywhere, with no links to a central power source.

- Fungibility: Its multiple usages are second to none. It is an energy source, lubricant, and key manufacturing ingredient for thousands of products.

- Scalability: Globally, it has been the prime source of energy for transportation systems for about a hundred years and cannot be easily replaced.

In his book *The Long Emergency: Surviving the Converging Catastrophes of the Twenty-First Century* (New York: Grove, 2005), James Howard Kunstler sums up the wonderful oil endowment we are in the process of depleting: "The oil endowment was an extraordinary and singular occurrence of geology, allowing us to use the stored energy of millions of years of sunlight. Once it's gone, it will be forever gone."

The geologic community sees this oil endowment as a finite resource subject to the immutable laws of geology, while economic technocrats look on it as a resource that can be extended almost indefinitely through new technologies that find, extract, and extend the productivity of old and new oil fields. Indeed, oil production has ramped up through horizontal and multipad drilling, fracking, enhanced oil recovery techniques, seismic mapping, deep-water drilling, and more. Though supply-siders believe we can drill our way into an oil nirvana—a possibility in the short run—it is not a sustainable long-term proposition.

A few basics to keep in mind: First, oil is finite. We may *discover* oil, but we can't *create* it. The easy-to-get oil is gone. Conventional crude oil peaked several years ago, and the new, unconventional finds—shale, tar sands, and deep-water oils—are far costlier to extract and process than conventional crude. Their lower net energy value (the EROEI: energy received over energy invested) means it takes more energy to produce energy. Hence, future costs have nowhere to go but up and could reach a point where production costs exceed the going market price for oil. It happened briefly in the past decade, when shale oil production costs exceeded the market price and shale oil production dropped.

As a finite resource, oil depletion and decline rates are also part of the story. Overall, conventional oil fields decline at a rate of about 5 to 7 percent or more per year. Shale wells, by comparison, deplete at rates as high as 40 percent or more in the first year. Over time, it will take a massive effort just to maintain current levels of production. Boosting net *new* production is even harder. Oil exploration efforts have slipped in recent years as oil companies, strapped for cash and struggling to remain solvent, cut back on their exploratory efforts.

Peak oil and peak production are of great concern to the oil markets. Peak oil, a geologic concept, declares that once an oil field reaches maximum production—usually when the field is about half used up—it will peak and then start to decline. Conventional crude oil peaked earlier in this century, and we now rely more on costlier unconventional oils for new production. Peak production injects above-the-ground inputs into the equation. Though there may still be plenty of oil left in the ground, these factors—and not geology—may limit what is produced.

Oil is not our only energy challenge. The list is long and includes reactor safety concerns and the disposal of nuclear waste from nuclear power stations; climate change and the carbon footprints of fossil fuels; aging energy grids and power infrastructures; and cyberthreats that could disable our energy systems. Meanwhile, new opportunities will arise in the areas of renewable energy, demand reduction, energy efficiency, and our energy mix.

The Energy Renaissance

As the new millennium progressed, global energy dynamics began to rapidly change. China had surpassed the United States as the world's largest consumer of energy, and oil prices reached record highs before crashing in 2008. New horizontal drilling and hydraulic fracking technologies in the United States created a surge in shale oil and natural gas production, and in 2016, natural gas surpassed coal in the United States as the largest baseload fuel for producing electrical power, a trend that continues as utilities convert their power plants over to natural gas to lower costs and reduce emissions.

On a macro level, energy needs are expected to grow by about a third from 2013 to 2040, and they will be met through a mix of fuel sources. As a legacy fuel, coal power is on the wane. Over time, natural gas, nuclear, and renewable energy systems will produce a growing share of all electrical energy. Renewable energy in particular will account for the lion's share of new energy coming online as gas eventually ebbs.

The biggest stories in this energy renaissance will be the rapid growth of renewable energy in a more blended energy portfolio and the growing emphasis on demand reduction and energy-efficiency programs. Both areas will be discussed in Part III of this book. For now, let's briefly look at each area.

Renewable Energy

Powerful new economic, political, and climate imperatives, cost factors, and technologies have burst the renewable energy floodgates. Solar, wind, biomass, geothermal, and a host of budding new systems are now surging, and the challenges of connectivity, energy storage, grid infrastructure, and intermittency issues are being systematically addressed. Chart 4.1: The Energy Matrix highlights several prominent energy forms and their respective characteristics.

As one measure of its success, renewable energy accounted for about 6.1 percent of the total energy generated in the United States in 2006. That number has now increased to about 10 percent of our total energy mix, a remarkable increase of over 65 percent in a little over a decade, and it will climb at a far higher rate in the coming years. Many US states—and world nations—now have aggressive energy goals, in which renewable energy is targeted to provide 20–25 percent of the baseload fuel for electrical power generation over the next few years. As price points drop and become more competitive—as has happened with wind and solar energy—and as grid systems and energy storage technologies improve, renewable energy will be our largest source of new energy production from here on in.

With growing traction in this new energy renaissance, we will see an explosion of new technologies, infrastructures, and cottage industries in a supportive role as well as a rapid emergence of new economic growth engines. In fact, it is already happening, and clean energy is now among the greatest new job creators in the world.

Demand Reduction

The energy needed for economic growth must come from either increasing the units of energy or decreasing demand so that more can be done with less. Demand reduction is the low-hanging fruit in this equation, and it can reap immediate benefits at a very low cost, a fact not lost on companies, building owners, utilities, and residential owners paying their monthly utility bills.

Chart 4.1: The Energy Matrix

Source	Key Usages	Supply Status	Pros	Cons
Oil	Transportation Manufacturing	Peaking	Best energy source available; ideal for transportation systems	Oil supply will peak; cost of new extraction is high
Tar Sands, Shale, Deep-water	Transportation	Large	Large supplies available	Pollutive; lower net energy value and higher costs
Natural Gas	Heating Electrical Power	Large	Clean burning and efficient; vast new supplies through fracking	Pollutive if fracking is not done right
Coal	Electrical Power	Large	Large supplies in USA; multiple purposes via coal gasification, etc.	Brutal greenhouse gas emissions
Nuclear	Electrical Power	Large supply with breeder reactors	Environmentally clean; large supply with breeder reactors; new-generation power stations are safer	Nuclear waste disposal; high capital and regulatory costs to build
Biomass	Transportation Electrical Power Heating	Renewable	Easy to integrate into existing fuel systems; good supply with switchgrass and other cellulosic fuel sources	Marginal EROEI and limited capacity with corn-based ethanol; also competes for corn as a food or feed source
Hydroelectric	Electrical Power	Renewable	Good, clean energy source	Supply limited to water and dam capacity; some eco effects

Source	Key Usages	Supply Status	Pros	Cons
Geothermal	Electrical Power	Renewable	Great potential; clean-energy EROEI improving with new technology	Limited access and availability, but used increasingly for houses and buildings
Wind	Electrical Power	Renewable	Rapidly growing, clean energy; major source of renewable energy	Requires large tracts of land; wind and storage issues; must be located in windy areas; energy grids needed
Solar	Heating Electrical Power	Renewable	Unlimited energy source; a clean-energy resource	Land usage; storage; and intermittency issues
Hydrogen	Multiple	Renewable	Nearly inexhaustible supply and clean burning	Negative EROEI at present and long technological curve to commercialize

Demand reduction comes in three forms: increasing energy efficiency so that less energy is wasted and more can be done with less; conservation efforts such as reducing waste, reusing, recycling, and repairing; and reducing demand with new technologies and by changing behaviors where possible with substitutes such as walking, biking, driving less, and using public transit.

Buildings are heavy users of energy, and efforts to retrofit lighting, heating and air conditioning, and insulation, along with new "smart" systems and conservation-minded behavioral changes, have proven to be highly cost effective over a relatively short period of time. Residential consumers are finding the same to be true.

Broader initiatives in the areas of energy savings and waste management are exciting. A move toward what is called a circular economy—discussed in Part III—in which resources are maximized and waste drastically reduced at a systemic level, is gaining traction.

New disciplines, such as biomimicry, look at ways to mimic nature by using low-temperature and low-pressure processes along with green chemistry to lower energy consumption and carbon footprints. A cornucopia of innovations is now being shared everywhere, which leads us to the second part of this E-Cell: Technological Forces.

E-2.2: Technological Forces

Technological evolution has been a slow, grinding process for most of our history—until recently. The earlier discoveries of fire, heat, the wheel, and primitive hunting and agricultural techniques were easily assimilated into the societies and cultures that employed them. The cycle of technological innovation started to accelerate and intensify as the first industrial revolution took shape in the middle of the nineteenth century. Centered around coal, water, and steam, the newfound power system bolstered productivity and reshaped our transportation and manufacturing systems. The second industrial revolution—from about the early 1900s through the 1960s—revolved around electrical power and the widespread incorporation of mass production processes. The third industrial revolution—from roughly the late 1960s to present times—was built around a new era of electronics, digitalization, computerization, and the internet, introducing processes that automated industrial production and connected the world.

The fourth industrial revolution—now in its infancy—will meld together a host of new physical, digital, and biological technologies. Its speed will outstrip our ability to absorb and assimilate change in a timely manner. This all-encompassing technological blitzkrieg promises to intoxicate us with ever-greater convenience, pleasure, productivity, and new life experiences. It will also reinforce an almost mystical belief that technology cures all ills with quick answers and painless panaceas. If only it were that easy.

To be sure, we have embraced and benefited from the Nuclear, Space, Biomedical, and Information Ages in the past few decades alone, so this isn't our first rodeo. But the fourth industrial revolution will feature artificial intelligence, quantum computing, smart systems, 3-D printing, robotics, and so much more. It will become more directly involved in decision making, warfare, command-and-control mechanisms, and other areas once controlled solely by the human mind.

Its all-pervasive reach will make life easier in many respects, but it has a dark side that must not be overlooked, aftershocks that linger long after the novelty of the "latest and greatest" technology wears off. History has taught us that whenever the scope and speed of a new technology outpaces our ability to assimilate it into our culture and economy, the chances of misuse and unintended consequences increase. The greater the scope of the technology, the more vulnerable we become.

This shouldn't come as a surprise, as we are hardwired to think in linear terms and apply linear logic to the exponentially growing technologies entering into our mainstream. We must fight that instinct or risk falling hopelessly behind the technological assimilation curve, opening a gap with profound repercussions.

Historically, there are endless examples of this phenomenon. Few people envisioned the cyberthreats, privacy, and other issues attendant to the internet in its early development stages. The carbon footprint of coal-powered energy systems was never a real consideration until well into the twentieth century, nor was the disposal of radioactive waste from nuclear power plants. New "superbug" bacterial strains resistant even to Colistin—the powerful antibiotic of last resort—have emerged partially because of improper or overuse of miracle drugs. The Human Genome Project, in mapping out our DNA, has asked a host of moral and ethical questions that baffle the greatest minds.

Indeed, the internet and social media have connected the world while diminishing personal interaction. Tweets and texting have replaced many of the more intimate face-to-face contacts of yesteryear, but being plugged in does not always mean being connected. Recent interventions in our elections through the social media, indiscriminate data sharing, and the ability to manipulate images and video to make a candidate appear to be saying something they didn't should send chills down our necks, but that doesn't seem to be the case. In a world that prefers a soundbite to a thoughtful inquiry, such technologies can be game-changers.

This is not an antitechnology commentary, but rather a reminder of the yin-yang nature of great technological advances. We will cover the challenges of the fourth industrial revolution in Part III. For now, let us ponder the words of social philosopher, author, psychologist, and inventor B. F. Skinner, who said, "The real problem is not whether machines think but whether men do."

Summary: Energy and Technological Forces

The behemoth Energy and Technological Forces have had a profound impact on modern society and will continue to shape the form and substance of the perfect storm as follows:

1. **A game-changing energy transformation is now underway; the outcomes are uncertain.**

   - Legacy fossil-fuel energy systems continue to produce most of the world's energy.

   - The energy continuum and infrastructures are built around these systems.

   - The imperatives of finite supply and carbon footprint concerns are changing dynamics.

   - Maintaining the accessibility and affordability of energy needed to meet growing demand will be a big challenge.

   - Replacing oil—the major transportation fuel—will be particularly difficult.

2. **A promising new energy renaissance is here, but the transition will be daunting.**

   - New renewable technologies with falling price points are encouraging.

   - Clean-energy development is now one of the fastest growth industries in the world.

   - Replacing a legacy fossil-fuel energy system with scalable alternatives will be formidable.

   - An energy renaissance could become a giant catalyst for economic growth.

   - Renewable energy will be our major provider of new energy.

3. **Demand-reduction initiatives are the low-hanging fruit for carbon reduction.**

   - Climate change and carbon footprint reductions will be a major driver.

   - Energy efficiency, conservation, and demand reduction provide rich targets.

   - Opportunities for quick returns, lower costs, and innovation are plentiful.

4. **The growth of new technological innovations will be promising and perplexing.**

   - The fourth industrial revolution will be both productive and disruptive.

   - The threat of technologies surpassing our rates of assimilation is serious.

   - The quest for global technological leadership will be a new battleground.

-5-

Environmental and Ecological Forces

Global warming isn't a prediction. It is happening.

—James Hansen

We are eyewitnesses to a game-changing saga of epochal proportions. The powerful forces of climate change and ecological degradation are grinding together like tectonic plates, creating shockwaves that far exceed the pace and intensity of typical cyclical adjustment. These forces are not easily understood, which may be why they have so often been ignored, denied, or dismissed as aberrations that technology will surely fix. However, it doesn't work that way. As we explore the insidious growth of these Environmental and Ecological E-Cell forces, the magnitude of the threat will become clearer.

E-3.1: Environmental Forces

The relatively new challenge of climate change is a blockbuster. Its insidious progress is escalating, ravaging the world in a multitude of ways. Though our military and intelligence agencies fear it and the international community gets it, response in the United States has been sluggish. Amid time-consuming debates over its causes or the validity of the science behind it, the climate-change juggernaut continues to worsen.

Our story starts high up in Earth's razor-thin security blanket, our atmosphere. This gaseous shell differentiates Earth from all other known cosmic bodies by providing a planetary equivalent of the human immune system. It shields us from deadly cosmic radiation; self-regulates temperatures, humidity, and other atmospheric components; shapes our weather patterns and other life-giving cycles; and sustains a delicate but essential blend of nitrogen, oxygen, carbon dioxide, and other gases. Its self-regulation of the precise mix of greenhouse gases (GHGs) needed to sustain life has worked beautifully throughout human history—at least up until now.

But something is happening; our atmosphere is changing. Aggressive feedback loops are intensifying, and we are approaching—or perhaps have even passed—a tipping point. The evidence is overwhelming, and the trajectories are ominous.

The scope and complexity of climate change boggles the mind. As a way of wrapping our arms around it in nonscientific terms, think of the human body battling a chronic disease. We are born with an immune system that develops over time to protect us from hostile intruders. Earth's atmosphere likewise wards off harmful radiation and nurtures a sustainable environment for its inhabitants. Our life-support systems—cardiovascular, muscular, neural, skeletal, circulatory, and other systems—keep us going, much as Earth's ecosystems, water cycle, and other systems sustain life. Both enjoy self-regulatory mechanisms that keep them healthy and operational—*under normal conditions.*

The game changes, however, when a toxic agent overwhelms the system. For us, it might be a virus; for Earth, it's a massive carbon dioxide overdose. Under normal conditions, our atmosphere self-regulates itself back to a desired equilibrium in much the same way that a human body recovers from a fever. Left unchecked, however, the fever threatens the entire immune system, just as global warming degrades our planet's atmospheric system.

As these feedback loops intensify, the chronic disease will worsen. The rising fever inflicts damage on the immune system and organs, and our capacity to recover is impeded. If it goes too far, even anti-biotics and the best medical care will fail to reverse the downward path. In a similar manner, our planet's health is compromised by the rising greenhouse gases that heat it, damage its ecosystems, and degrade the self-regulating atmospheric systems that sustain life. Eventually, life will be forever changed.

The closer we get to that tipping point, the more precarious our situation becomes. We can quarrel about the epidemiology of our fever or the causes of climate change, but our unwillingness to act—until we get more information—will most certainly jeopardize the outcome. The consequences for the inhabitants of Planet Earth could be dire.

Our planet's self-regulating mechanisms are straining under the impact of the greenhouse effect, a chemical umbrella that locks in a mixture of such heat-retaining GHGs as carbon dioxide, methane, nitrous oxide, ozone, and water vapor. Not all elements are created equal. Human-made gases, like chlorofluorocarbons (CFCs), are infinitely more toxic. For now, we will stick mainly to the role of CO_2 in this equation.

The higher the CO_2 levels, the warmer the temperatures and the greater the threat. The direct correlation between CO_2 levels and global temperatures provides a good metric for monitoring our atmosphere over time. Core ice samples dating back over 650,000 years reveal that the CO_2 parts per million (ppm) count did not exceed the 300-ppm threshold until recently. It registered about 280 ppm at the start of the industrial revolution in the mid-nineteenth century and climbed to about 315 ppm by 1961—an increase of about 12.5 percent. By 2016 it had risen to over 400 ppm, a stag-gering increase of over 27 percent in less than 60 years and of a magnitude well beyond the range of a cyclical variation; it clearly was of anthropogenic origin. As of 2020, it reached a level of over 411 ppm.

Chart 5.1 provides a step-by-step schematic of how this toxic GHG effect works. As the primer suggests, solar radiation from the sun powers our climate system. Upon reaching Earth's atmosphere, the sun's rays are either reflected back into space or absorbed by the planet. (The reflection factor is called albedo.) The absorbed radiation heats the planet's surface, and some of the heat is emitted back into the atmosphere as infrared radiation. A good portion of this is absorbed and reemitted in all directions by the "greenhouse umbrella."

Chart 5.1: A Primer on Climate Change

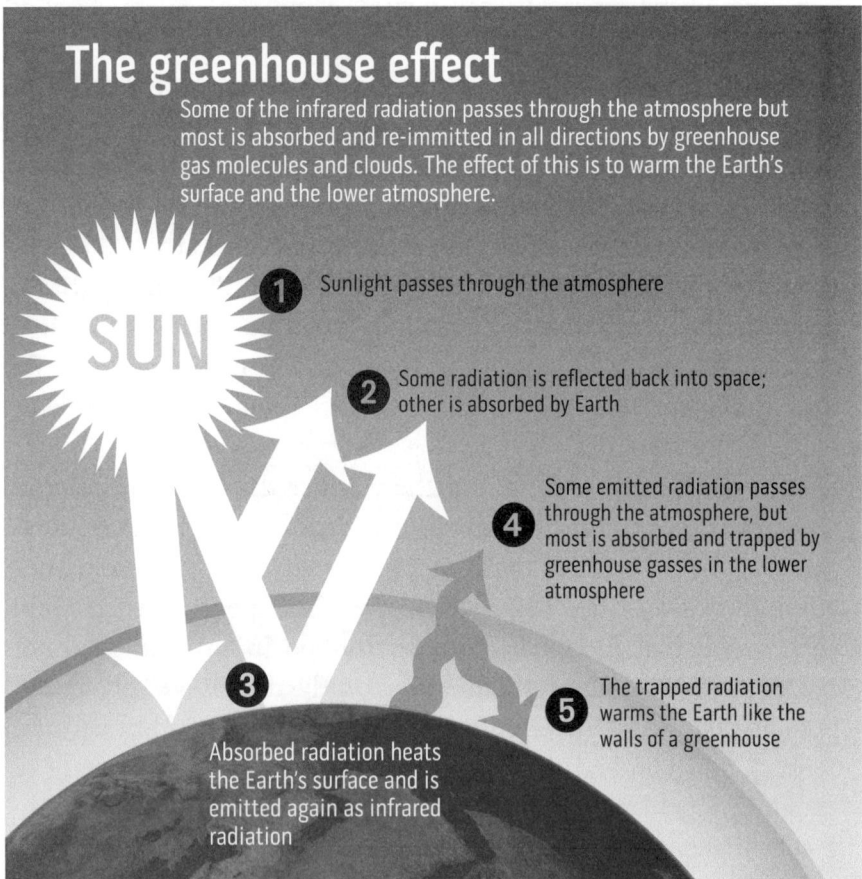

The greenhouse effect

Some of the infrared radiation passes through the atmosphere but most is absorbed and re-immitted in all directions by greenhouse gas molecules and clouds. The effect of this is to warm the Earth's surface and the lower atmosphere.

SUN

1 Sunlight passes through the atmosphere

2 Some radiation is reflected back into space; other is absorbed by Earth

4 Some emitted radiation passes through the atmosphere, but most is absorbed and trapped by greenhouse gasses in the lower atmosphere

3 Absorbed radiation heats the Earth's surface and is emitted again as infrared radiation

5 The trapped radiation warms the Earth like the walls of a greenhouse

Continuing the metaphor of climate change as a chronic disease, chart 5.2 compares a few key features and vital systems of Planet Earth with those of the human body. The comparisons are revealing.

Chart 5.2: Climate Change as a Chronic Disease

Feature	Planet Earth	Human Body
Chronic Disease	Climate change	Diabetes, high blood pressure, etc.
Protective Shield	Atmosphere	Immune system
Life-Support Systems	Energy cycle, water cycle, food chains, ocean currents	Circulatory, muscular, digestive, and other systems
Self-Regulating Systems	Regulate atmosphere and sustain planetary life	Regulate life of human body
Feedback Loops	Planetary conditions that help or harm	Habits: good and bad
Harmful Loops	GHG buildups, diminished capacity to absorb GHGs	Systemic damage from illness or injury if left untreated
Tipping Point	Climate change intensifies until food chains and global systems collapse; change is irreversible	Chronic disease worsens; patient is disabled or dies

When facing a life-threatening diagnosis, we would most certainly want a second opinion; we already have thousands of second opinions on the diagnosis of climate change. Consulting on Earth's health, 97 percent of climate scientists[1] have already agreed not only that climate change is happening, but also that it is occurring at a more rapid pace than first expected and is largely caused by anthropogenic forces. Yet, despite this nearly unanimous diagnosis by virtually every major scientific body in the world, some still call climate change a hoax.

In human terms, this is like visiting the Mayo Clinic and consulting one hundred top specialists in the chronic illness being diagnosed. At the conclusion, ninety-seven of them confirm the diagnosis, two of them want more information, and one claims there is no problem. With our health on the line, most of us would opt for immediate treatment. And yet, when it comes to the planet's health, special interest groups are asking us *not* to take the obvious step. Like the tobacco lobbies preceding them, these groups admonish us to stay the course and not act precipitously "because the data and science is not all in yet." What is wrong with this picture?

Earth's Medical Chart

Sticking with our medical analogy, let's assume Earth is running a low-grade fever with a host of chronic respiratory ailments. What information is available to confirm the diagnosis? A quick look at the Earth's medical chart reveals a disturbing picture.

Global Temperatures: While our planet has been warming since the 1880s, most of it has occurred over the past thirty-five years. The years 2015–2019 were the warmest in recorded history. Global temperatures have risen by over 1.4 degrees Fahrenheit since the beginning of the previous century. Oceanic temperatures have also risen as oceans absorb the sun's heat at an increasing rate, with ecological consequences that will be discussed later. Arctic temperatures are now rising at even higher rates than previous averages, and, without doubt, our planet's fever is trending upward.

Atmospheric "Blood Counts": The crucial diagnostic metric here is the GHG level, and we need to know that not all greenhouse gases are created equal. While the bulk of GHG emissions are in the form of carbon dioxide—with ppm of CO_2 in the atmosphere the most common measurement used—other greenhouse gases have a far greater heat-retaining capacity than CO_2 and/or longer shelf lives in the atmosphere. They are expressed as carbon dioxide *"equivalent"* gases to help establish their heat-retaining capacity on a consistent basis. When aggregated with carbon dioxide, the GHG level is expressed as "CO2e," the carbon dioxide equivalency value.

Methane, for instance, has a heat-retaining capacity over twenty times greater than CO_2 but it remains in the atmosphere for only about seven years, compared to up to two centuries for CO_2. Nitrous oxide has a heat-retaining ratio almost three hundred times that of CO2. The most toxic of all are human-made fluorinated (F) gases, such as hydrofluorocarbons, CFCs, and others with heat-retaining characteristics that are thousands of times higher than CO2. The bottom line is this: while CO2 levels have increased by over 45 percent since the first industrial revolution, anthropogenic gases are far more toxic and could rapidly accelerate GHG levels as they accumulate.

The atmospheric "blood counts" on Earth's medical chart are sending out other warning signals that are confirming the threat.

Ice and Glacial Melts: Every kid knows an ice-cream cone will not fare well in a heated room. This holds equally true for the massive ice sheet and glacial melts in Greenland, the Antarctic, the Himalayas, and the Arctic Sea. Satellite data confirms the accelerated melts almost daily. Pictures of the ice shelves the size of Delaware breaking up in the west Antarctic and the rapid movement of melting ice sheets in Greenland are frightening; the discovery of huge troughs of ice streams beneath these ice sheets, lubricating their movement toward the sea, confirms the diagnosis.

Rising Sea Levels: While sea levels rose about 6.7 inches in the past century, the annual rate of increase over the past twenty years has been five times higher than that of the rate over the preceding eighty years. Sophisticated tide gage readings and satellite measurements are confirming the pace. The increase is due primarily to thermal expansion, in which the water in warming oceans expands, as well as increased melting of land-based ice sheets, glaciers, and snow. The IPCC—covered in chapter 11—has projected sea level rises of 11–38 inches by the end of the century.

The global consequences are enormous. Roughly 40 percent of the population in the United States resides in or near coastal areas. Rising sea levels and massive storm surges are eroding shorelines, causing widespread flooding, contaminating agricultural and freshwater areas, and devastating infrastructures. Globally, eight of the world's ten largest cities are near a coast, and several island nations will be wiped out or rendered uninhabitable.

Organic and Systemic Damage: Earth's life-supporting organic systems are under attack from both climate change and wasteful anthropogenic practices. Weakened, these systems have combined to form a gigantic feedback loop that is damaging Earth's capacity to self-regulate and nurse its atmospheric and climate systems back to a healthy state. The warning lights are flashing everywhere, and we can readily see the destructive hand of mankind in both direct and indirect ways—a topic covered in the "Ecological Forces" section that follows. Meanwhile, a few brief examples of the land- and water-based threats involved in climate change paint a disturbing picture:

Land-Based Threats

Deforestation: The mass destruction of rainforests and other wooded areas releases more CO_2 into the atmosphere as trees are cut down and destroys the carbon "sinks" that absorb CO_2 in the photosynthetic process.[2] The carnage is breathtaking: between 1990 and 2015, trees covering an estimated 129 million hectares (about 320 million acres)—a space roughly the size of South Africa—were chopped down. In addition to the atmospheric threat, the impacts on the topography were devastating.

Desertification and Topsoil Erosion: The transformation of arable land to deserts or wastelands through climate change and unsustainable agricultural and forestry practices continues unabated. The conundrum of feeding a growing population on a shrinking base of productive land is sobering. The desertification process is particularly severe in northern China and large parts of Africa. The erosion of productive topsoil is widespread and puts a tremendous strain on agricultural production and water supply.

Permafrost Melts: Vast areas of permafrost in Siberia, Canada, and Alaska, frozen for thousands of years, are now thawing and releasing huge quantities of methane and carbon dioxide. The high heat-retaining characteristics of methane will exacerbate GHG buildups.

Water-Based Threats

Saltwater Degradation: Our oceans and seas are huge carbon sinks that absorb heat and CO2. Ocean temperatures are rising, and NASA estimates that the acidity of surface ocean waters has increased by about 30 percent since the first industrial revolution. Rising acidification prompted by excessive CO2 buildups and other human offenses contribute heavily in turn to coral reef destruction, undermining life-giving ecological systems vital to marine life. Over time, the ocean's circulatory conveyor belt—thermohaline circulation—could be compromised, with devastating effects on Earth's weather.

Fresh-Water Challenges: As the planet warms and draws more water into the atmosphere through evaporation, ice melts, and altered hydrologic patterns, weather patterns are becoming more severe. As conditions escalate, larger areas will face the increasingly severe and costly effects of too much or too little water, in the form of floods and droughts. Decreased snowmelt at higher altitudes— with a commensurate loss of runoff to the regions below—will exacerbate the problems of massive water-starved populations. As one example, a severe decrease in levels of Himalayan runoff, which currently provides drinking water for over 40 percent of the world's population, could result in catastrophic losses of human life.

E-3.2: Ecological Forces

Question: What do a 747 passenger jet, Otis elevators, and Tylenol bottles have in common?

Answer: They all have warning labels that state the maximum levels at which they can be safely used. The 747-400, for instance, lists a gross takeoff weight of about 830,000 pounds; an Otis elevator posts a capacity limit of, say, twelve passengers; and Tylenol admonishes users not to take more than twelve pills per day. In effect, they all say, "This is the carrying capacity of our product. If you exceed this limit, you will do so at your own peril." The greater the extension beyond the threshold, the greater the risk.

Our planet also has a finite carrying capacity, though the exact numbers and mix of species is unclear. As a mega-system, Earth has a finite supply of fixed resources, such as land, water, and minerals, along with a regenerative supply of food, recyclable water, renewable energy, and other resources, within certain parameters and constraints.

In a perfect world, our planet maintains an equilibrium in which its resources and supportive systems operate at optimal efficiency and in balance with the requirements of its human population. But this is not a perfect world. Anthropogenic forces are skewing the balance, disrupting the equilibrium, damaging eco-support systems, and exploiting finite resources in an unsustainable manner. It will be difficult to reverse this troublesome trajectory.

Our insatiable appetites for growth are colliding with Earth's capacity to sustain life at the levels we have come to expect. Through technology, heavy expenditures of energy and capital, and a relentless assault on our finite resources—from oil to aquifers—we have kept the ecological Ponzi scheme going. In this zero-sum game, the first to lose are often underdeveloped nations without the capacity to adapt, but the immutable laws of supply and demand will eventually catch up with everyone.

This section focuses on the forces leaving the heaviest ecological footprint and includes a growing global population with an aging demographic, rising levels of per-capita consumption, and wasteful and destructive behaviors. This troubling trifecta presses hard against our planet's capacity to sustain growth. Our ecological footprint is taking a toll, and our days of drawing down on our future to support our unsustainable ways are limited. The IOUs are already coming due.

It isn't rocket science and shouldn't come as a surprise. Over two hundred years ago, Thomas Malthus, an English scholar, sounded the alarm in his 1798 book *An Essay on the Principle of Population,* in which he claimed that the population would increase faster than food supply and would end in disaster unless some form of constraint was implemented to reverse the trend. His warnings may have been premature, given that the population in his time was only about one-eighth its current size, and the new technologies, energy sources, and fertilizers that allowed for soaring agricultural production were not yet discovered, but he understood the delicate balance between human consumption and Earth's finite carrying capacity.

As we watch the forces of growth collide with our finite capacity to support it and then factor in the ecological damage we are inflicting to perpetuate it, we can begin to appreciate the devastating impact of our ecological footprint. Consider just three:

Population Growth and Changing Demographics

Throughout human history, the population growth rate has been slow, but steady. The huge spike over the past 60 years bears little resemblance to growth patterns of the past. The human population did not reach one billion until the early 1800s. It took another 127 years to reach two billion in 1927 and 33 years to reach the three-billion mark in 1960. But then, in just the last four decades of the twentieth century, the population doubled to over six billion people, a massive number of new mouths to feed, clothe, educate, employ, and assimilate into our global society.

Chart 5.3: Global Population

Years Passed	Year	Pop. in Billions
—	1800	1
127	1927	2
33	1960	3
14	1974	4
13	1987	5
12	1999	6
12	2011	7

Source: UNFPA

Current estimates suggest the population will climb to about 9.7 billion people in 2050 from a level of 7.4 billion in 2016. About 60 percent of the global population lives in Asia; 16 percent in Africa; 10 percent in Europe; 9 percent in Latin America and the remaining 5 percent in North America. While the largest growth rates are occurring in underdeveloped nations, the lower increases in developed nations are offset by their higher per-capita consumption rates and oversized ecological footprints.

The second part of the population challenge is an aging demographic. In earlier times, young children greatly outnumbered their elders; fertility rates were high, and life expectancies were low. The inverse has occurred in many nations over the last few decades: fertility rates are lower and life expectancy greatly extended.

As one measure, the global median age—the age at which half the world's population is older and the other half younger—climbed from 23.5 years in 1950 to 29.6 years in 2015. Estimates are that it will increase to 33.1 years by 2030. The median age varies from country to country, with a current high of 46.5 years in Japan and a low of 14.8 years in Niger. The median age in the United States climbed from 30 years in 1950 to 38 years in 2015. Percentagewise, the fastest-growing age group in the world is the oldest—those 80 years or older.

The implications are dramatic. Economically, it will impact growth, savings, productivity, and utilization of healthcare and pension benefits. With fewer active employees supporting a larger base of retirees, the discretionary purchasing power of a younger citizenry will be dampened. In the United States, where roughly ten thousand baby boomers retire daily, the intergenerational impacts will be profound. China recognized the demographic time bomb of its 1979 one-child-per-family policy and initiated a two-child family policy in 2015 to bring more young people into their population mix. Japan's situation is the most severe of all developed nations, creating a long-term threat to their economy.

Per-Capita Consumption Levels

The carrying capacity of our planet has its limits. Though those limits are difficult to predict with precision, ecologists have micro-modeled our per-capita bioconsumption levels and waste patterns and tracked them against the planet's biological capacity and ability to replenish resources and absorb waste. Our ecological footprint—the amount of nature it takes to support people—can then be tallied to provide a rudimentary ecological accounting system.

The Global Footprint Network—an independent think tank specializing in our global ecological footprint—estimated in 2016 that it would take the equivalent of 1.6 Earths to sustain current consumption levels. Put another way, we are using up resources at a rate that is 1.6 times greater than the rate of replenishment. Once nonrenewable resources, such as fossil fuels and minerals, are gone, there is no replenishment. This unsustainable trajectory will worsen as a growing population with insatiable appetites and wasteful practices continues to consume at current levels.

Fresh-water shortages pose the most immediate and perhaps greatest challenge for humankind. Simply put, it is the one indispensable resource for which there are no substitutes. While about 70 percent of Earth is covered by water, only 2.5 percent of it is fresh-water. Of this amount, less than 1 percent of it is easily accessible, and it is unevenly distributed throughout the world. Roughly 70 percent of all useable water is used for agricultural production, 20 percent for industrial purposes, and the remaining 10 percent for domestic usage. About 85 percent of the world's population lives in the driest half of the planet.

As global living standards improve, our per-capita consumption rates will climb. Richer countries will consume up to ten times more natural resources than the poorest ones, and the difficulty of fresh-water management, already a significant global challenge, will only intensify as the population increases, consumption rates climb, and expectations continue to rise.

Waste and Destructive Behaviors

A toxic byproduct of overconsumption is the waste that is left behind. In our quest for convenience, fostered by modern technologies and globalization, our plasticized, overpackaged, throwaway culture is generating prodigious amounts of liquid, solid, and gaseous wastes that contaminate our water supply, gorge our landfills, and pollute the air we breathe. A considerable amount of energy and resources are expended just to remediate the toxic effects.

Our concrete urban jungles fail to capture and retain rainwater, sending it downstream instead in a more polluted form. Our crumbling pumping and distribution infrastructures—a la Flint, Michigan—are aging and leaking, and waste and contaminated water from farming, sewage, and industrial processing are now reaching crisis proportions in many areas. We have a serious domestic problem, but the water problems in underdeveloped countries are far worse. At least a third of the world's population lives with an inadequate supply of sanitized water, leaving them exposed to cholera, typhoid, and other waterborne diseases. The pollution of our oceans is reaching crisis proportions as well.

Solid waste from food, overpackaging, manufacturing, and other industrial processing, as well our preoccupation with "stuff," is filling and often contaminating our landfills. It is estimated that solid wastes have increased tenfold over the past five decades and are projected to double by 2025. While waste management and demand-reduction efforts are easy targets in our quest for sustainable growth, and efforts to create zero-waste systems, along with strong grassroots efforts to repair, recycle, and reuse, are gaining traction, waste will continue to compromise the carrying capacity of our planet.

Air pollution is the third leg of the pollution stool, and a deadly one it is. The World Health Organization (WHO)—a UN agency specializing in international public health—calls it a global health emergency. The United Nations estimates that more than 3.3 million people—a lowball estimate compared to many others—die prematurely from air pollution, and the medical and economic costs are staggering. The WHO estimates that only one in eight people live

THE PERFECT STORM PRIMER · 71

in cities that meet recommended air-pollution levels. The cumulative impact of breathing in ozone, nitrous oxide, pollens, dust, and a toxic mix of smog or smoke from wildfires has yet to be fully appreciated. While the stats are alarming, it often takes a visual event to awaken the public.

One such event occurred during the 2008 Beijing Olympic Games, perhaps the most polluted Olympic Games ever witnessed. Despite draconian efforts by the Chinese government to reduce pollution prior to the games by restricting car usage, shutting down factories, and slowing construction projects, the optics were terrible. The athletes and spectators were exposed to air-pollution levels that exceeded safety limits throughout the event, and billions of global television viewers caught a glimpse of the festering ecological Armageddon that awaits, should we decline an aggressive response.

The mass extinction of nonhuman species—plants, animals, fish, fowl, and other species all up and down the food chain—is a work in progress. Some have dubbed it the sixth wave of extinctions to occur over the past half-billion years, and this one—unlike the meteorites, volcanoes, or floods that triggered past extinctions—is of an anthropogenic nature. Simply put, climate change and the destruction of habitats now exceed the speed at which many ecosystems and species can adapt or replenish. Once they are gone, they're gone.

There is now a growing movement in the scientific community to designate a new geological period based on humankind's influence on Earth and its species: the Anthropocene Epoch. The name is derived from the Greek word *anthropo,* meaning "human," and *cene,* meaning "new" or "recent." The very fact that it is being considered speaks volumes about the growing impact of our human footprint. The environmental and ecological threats covered in this chapter barely scratch the surface, but they are more than enough to warrant the name.

In later chapters, we will explore many of the contentious ecological and environmental threats and policy issues now confronting us:

- Intergenerational actions: short-term "fixes" versus long-term, sustainable solutions

- Nationalistic versus global approaches to planetary challenges

- Optimal balancing of energy, economic, ecological, and environmental forces

- Agricultural production and the morality of using crops for fuel and not food

- Fresh-water conflicts and the conundrums they will trigger

- Climate mitigation or adaptation strategies and their fight for attention

- Geopolitical flash points in a titanic clash for scarce resources

Summary: Environmental and Ecological Forces

The insidious and aggressive growth of climate change has now escalated into an existential threat. The threat is aggravated by our wasteful and destructive ecological practices. Taken together, environmental and ecological forces land a toxic one-two punch that will significantly contribute to the perfect storm.

1. **Climate change is increasingly recognized as an existential threat.**

   - It is growing aggressively at rates now exceeding earlier projections and expectations.

   - It is observable and quantifiable, no longer a product of abstract computer models.

- We are approaching tipping points, and the time remaining for dramatic turnaround actions is limited.

2. **Climate change is a metaphorical equivalent to a chronic disease—on a massive scale.**

   - Its insidious growth conceals its systematic degradation of the planet's organic systems.

   - Dangerous feedback loops are hastening its exponential development.

   - Its impacts, now widely felt, will intensify further at great cost and peril to humankind.

3. **An ecological tsunami is co-occurring with climate change; threat levels are rising.**

   - A growing population, overconsumption patterns, and wasteful practices are contributors.

   - Pollution of air, water, and land and depletion of resources are exacerbating conditions.

   - Ecological destruction of plant, sea, and animal life will endanger global food chains.

4. **Environmental and ecological degradation are threat multipliers to humankind.**

   - Climate change and resource shortages will be increasingly disruptive to societies.

   - Fresh-water and food shortages are becoming immediate threat multipliers.

   - The economic costs of adaptation to storms, fires, droughts, and floods will skyrocket.

- The quality of life will suffer, and public unrest and disruption will intensify.

5. **Our application of linear thinking to exponential risks in these areas puts us in jeopardy.**

   - Solutions cannot be found in quick fixes; concerted long-term efforts are required.

   - The clock is ticking, and our lack of progress is further aggravating the problem.

   - The consequences of inaction are too awful to imagine: will we awaken to the call?

6

Expectations and Behaviors

Change is inevitable. Growth is optional.

—John Maxwell

Life is a continuum, and change, an integral part of it, is not always embraced. We cling to cherished times and resist unwanted intrusions upon them. One such beloved paradigm is the American Dream and its vision of unlimited opportunity and promise of a better life. It was almost a given that the standard of living for each successive generation would be better than that of its parents. It was hard not to be optimistic about such a future.

But alas, dreams end, and we awaken to the hard realities of life. Some bubbles, like the Great Recession in 2008, burst abruptly. Though painful at the time, it at least had an identifiable beginning and end, with targetable solutions in between. The more insidious bubbles spring slow leaks that can take years, decades, or even generations to play out, their beginnings and ends blurred by a mushy middle that puts us in a twilight zone of transitional uncertainties.

Like it or not, we are now floundering in such a twilight zone. The deeper we get, the murkier it becomes. Something's not right, but what? We may choose to ignore or deny our shifting paradigm, but we can't escape it. Understandably, we cling to the familiar expectations and behaviors of the past, but the pressures on them keep building.

This is not to suggest that the American Dream has come to an end. Rather, it is a recognition that the dream enablers that made it all possible—cheap energy, abundant resources, and unlimited opportunities for growth—are eroding. As a reality check, ask a Millennial with a mountain of student-loan debt and a questionable job market how they feel about their access to the American Dream, and you are likely to discover it falls far short of the expectations of previous generations.

When our political leaders proclaim that "our greatest days are still ahead of us," are they defining "greatest" as a continuation of the American Dream we have always known? If so, do they really believe it? Further, is this the only measuring stick we can use to define greatness?

Let's be clear: though our American Dream is morphing into something different from what we have known, it does not have to be a guaranteed plunge into the abyss. To be sure, it will require a shift in our thinking and recalibration of our expectations and behaviors toward a new reality based on doing more with less, but the shift is not necessarily bad, only different.

This chapter examines the fourth E-Cell of our perfect storm model: Expectations and Behaviors. We will examine some of the structural mechanisms that have shaped our lifestyles and suggest how even small, incremental changes can magnify intergenerational outcomes over the course of several decades. Further, it provides a continuum of changing realities from the present to the future and a list of eight game-changing megatrends that will shape our future.

As we look at the past, compare it to the present, and then project how our expectations and behaviors might stack up against future realities, we will see a widening gap that will make our encounter with the perfect storm that much more difficult. In this effort, we will be looking at three things: generational branding, paradigm shift mechanics, and the new paradigm.

Generational Branding: Every generation has been endowed with unique timeframes, challenges, demographics, cultural norms, seminal events, and trends that brand it with a distinctive DNA. This genetic code is constantly shaped by circumstances and passed on as a new norm to succeeding generations. We need to understand the DNA of previous generations to truly understand our own, and a brief generational summary is provided in chart 6.1 to aid in making the comparisons.

With this context in mind, we will focus on the unique brands and shifting behavioral paradigms of four generational cohorts, with reference to two others. The four main cohorts will be the Silent Generation, born between 1928 and 1945; the baby boomers, born between 1946 and 1964; Generation X, born between 1965 and 1980; and the Millennials, born between 1981 and 2000. Two generations bookend this foursome: The Greatest Generation, those born before 1928, and Generation Z, born in the twenty-first century. Chart 6.1: Generational Branding provides a thumbnail sketch of the four main generations discussed here.

The chart provides only a rough approximation of each generation. The timeframe for each varies by sociologist, as do the key events and attributes assigned to that generation. In addition, the views and life experiences of individuals vary by virtue of their chronological placement within their generational cohort. For instance, a baby boomer born in 1946 will see the world differently from one born in 1964. Nonetheless, the chart provides a helpful starting point. The following synopsis will help describe the transitional process within all six cohorts.

Chart 6.1: Generational Branding

Generation	Silent	Baby Boomers	Gen X	Millennials
Birth Years	1928–1945	1946–1964	1965–1980	1981–2000
Population in 2015	28 million	75 million	66 million	75 million
Key Events	Depression WWII Atomic Age	Cold War Space Age Vietnam War	Watergate Civil Rights Social Unrest	Digital Age Globalization Internet
Family	Traditional	Dispersed Divorces up	Two-parent Workers Latchkey kids	Blended families Looser structures
Attitude toward Authority	Respectful	Impressed	Unimpressed	Relaxed
Technology	Cope with it	Master it	Enjoy it	Employ it
Work Style	Hard work Duty Loyalty	Workaholics Team players	Entrepreneurial Skeptical	Participatory Balanced
Money	Save Pay cash	Play now, pay later	Hedge it Be cautious	Earn to spend Optimistic
Education	A dream	A birthright	A means to an end	Expensive Loan debt
Core Values	Conformity Patriotic Conservative	Self-gratification Optimism Rebelliousness	Diversity Tech literacy Self-reliance	Confidence Street smarts Independence

Greatest Generation: Born before 1928, they are rapidly becoming extinct. They led the way, suffered through the Great Depression, and won World War II. Selfless, stoic, and resilient, they laid the groundwork for the American Dream, and we owe them a huge debt of gratitude.

Silent Generation: The class of 1961, born in 1943, fell into the latter part of the Silent Generation. While we didn't directly participate in the seminal events of that era, they were integral parts of our growing up, the generational DNA we inherited from our parents. The hammer-and-sickle flag of the Soviet Union, McCarthyism, and the launch of Sputnik—events framed in the ideology of the Cold War—shaped our lives and those of our close relatives, the baby boomers.

Baby Boomers: The boomers rode a tidal wave of unparalleled economic growth following World War II. The pent-up austerity of the war years erupted into an insatiable consumer buying frenzy. Good jobs, educational opportunities, and material possessions were plentiful, and boundless optimism filled the air. Young boomers were huge beneficiaries. As the boomers came of age, a touch of self-absorption and rebelliousness set in and became part of the DNA they passed on to Generation X and the Millennials.

Generation X: This post-boomer cohort was the first to feel the backlash of years of growth and excess. With both parents often working, they were the latchkey generation that came home from school to an empty house. Both the economy and political institutions—a la Watergate—were often in question, and Gen Xers sometimes experienced a greater wariness and skepticism than previous generations. They also became more self-reliant and entrepreneurial and openly embraced the flourishing technological revolution, but there were compensating balances, to be sure.

Millennials: Now the largest generation, the Millennials are the product of a digital age, globalization, terrorism, rising college-loan debts, and what many feel is coddling by concerned parents. They seek a more balanced reality between work and nonwork endeavors and are more socially aware than other generations. They live more for the moment and are, perhaps, more optimistic than warranted—though many no longer expect to live as well as their parents.

Generation Z: Born in the twenty-first century, their brand has yet to be determined. Growing up in a technological nirvana of instant messaging, artificial intelligence, and smart everything, they are technologically connected. Their quest for instant information and the manner in which they receive and process information will undoubtedly help shape their future brand. Many will be first-time voters in the 2020 election.

As we move forth in the third decade of the twenty-first century, the American Dream of old is being challenged. The incremental changes and trajectories of previous generations have altered the playing field, and we are now caught somewhere between the good old days and the vast unknown ahead. Floundering in this twilight zone, many are befuddled, disconnected, and at odds with what the future may hold. Fortunately, we can take some of the mystery out of this by understanding how a paradigm shift works.

Paradigm Shift Mechanics

The *American Heritage Dictionary* describes a *paradigm* in part as "a set of assumptions, concepts, values, and practices that constitute a way of viewing reality for the community that shares them, especially in an intellectual discipline." A shift in paradigms constitutes a move from an old to a new order, and these transitions, manifested through smaller incremental changes, are often difficult to recognize. The scope and complexity of the changes, the triggering events that set them in motion, and the duration of the transition will vary. For example, an individual can immediately identify and feel the changes triggered by something like a divorce, loss of job, relocation, or death of a loved one. Though difficult, there is little doubt that a transition has taken place. Generational, demographic, and cultural paradigm shifts are more subtle and of longer duration, and the cause-and-effect forces driving them are less easy to detect. We will focus for now on this latter category.

Despite variances in the types of transitional shifts, there is common ground in their structural mechanics. The following authors, respected authorities on the dynamics of personal, cultural, and demographic changes, offer interesting insights on the topic. Consider the following vignettes:

In *The Next America: Boomers, Millennials, and the Looming Generational Showdown* (New York: BBS Public Affairs, 2014), author Paul Taylor, with the Pew Research Center, writes, "Demographic transformations are dramas in slow motion. They unfold incrementally, almost imperceptibly, tick by tock, without trumpets or press conferences. But every so often, as the weight of change builds, a society takes a hard look at itself and notices that things are different. The 'aha' moments are rare and revealing."

William Bridges, in *Transitions: Making Sense of Life's Changes* (Boston: Addison-Wesley, 1997), gets at the importance of process and awareness: "In human life, as in the rest of nature, change accumulates slowly and almost invisibly until it is made manifest in the sudden form of fledging out or thawing or leaf-fall. It is the transition process rather than a thing called a mid-life transition that we must understand."

The inevitability of change and the need for a transitional process to accommodate it is evident in the above passages. While transitions are often messy and unpredictable, an understanding of the process will help eliminate some of the ambiguity. The structural underpinnings of almost every paradigm shift include four major parts:

1. Base reality: The foundational starting point for measuring a paradigm shift

2. Triggering event: The occurrence that sets off the move to a new order

3. Transition process: The series of shifts taking us from one reality to the next

4. New reality: The arrival into a new paradigm and the solidification efforts that follow

Before reviewing each phase, it is important to know that the very act of sorting a life event or trend into one of four buckets is, in itself, a giant step toward increasing our level of awareness and getting positioned for the steps that are likely to follow. Now, let's take a closer look at the key phases.

Base Reality: First, we need a baseline paradigm from which future shifts can be measured. Paradigm changes can more easily be seen in the rearview mirror than at the time of occurrence. Hence, in measuring change, it is best to allow for a longer gestation period through which events and trends can be tracked. The start date could be the beginning of the new millennium, the decade in which the reader was born, or, in the case of this book, the birth year of the class of '61, which is 1943.

After establishing a reference point, the next step is to map out the metrics that will be used to plot shifts based on what it is we want to measure. For example, to track climate change, metrics such as global temperatures and the carbon ppm level should be included. The seven-point methodology for identifying and tracking events and metrics outlined in chapter 2 provides a model for constructing transitional metrics.

Triggering Events: With a baseline reference point and a sense of direction established, the diagnostic process of working backward to locate and identify the key triggering mechanisms becomes easier. Unlike personal transitions, which are often triggered by a singular event, generational changes are triggered by colliding events that multiply and subdivide, like the cellular process within the human body. For example, baby boomers' generational experiences were partially shaped by the Cuban missile crisis, the civil rights movement, and the first moon landing, each event a single outcome of larger social and civic processes. The missile crisis brought home the gut reality that a nuclear holocaust was a distinct possibility, the civil rights movement changed the tone and character of our nation, and the moon landing opened a vast new arena of exploration never before imagined. Over time, these event algorithms transmuted distinctive features that helped create future trends.

Transition Process: The journey from point A to point B involves three general steps:

- Develop a sense of awareness of the change, where we are in the transition, and the need for action to complete the transition.

- Respond to the need for change with practical solutions, seeking singles rather than grand slams and working with others for greater leverage.

- Recognize that change is difficult and that resilience, flexibility, and acceptance of the things we cannot change are our best tools.

New Reality: At the completion of the paradigm shift, we accept and enter the new paradigm. The new reality will arrive whether we want it or not: if we stumbled through the process, unwilling and resistant, we will be poorly prepared for the inevitable. However, if we have navigated the transition process with intention, we will be well positioned to move forward.

The New Paradigm and the Perfect Storm

Yogi Berra is reputed to have said, "It's tough to make predictions, especially about the future," and this certainly applies to predicting the new paradigm that will follow the perfect storm. Still, we can make educated guesses, and have done so in chart 6.2: The Continuum of Realities. It highlights the changes we might see using a before-and-after format that purposely contrasts potential extremes. Statistically, the likely outcomes probably lie somewhere in between.

The long-term picture becomes clearer when we review a timeframe of several generations. It enables us to plot out the trajectories with greater accuracy and extrapolate their future pathways. The shifts in expectations and behaviors outlined demonstrate the widening gap between our perceptions and the new realities that are rapidly emerging. The snapshot of current to future realities and the list of eight megatrends that follow show the forces that are already shaping our expectations and behaviors.

Chart 6.2: The Continuum of Realities

Current Realities	Potential Future Realities
Globalization	Deglobalization
Dollar-based reserve currency	Gold and hard assets the new reserve
National debt—controllable	Red ink; a catastrophic anchor on growth
Growing economic prosperity	Economic stagnation and decline
Rising standards of living	Declining standards, perhaps severe
Entitlement safety nets	Significant cutbacks; loss of safety nets
Cheap and abundant natural resources	Resource scarcities (e.g., water)
Global population growth	Population ages and declines (famines, wars)
Global health somewhat adequate	Health pandemics (drug-resistant microbes)
Growth-oriented mindsets	Downsizing, downscaling, and rightsizing reign
Complex; automated systems	Regression to simpler systems
Fossil-fuel energy systems	Renewables with a demand-reduction focus
Unlimited mobility	Constricted mobility (costs and resources)
Growing suburbs and exurbs	Migration to city hubs (public transit, water)
Vehicle-oriented transportation	Public transit, rail, and bikes
Decline of rural America	Migration back to crop-producing farmlands
Global/national economic focus	Regional and local economic focus
Mega-agricultural systems	Smaller farms for local/regional production
Luxurious, throwaway culture	Back to basics: reuse, recycle, and repair
System-based dependencies	Greater self-reliance (new skill sets needed)
American Dream still strong	Dream recalibrated, scaled back, and downsized

Do not focus too much on these projected worst-case scenarios. Instead, consider the transitional process that could lead to them. Humankind could exercise a number of actions to mitigate many of the sharper edges, a topic covered in Part III of this book.

Many future realities are based on the fact that nations will compete for fewer resources. There will be a growing divide between have and have-not nations and divisions within their respective populations. Loss of opportunity, dwindling natural resources, and a mountain of debt will collectively work to limit the choices, mobility, lifestyles, and safety nets for large segments of the population. Harsh realities will drive what we do and how and where we do it until we finally learn how to do more with less. It will be a huge cultural shock, and the process of adaptation will be long and hard.

No one said it would be easy; paradigm shifts never are. In her book *New Passages: Mapping Your Life across Time* (New York: Random House, 1995), Gail Sheehy equates the vulnerability of people transitioning through a new stage in life to that of lobsters shedding their protective shells to grow: "We, too, in each passage from one stage of human growth to the next, must shed a protective structure. We, too, are left exposed and vulnerable—but also yeasty and embryonic again. At such points, we enjoy a 'heightened potential' for making a real stretch of growth. But we can also fall back, lose ground, give up, or simply ignore the impulse to change and remain stuck in our shells. Whatever we do, the future will be rendered better or worse but, in any case, restructured."

Eight Megatrends

The following eight megatrends—each in different stages of development—are currently interacting with one another and producing new mutations that will shape our behaviors and expectations for decades to come. Each trend closes with a prognosis that suggests future movement.

1. **Climate Change:** The rapid buildup of atmospheric GHGs is intensifying, and the impacts are becoming more pronounced. Climate-induced droughts, floods, rising sea levels, and natural disasters are occurring with greater frequency and severity, becoming threat multipliers across a large spectrum of the globe. *Looking ahead, without an all-out effort to meaningfully address climate change now, we will soon reach tipping points that will render it irreversible.*

2. **Ecological Footprints:** The world's finite supply of fresh-water, arable land, and other physical and natural

resources is bumping against an unsustainable demand curve. Wasteful behaviors and lavish consumption patterns exacerbate the threat. *Looking ahead, our ability to recalibrate expectations, change behaviors, and reduce our ecological footprint may be the only viable alternative left to address this challenge. The outcome is in question.*

3. **Population:** The global population has more than doubled over the past half century, and its demographics are shifting. The increases are straining our planet's capacity to sustain life as we know it and threatening the social systems that provide for a needier population. *Looking ahead, with a growing and aging population, there is little margin left in the system for contingencies; the physical and financial strains on our carrying capacity will become severe, frequent, and destabilizing.*

4. **Energy:** The endless demand for energy is coinciding with a gradual shift from legacy fuel systems to renewable and alternative energy systems—all part of a growing new energy renaissance. Climate change and the quest for cleaner fuels will accelerate the process. *Looking ahead, the challenge of transitioning away from one mainstream energy system to another without major economic disruptions is daunting. The move from our oil-based transportation system could become a race against time if finite oil supply can no longer meet demand.*

5. **Global Economy:** The global economy has evolved into an intertwined network of interdependent systems. With massive debt, fewer protective international firewalls, and a massive debt bubble of unfunded entitlement liabilities coming due in the United States and elsewhere, the threat of a global meltdown is escalating. *Looking ahead, bursting economic bubbles, sovereign debt defaults, trade wars, or even an unforeseen black swan event could trigger a chain*

reaction leading to a global economic meltdown that dwarfs the Great Recession of 2008.

6. **Geopolitical:** Global power structures are rapidly changing as we plunge into a new cold war fought over the control of scarce resources and markets. With China as the newest superpower and the spread of nationalistic movements, the playing field has changed. The specter of nuclear proliferation, asymmetric warfare, and a dangerous new arms race will add to the destabilization. *Looking ahead, geopolitical flash points are intensifying and taking us into uncharted waters; the world has become a more dangerous place in which to live. The threats of miscalculations—with unintended consequences—are escalating.*

7. **Technology:** The digital revolution, quest for connectivity, artificial intelligence, robotics, quantum computing, 3-D printing, and smart everything has changed the way we work, think, play, and interact with others. Our inability to adjust to rapidly changing technologies in a timely manner has created a new set of challenges as we enter the fourth industrial revolution. *Looking ahead, the challenges of cybersecurity, privacy issues, national security, and technological disruptions—natural or otherwise—are formidable. Worksite mismatches between the new technological skill sets needed and those available will pose an ongoing challenge to future economic growth.*

8. **The American Dream:** The American Dream—now a global aspiration—was based on abundant resources, cheap energy, economic opportunities, a can-do spirit, and rising expectations. As expectations continue to rise and clash with a diminished capacity to provide, the dream we knew is at risk. *Looking ahead, the great unknown will be in our resilience and ability to adapt once the dream enablers no longer support our expectations. Our future hangs in the balance.*

Summary: Expectations and Behavioral Forces

Our expectations and behaviors shape and are shaped by the world we live in, and the paradigm shifts—large and small—that frequently occur have common characteristics. An understanding of them will help us to weather the storm.

1. **Every generation has a unique brand that best describes its circumstances.**

   - It provides an approximate DNA that helps frame and identify generational dynamics.

   - It carries with it the general expectations and behaviors of its generational cohort.

   - In a state of constant change, it provides a baseline for each respective generation.

   - The degree of change will intensify as we grow nearer to the perfect storm.

2. **The process of transition has definable, but destabilizing, characteristics.**

   - Paradigm shifts from one set of norms to another are, by nature, destabilizing.

   - A murky process, the transition leaves us in periods of uncertainty.

   - An understanding of the dynamics will ease, but not eliminate, the process.

   - The transitional time period will vary based on the complexity of change.

3. **The quality of our pre–perfect storm planning will directly impact our chances.**

   - The planning tools and forecasts provided in this chapter will facilitate planning.

   - The sooner we awaken to the threat and act, the better our chances.

   - Our ability to face reality as it is and act with resiliency is critical.

   - Willingness to recalibrate our expectations and behaviors is crucial.

4. **The new realities following the paradigm shift will be severe and daunting.**

   - The Continuum of Realities and Eight Megatrends provided offer a glimpse of potential futures.

   - An awareness of current and future expectations and behaviors will help the outcome.

   - Our adaptability can be enhanced by understanding transitional dynamics.

   - Our capacity to change and adapt will be crucial.

PART II

Pathway to the Perfect Storm

What is past is prologue.

—William Shakespeare

The perfect storm has been building for decades, but we have missed the signs and ignored the warnings. The thought of anything so menacing was simply beyond our imagination. How could it happen? Where will it take us? Part II will explore these issues and more.

Shakespeare's claim that "what is past is prologue" suggests we can learn from the past. We will test his assertion in Part II as we longitudinally track, on a decade-by-decade basis, both the perfect storm and the assault on the American Dream from infancy to the existential threats that they pose today.

As we examine seemingly random events with a focused eye on connectivity, we will begin to see the damage done in each progressive decade and how it contributed to the perfect storm and the stifling mortgage that we continue to take on the American Dream. The change differentials become far more visible when viewed over a long span of time.

History suggests that we have consistently glossed over the important things with our fixation on the here and now. Worse, our myopic preoccupation with painless, quick-fix solutions has done little to address our deeper challenges, which have grown into a deep-rooted system that will be difficult to weed out.

The storm clouds are already gathering. By taking a long, hard look at how this looming storm developed, we can learn from the past and find constructive strategies to mitigate its sharper edges, a topic covered more fully in Part III. Perhaps, in the process, we may even find ways to curtail future mortgages on the American Dream so that those following us will have a better chance for a better future.

We'll see.

-7-

The 1940s

Remember Pearl Harbor

I n the wee hours of January 1, 1943, the first of more than 2.9 million babies born in America—future members of the class of '61—took a first breath. We entered the scene, as war babies, during a crucial time in America's titanic struggle with fascism; the outcome was still in question, and we finished the decade as newly minted first graders just learning to read.

The total population of the United States in 1943 was about 136.7 million people, and more than 15 million of them would wear the uniform of their country at some point in the war. Those not fighting often served in a critical war industry or farmed, and millions of women not in the armed forces worked in factories to produce a prodigious amount of military arms and supplies, making America the "arsenal of democracy" that President Franklin D. Roosevelt had proclaimed it to be.

Within months, following the attack on Pearl Harbor on December 7, 1941, America had breathtakingly transformed its entire economy from a peacetime to wartime footing. The production of consumer goods was put on hold as plants and industries were redirected toward producing tanks, planes, ships, cannons, ammunition, railroad cars, and other wartime goods. In addition to equipping our own armed forces, we were also major military suppliers and food producers for our allies.

Engaged in a cause greater than ourselves, the war effort superseded personal hardships and deprivations. The list of rationed goods and services was long: gasoline, rubber, sugar, meats, canned goods, shoes, and a vast array of consumer products and services. Personal savings were redirected into war bonds, and household metals were collected and melted down to produce weapons of war. Patriotic movies filled the theaters, and trains, ships, and planes carried our troops to bases throughout the country and around the world.

In this wartime environment, it was commonplace for the newborns of 1943 and their siblings to find Dad off fighting the war and Mom holding down a wartime job while caring for the family as best she could between work shifts. Air-raid drills and nighttime blackouts were routine protocols, and listening to the news on the radio embedded in a large console in the living room was a regular part of each day.

As infants, we had no clue about the draconian efforts underway to mobilize and transform an entire economy almost overnight. It meant recruiting, training, and equipping the largest and most powerful armed forces in the world, inventing the atomic bomb, producing a massive fleet of B-29 bombers that could carry it, and building the mightiest naval armada in history. The gargantuan effort to organize the cohesive military-industrial complex that won the war was accomplished within a span of only forty-four months following the attack on Pearl Harbor.

President Roosevelt was deep into his third term in office as the class of '61 entered the world in 1943. The average life expectancy was 62.9 years, and the number of Americans collecting Social Security benefits—a program that was only eight years old at the time—was minuscule.

On the home front, *Casablanca* captured the Academy Award for best picture in 1943, and Bob Hope and many other stars entertained our troops all over the world. Though consumer goods and food products were rationed, a loaf of bread cost a dime, a gallon of milk cost 62 cents, and a gallon of gas went for 15 cents. The average income was $2,041, and an average new house cost about $3,600. America acclimated to a full wartime footing well before Christmas 1942.

The war started to turn against the Axis powers in 1943, though the news was still touch-and-go. The German Wehrmacht was pushed out of North Africa; Mussolini was deposed and Italy surrendered in 1943. The American Eighth Air Force efforts to bomb Nazi Germany and challenge the German Luftwaffe over the skies of Europe picked up steam. The Russians were heavily engaged in gargantuan infantry and tank battles on the eastern front, and America began its counteroffensive in the Pacific theater of war. Following the crushing Japanese naval defeat at Midway in 1942, Guadalcanal was taken and the Marine Corps started its island-hopping campaign with the bloody battle of Tarawa in the Gilbert Islands, an effort, made concurrently with General MacArthur's advance through the Philippines, that would culminate in the bloody battles of Iwo Jima and Okinawa prior to the war's end.

Though the war news delivered in the ten-minute headline news briefs in local theaters improved, the twenty months remaining in the war at the start of 1944 were a tough slog. By war's end, more than four hundred thousand Americans had been killed in action. All told, more than forty-eight million people are estimated to have been killed—far more by some estimates—in World War II, the greatest conflict ever experienced by humankind.

The Germans surrendered on May 7, 1945. Following the dropping of atomic bombs on Hiroshima and Nagasaki on August 6 and 9 respectively, and the Soviet Union's declaration of war and subsequent attack on Japanese-held Manchuria on August 9, the Japanese gave notice that they would surrender on August 15. The formal surrender of Japan, on the deck of the battleship USS *Missouri*, took place on September 2, 1945, and the massive challenge of rebuilding a war-torn world began in earnest. Europe was in shambles, the Soviet Union heavily damaged, and Germany and Japan devastated. China was engaged in a civil war that was ultimately won by the communist forces of Mao Tse-tung. The British Empire was spent, and the United States emerged as the only unscathed great power.

The Greatest Generation—those born before 1928—fought and won the war. The Silent Generation, of which we in the class of '61 were tail-end members, were young bystanders, and the baby boomers born after the war were recipients of the prosperity that followed. Clearly, a debt of gratitude will always be owed to the Greatest Generation for their remarkable efforts in winning the war so soon after surviving the Great Depression.

Captain Robert L. Wieman was one of the more than fifteen million Americans in uniform, and his story, while not unique, reflects the can-do spirit of the Greatest Generation. He was a fighter-bomber pilot in the Pacific theater of war and was stationed in Japan immediately following the war as part of the Allied occupation forces. In the "Reflections and Profiles" sidebar below, Bob shares his story with a special emphasis on one of the great controversies following the war: should we have dropped atomic bombs on Japan?

Robert L. Wieman

Bob Wieman was in trouble. While landing his P-38 fighter plane at Clark Field in Manila, his left engine quit just short of touchdown. He immediately chopped power in his right engine to stabilize the plane just enough for a crash landing that tore off the landing gear at the nose and left-wing positions and half of the left wing. A fuel tank ruptured, flooding the cockpit with gas. The twisted airframe made the exit from the cockpit difficult, but Bob survived thanks to his quick actions, good luck, fate, or whatever. Though the plane was totaled, Bob impishly wrote in his debrief report, "Check landing gear—last landing was rougher than normal."

In a larger sense, Bob's near-fatal crash reflected the stoicism of the Greatest Generation. They had lived through so much in the Great Depression, with its dust bowl droughts, economic misery, and sky-high unemployment rates. Adversity was almost a way of life, and, like Bob at the control of his plane, they didn't waste time bemoaning their plight; they just dealt with it.

Bob's life was forever changed when, as an eleven-year-old farm boy, he was treated to a ride in a World War I Curtiss Jenny biplane at the county fair. A transformational experience, Bob knew from that time on that he wanted to fly—and not farm—but who could afford flying lessons during the Depression? No credit cards, no cash, no flying; it was as simple as that.

Japan changed all that on December 7, 1941, at Pearl Harbor. Overnight, the recruiting stations were filled with young men and women eager to enlist, not look for deferments. A sense of duty and patriotism was part of the Greatest Generation's DNA, and Bob fit the mold, enlisting in the Army Air Corps Pilot Training Program while still a student at Gustavus Adolphus College. After a long and intense period of flight training, Bob earned his wings and was assigned to the hottest bombers in our nation's arsenal, including the B-25 Mitchell bomber, the B-26 Marauder, and the A-26 Invader. The war needs were great, and flight training was hazardous. Bob lost good friends in training accidents and had a few close calls of his own.

Assigned to the Fifth Air Force, 319th Bomb Group, 90th Squadron, in the Pacific, Bob's final assignment—providing tactical air support for ground forces invading Japan—was scratched with the surrender of Japan following the A-bomb drops on Hiroshima and Nagasaki. Shortly after, Bob was stationed at Atsugi Air Base in Japan—only miles from Mount Fujiyama—where he saw firsthand the massive defensive systems that Japan had built in preparation for an Allied invasion. In his book, *A Farm Boy Takes Flight: True Stories,* Bob wrote,

> If we had been forced to invade the Japanese mainland—and we were very close to doing that—the loss of life on both sides would have been in the millions. The system of inter-connecting caves between the Tokyo/Yokohama area that I viewed was a marvel of engineering. It would have been next to impossible to get them out alive. They would have fought to the death, as they did on most of the small Pacific islands we invaded on our way to Japan.
>
> I shudder to think of what an invasion of Japan would have been like. My A-26 attack bomber squadron was scheduled to be one of the first units to hit them in an effort to make it easier for the marines to make their landing. Had that scenario taken place, I might not be here writing this story. All I can say is I'm glad there was no invasion.

Bob mustered out of active duty in July 1946 and remained in the reserves. Like millions of returning vets, Bob spent almost a half decade of the 1940s in the military. With optimism and hope for a better future and the GI Bill, Bob completed his undergraduate degree at Gustavus Adolphus and then got his master's degree in analytical chemistry at Utah State. After working for corporate giants Baxter Laboratories and 3M, Bob retired from 3M in 1982 and then began a series of new ventures in real estate and other interests.

An avid motorcyclist, glider pilot, and private pilot, Bob took his last cycle ride at age ninety-three before selling it. He relished new challenges, and in his late eighties, he took up writing. Several of his stories have been published in the *Arlington Enterprise, Flying Magazine, Aviation History,* and the Smithsonian's *Air & Space Magazine.* Still living in his house of many years, with a mini museum of the many planes he has flown, Bob and his lovely wife, Barbara, are now in the process of moving to a new place this year—at about the time he turns ninety-eight.

Bob's Greatest Generation values were shared by many: hard work, guts, determination, and a stoic tendency toward action—getting things done and not just talking about them. Truly remarkable, they paved the way for our future and earned their title as the Greatest Generation—and we are all the better for it.

The atomic bomb controversy may look different to the generations twice removed or more from the war, but an invasion of Japan would have been an Armageddon. Casualty rates for the military forces and civilian populations would have been catastrophic. Sadly, the Atomic Age, and the nuclear proliferation that it ushered in, remains one of the great existential threats to humankind.

The Postwar Years

The shattered world was desperate for order, and significant efforts were initiated during the war to help stabilize postwar international financial and governance systems. First, the Bretton Woods Conference established a monetary exchange rate system, the International Monetary Fund (IMF) and the World Bank. Currency was pegged to gold, with the US dollar being the new world reserve currency. Second, the United Nations Charter was drafted at Dumbarton Oaks in Washington, DC, in 1944, and the United Nations came into existence on October 24, 1945. These institutions—spearheaded by the United States and clearly skewed to our advantage—would play a significant role in global governance in the decades to come.

Despite these efforts, our focus quickly shifted to our newest adversary, the USSR and the communist ideology it represented. Winston Churchill described the line dividing Russian occupation of Eastern Europe from the rest of Europe as the Iron Curtain in 1946.

The massive new conflict that developed between the Soviet Union and the United States and its Western allies was now officially called the Cold War.[1] Based on America's policy of containment, it was fought mostly on economic, political, and ideological fronts with a smattering of so-called proxy wars that could easily have turned hot.

In this cold-war arena, the superpower status of the United States was confirmed in April 1948 by the Marshall Plan to rebuild Europe. It provided over $12 billion—worth over 120 billion in today's dollars—in economic aid and was immensely successful in restoring Europe and highlighting the economic contrasts between the two competing systems. Quite simply, no other nation on Earth had the financial muscle to pull this off. It cemented thereafter an expectation that the United States would take on the role of global leadership throughout the Cold War, a position we have more or less held ever since.

The Soviet dictator, Joseph Stalin, tested our resolve on June 24, 1948, by blockading Berlin. The West responded with the now-famous Berlin Airlift, which yielded a huge PR victory for the Western powers as the beleaguered population of Berlin was supplied by air until the blockade was lifted on May 12, 1949. Militarily, America's superpower status in the late 1940s was reinforced by its monopoly on the atomic bomb, a condition that would soon change.

In the meantime, as the "tweener" generation connecting the pre- and postwar generations, we represented an America in transition. It was a transition from a rural to an urbanized society, from a regional to a world superpower, and from relatively simple regional leadership to complex, high-tech global leadership. Charlie Darth, a member of the class of '61, is a living example of this transition. Consider the lifestyle changes he experienced within a few years following World War II.

Charlie Darth

I spent most of the first ten years of my life living in Westby, Montana. It was a small town of about four hundred people located on the eastern border of the state, only a few miles from the Canadian border. As you might imagine, it was brutally cold and windy, and its elevation of three thousand feet seemed to make it even colder. It was fun to watch the Great Northern steam locomotives running through town, but there wasn't an awful lot to do. I guess the two biggest attractions were the Friday-night gatherings in the town to watch the high school basketball games and the real biggie, the annual fair in Westby.

We lived in a small, four-room house with a porch. We had electrical power but no running water. Our "bathroom" was the outhouse in the backyard, and our weekly bath was taken in a washtub on the kitchen floor in which we all used the same water. My job, every morning, was to go out on the porch and pump a pail of water from the well for household usage. My brother, Cal, and I slept in one room, and my folks in the other bedroom. Our oil-fueled stove in the living room was our only source of heat, and it left us waking up on many a cold morning with frost on the wall.

We had no telephone but stayed connected with the outside world by way of our big radio in the living room and trips into town, where my uncle owned a grocery store. Dad had a car, but with no garage to shelter it from those cold Montana nights, it took some doing to keep it going. With no doctors or dentists in town, timely medical care was no small problem. We had one school that combined all grades, and without the critical mass to support each grade level, we combined two grade levels per classroom. I was one of six cousins that helped fill our classrooms. While it all seemed normal at the time, there wasn't, in retrospect, much of an opportunity to get ahead in Westby.

In 1953 we moved to the big city of Minneapolis and lived in a small, three-bedroom house in North Minneapolis. With its running water, indoor plumbing, and a ventilating system to heat the house, it gave me a taste of the good life. My folks even bought our first television set around that same time. Cal and I still shared a room, and my grandmother had the spare bedroom. In those days, families took the responsibility of caring for their elderly parents. I started my fifth-grade year in North Minneapolis and can still remember getting under my desk for air-raid drills and being forewarned not to look up for fear of getting blinded by an atomic explosion. Still, it was a less complicated time, and life in those early years was good.

Charlie's story is unique in at least one respect: he lived through a significant shift in lifestyle, gaining access to modern conveniences and new opportunities almost overnight. The transition from a simpler to a more complex lifestyle was elongated over a longer time-frame for most of us in the class of '61. Still, when we entered the first grade in 1949, the challenge of learning to read and write was about as complex as we ever wanted life to be.

The Baby Boomers Arrive

By and large, the last half of the 1940s was an era of high energy for the United States. The new GI Bill[2] helped finance the delayed college education of millions of returning servicemen and women, and new housing and a massive economic transformation to a peacetime, consumer-based economy created a job-rich market. America was on the move, and the table was being set for a bright future.

The great baby boomer generation launched in 1946 would tally over 71 million people by its end in 1964. While young in the late 1940s, it would hold the title of the largest generational cohort until the Millennials arrived about seventy years later. The early boomers would be movers and shakers in America for much of the second half of the century, and their subsequent retirement, starting in 2011, has become part of a huge entitlement challenge for the generations following them.

For the class of '61, our age of innocence was coming to a close. We were about to enter the second half of the twentieth century, and it started with a bang.

Mike Conley

I don't remember World War II at all, but I do remember some of the artifacts of the war, like the used military equipment rusting in the junkyards along Washington Avenue in Minneapolis and the music of that era, sung by the Andrews Sisters and others, playing over our big radio console in the living room—maybe even singing one that my dad taught me about *"Lili Marlene,"* a favorite of soldiers from all sides during the war.

I started kindergarten at the old Lowell School in North Minneapolis and was halfway through first grade by the end of the 1940s. In those formative years, I developed an intense interest in aviation and World War II, which would become almost part of my DNA throughout my entire adult life. The neighborhood was full of kids, and it seemed like everything was new and interesting; boredom was never a problem for me. The one crisis that terrified parents at that time was polio. There were real concerns with letting us play in unknown public areas and movie theaters, particularly in the heat of summer, and a mild cold or aching joint could easily lead to polio fears. With this exception, growing up was a time of carefree fun, curiosity, wonderment, and innocence.

Summary of the 1940s

One of the most transformational decades in history, the 1940s—shaped by World War II and its aftermath—molded and codified the world structures and norms through the remainder of the century and into the new millennium. Indeed, the origins of the perfect storm trace back to this remarkable decade.

1. **World War II shattered the status quo and reshaped the world and the way it operated.**

   - It was a grim reminder of destructive modern weapons and humankind at its worst.

   - It advanced amazing new technologies, ushering in jet travel and the Atomic Age.

   - It realigned the global power structures, often in divisive and contentious ways.

   - It transformed the aspirations and expectations of nations and peoples.

   - It launched early globalization and the interconnected world we live in today.

2. **The global institutional structures that prevail today were set up during and after the war.**

   - The United Nations was established along with a stream of special world organizations.

   - The trade, currency, finance, and world banking systems were established.

   - The United States, a key architect and backer of these structures, benefited handsomely from them.

   - The United States became the go-to rebuilder of nations decimated by the war through the Marshall Plan.

3. **The Cold War that followed dominated the global arena for the next fifty years.**

    - The United States and USSR emerged as superpowers in a West versus Iron Curtain confrontation.

    - Multilateral treaty alliances were made around NATO, the Warsaw Pact, and others.

    - Spheres of influence and unwritten rules of the road helped govern the adversaries.

    - Two Chinas, the reconstruction of Japan, and later wars would change the Pacific Rim.

4. **The Greatest Generation led the way with its resiliency and can-do persona.**

    - The American economy transformed from a peacetime to a wartime status overnight.

    - The United States became the world's "arsenal of democracy" and financier of reconstruction.

    - The US postwar boom set the stage for continued economic growth.

    - The postwar baby boom would become a dominant force in the population.

    - The blessings received would later drift into platforms that promoted a perfect storm.

SNAPSHOT: *1940–1950*

	1940	1950	1960	1970	1980	1990	2000
Population in Millions							
World	2,300.0	2,557.6	3,033.2	3,700.6	4,458.4	5,330.9	6,145.0
USA	132.1	152.3	180.7	205.1	227.2	249.6	282.2
US Financials in Billions							
GDP	$98.2	$278.7	$534.3	$1,046.7	$2,791.9	$5,898.8	$10,117.5
Fed. Receipts	6.5	39.4	92.5	192.8	517.1	1,032.0	2,025.2
Fed. Outlays	9.5	42.6	92.2	195.6	590.9	1,253.0	1,789.0
Surplus / (Deficit)	(2.9)	(3.1)	0.3	(2.8)	(73.8)	(221.0)	236.2
Gross Fed. Debt	50.7	256.9	290.5	380.9	909.0	3,206.3	5,628.7
Interest on Debt	0.9	4.8	6.9	14.4	52.5	184.3	223.0
US Domestic Averages							
Wages	$1,725	$3,210	$5,315	$9,400	$19,500	$28,960	$40,343
Cost of new house	3,920	8,450	12,700	23,450	68,700	123,000	134,150
Cost of new car	850	1,510	2,600	3,450	7,200	16,950	24,750

Points of Interest

- End of Great Depression; World War II; postwar recovery and advent of the Cold War

- The United States becomes a superpower under Presidents Franklin Delano Roosevelt and Harry Truman

- GDP nearly triples from 1940 to 1950; debt increases over fivefold

- Huge postwar recovery and birth of the baby boomers from 1946

Snapshot Road Map: *The Snapshot compares key data points from the beginning of one decade to the beginning of the next. Sources are provided under Part II in the endnotes.*

8

The 1950s

When the Blast Goes Off,
Don't Look Up!

At 7:00 a.m. on the morning of August 29, 1949, the world was forever changed. In the forlorn steppe of Northeast Kazakhstan, the USSR detonated its first atomic bomb: a 22-kiloton device with the approximate power of the A-bomb dropped on Hiroshima. The United States no longer had a monopoly on atomic power; the nuclear arms race was on.

In a blink of an eye, the Cold War got uglier. The arms race escalated as the two great superpowers scrambled to build bigger and better atomic weapons with sophisticated new delivery systems. Less than one year later, on June 25, 1950, the war turned hot when North Korea invaded South Korea. The Korean War quickly escalated as the People's Republic of China joined forces with North Korea, and the United States and USSR lined up on opposite sides. The great powers were on a collision course, and the challenge of keeping it contained was huge.

For the class of '61—soon-to-be first graders in 1949—the nuclear explosion meant little. We were too preoccupied with our Tinkertoys, Lincoln Logs, and electric train sets. The more affluent might even be found watching a grainy picture on a seven-inch TV screen embedded in a monstrous console, but they were rare exceptions. For most, radio was still the only game in town.

As the Korean War escalated, local school boards felt the need to conduct air-raid drills to "protect" students against a nuclear attack. At the commencement of each drill, we would scurry under our desks and cover our eyes at a stern warning not to look up at the flash of blinding light that would indicate our city had just been destroyed by a nuclear blast.

No one mentioned we would be vaporized by the blast before we had a chance to look up. In fact, no one knew much of anything about atomic weaponry and its lethal side effects. It was all so new, and like so many other technologies that would spring up in the decades to come, it surpassed our speed of comprehension and ability to adapt. Over the course of the 1950s, the nuclear threat reached doomsday proportions, with both major powers possessing enough firepower to destroy the world several times over. Still, the horrors of a nuclear holocaust were not fully understood, and aboveground testing went on and on.

What we did know was that Joseph Stalin and the communist bloc countries he led were the bad guys. The red flag with its hammer and sickle evoked in us the same kind of fears that the Nazi swastika or Japanese rising sun must have triggered in the hearts of citizens living in the territories occupied by Germany and Japan only a few short years earlier. We feared the "red menace" over-running Europe and the rest of the world. Political careers were made—and broken—by the likes of such people as Senator Joseph McCarthy and his senate hearings on the communist infiltration of our government. At ground level, we were riveted by the bravery of secret double agent Herb Philbrick as he infiltrated communist cells in America and prevented mayhem every week in the hit TV series *I Led 3 Lives*.

We trusted our government to do the right thing and pretty much believed whatever the government told us was true. We trusted our major institutions almost as much as we distrusted the "commies." We believed in the American Dream and the upward mobility it represented, and we saw our ticket to success in a good education and hard work. Indeed, it was a model that would work well for decades to come.

In retrospect, the mid-1950s represented a simpler time. We were mesmerized with the coming age of television, 3-D movies, and the latest top-ten songs on the Lucky Strike *Your Hit Parade* show. The unveiling of new car models by the Big Three automakers—Ford, Chrysler, and General Motors—each fall was a much-anticipated event. Cloaked in secrecy, dealers unveiled new models with the latest gadgetry, colors, and chrome schemes, with tail fins that grew gaudier every year. Bigger was better, and residents of the snowbelt states were willing to overlook the rusted-out fenders and rocker panels that quickly marred those shining beauties. The thought of purchasing a foreign car was all but nonexistent.

It was good to be a preteen kid in the early 1950s. Somehow, we survived despite not wearing seat belts or biking helmets. We played with little red balls of mercury and were exposed to lead paint. We could go to the movie theater on Saturday mornings to watch our favorite Buck Rogers serial for a dime, and some of us were among the lucky few to own a rare Ted Williams, Stan Musial, or Mickey Mantle baseball card. A long-distance phone call was a major— often ominous—event, and a private phone number without a party line was a rare luxury. The ultimate dream of every kid was to visit the new Disneyland theme park that opened on July 17, 1955, but most of us settled for watching Disney's *Davy Crockett* series on TV. In Des Plaines, Illinois, on April 15, 1955, a new takeout place called McDonald's opened for business. As a kid growing up in this era, Curt Lange shares a few thoughts on the times.

Curt Lange

Curt Lange thoroughly enjoyed the freedom his bicycle gave him as a kid growing up in the 1950s. It was the all-purpose vehicle of his time, and he used it for transportation, riding in a "wolf pack" with his friends or making deliveries in his first real job in the ninth grade.

Curt was the prototypical kid of that time. He hopped on his bike after breakfast and was often gone until dinner. Ah, the freedom and options: the Camden swimming pool, Fairview Park, or whatever new adventure the wolf pack picked for the day. With few structured events, it was a time when kids could be kids. In these formative years, kids honed their own life skills—a.k.a. street smarts—and the ultimate authority of parents, though skirted on occasion, was never questioned. Like many peers, Curt grew up with this respect for authority.

At home, Curt and his older brother, Dave, enjoyed listening to *Fibber McGee and Molly* on the big radio console in their living room—that is, before they got their first TV set. After that, Curt was plugged into *Howdy Doody, Captain Midnight, Flash Gordon,* and all the other "can't miss" shows. Eavesdropping on the family party line telephone was keen fun, as was looking at the toys in the Sears, Roebuck and Company Christmas catalogue. Going to church on Sunday was part of the routine, and playing hooky was not an option.

Curt received a weekly allowance for his assigned set of chores, and that was it; spend it all in one day and go without the rest of the week. If he wanted something special, he saved up for it. No money, no purchase—though his dad once helped him pay for a football helmet with an attached face mask, the talk of the neighborhood. He also remembers his top three gifts as being his Marx electric train, a BB gun, and a portable 45 record player.

On a rare occasion when he decided to splurge, an extravaganza might be hopping a bus downtown by himself—something an eight-year-old did back then—and taking in a movie with an ice cream treat after at Bridgeman's. A hike up the Foshay Tower, the thirty-two-story skyscraper, was frosting on the cake. Without bus fare, Curt would often walk home, but that wasn't so bad, particularly in the fall, when the aroma of the burning elm tree leaves filled the air.

They were fun years, and the importance of family and friends, decency, hard work, and commitment stuck with Curt throughout college, the army, and a long career at Tennant Company, from which he retired in 2008 after a career of over thirty years.

Married for over fifty-three years to Monica Drossel—a remarkable lady Curt has known since childhood—and with three amazing daughters, Elizabeth, Sara, and Jessica, and their respective families, two grandkids, and friends galore, Curt and Monica have made their mark on the world and touched the lives of many people in such a positive way.

Working together, they have achieved the American Dream in a quiet but effective manner that so beautifully represents the better angels in our generation.

Our musical spirits were lifted by the birth of rock 'n' roll as we listened to Bill Haley and the Comets and others in the earlier 1950s. We listened on our car and transistor radios, the record hops, and at home on the single-play 45 records we purchased for ninety-eight cents. We knew the top-forty hits, hummed the lyrics, and "rated" the records from zero to ten while watching Dick Clark's *American Bandstand,* which debuted in 1957. We played Elvis Presley, Pat Boone, Fats Domino, Buddy Holly, and Jerry Lee Lewis records at our parties, and we listened to "the Singing Rage," Miss Patti Page, ask, "How much is that doggie in the window?" A five-minute slot on *The Ed Sullivan Show* was an almost-guaranteed ticket to success for any new talent. In 1958, The Kingston Trio brought folk music to new popularity with their hit song "Tom Dooley."

But all was not good. We were puzzled by our parents' mortal fear of polio and reluctance to let us play in public areas in the midsummer heat, the polio epidemic of 1952 still fresh in their minds. Just as the iron lung was a symbol of polio's destructive force, the advent of the Salk polio vaccine—developed by Dr. Jonas Salk— in 1955 was cause for great hope and jubilation. A few embryonic efforts in the areas of open-heart surgery, transplants, and DNA research, unnoticed at the time, would open the way for major new medical innovations in the decades to come.

Consumer purchases were usually made in some combination of cash, layaway plans, or direct credit arrangements with a major retailer, such as Sears or Montgomery Ward. Credit cards were simply not available, and it was not until the fall of 1958 that Bank of America launched the BankAmericard in Fresno, California, which would become the first successful and recognizable, all-purpose modern credit card. It was a portent of things to come, but for almost the entire decade, credit-card debt was not something you would find on a household's balance sheet.

Americans were also becoming more mobile. The launch of President Eisenhower's new Interstate Highway System[1] construction program in the mid-1950s changed the face of America. "See the USA in Your Chevrolet" became a household tune, and families were on the move. An entire new industry of motels, truck stops, and service stations emerged to accommodate America's new age of mobility. With a car in every garage, cheap energy, and good roads, the migration to suburbia (further encouraged by resistance to desegregation) began. The American Dream was alive and well; home ownership and a plot of land to call our own was finally within our reach. The massive postwar housing boom was well underway, and the pieces seemed to be falling into place.

It was also the golden age of commercial aviation and the birth of the Jet Age. The British De Havilland Comet made its first commercial appearance with the British Overseas Airways Corporation on May 2, 1952, and the Boeing 707 opened commercial service with Pan American Airways on October 26, 1958. While still outside the price range of most families, the possibility of seeing those faraway places with strange-sounding names was drawing closer. Without realizing it, we were tiptoeing into the early stages of a global economy.

The first nuclear submarine, the USS *Nautilus,* was launched and running under its own nuclear power on January 17, 1955. A little over three years later, on May 26, 1958, the first commercial nuclear power station in the United States was activated. The first commercial computer, the UNIVAC I, was sold to the US Census Bureau in 1951, and the transistor radio—introduced in 1954—became the fastest-selling commercial product of the time. The technological seeds of the future were sown without fanfare, and few of us recognized the significance at the time.

The United States was the economic powerhouse of the world, and President Dwight David Eisenhower was the world's go-to leader when times got rough. To be sure, the Soviet Union was a formidable adversary—at least militarily—but we heard and dismissed Nikita Khrushchev's words, that communism would bury us as just more "commie" propaganda. Though they had the power to end civilization with their powerful thermonuclear arsenal, it seemed impossible they could ever surpass us in technological, economic, or military power.

Sputnik and the Space Age

Our complacency was shattered when we learned that the Soviet Union had launched the first artificial satellite on October 4, 1957. A 184-pound spacecraft with a 22-inch diameter, Sputnik circled Earth in an elliptical orbit every 96 minutes. Transmitting radio signals back to Earth, its bleeps could be picked up by amateur radio operators. This was for real; there was now a human-made object in outer space, and we were officially living—and competing—in a new Space Age.

Sputnik shocked us to the core. As a nation, we were stunned to have been beaten so badly by the Soviet Union and fearful that the Soviets would soon be able to convert their peaceful satellite payload into an intercontinental ballistic missile (ICBM) that could quickly reach any defenseless city in the United States. We had fallen behind, and some questioned whether or not we could ever catch up.

But, like Pearl Harbor, it was a catalyst that energized the nation. Within a year, Congress enacted the National Defense Education Act,[2] a four-year program that poured billions of dollars into our educational system with a heavy emphasis on math and the sciences. NASA was also created and formally launched in 1958, replacing previous agencies on a larger and more focused scale.

After several failures to launch a Vanguard satellite into orbit, the United States launched its first successful satellite, the Explorer, on January 31, 1958. The space race was on, and it ushered in a new arms race for ICBM delivery systems. Within only a few short years, the nuclear, space, and arms races converged as the new battleground of the Cold War, an era that would dominate the global tapestry for the next several decades.

Our national confidence was further shaken toward the end of the decade. About ninety miles south of Key West, Florida, another event was unfolding that would change the dynamics of the western hemisphere for the remainder of the twentieth century and beyond and bring the world to the brink of a nuclear holocaust a short time later. The Batista regime fled Cuba on January 1, 1959, opening the door for Fidel Castro's communist-led coup shortly thereafter. The Soviet Union had established a beachhead in the West; the Cold War was suddenly right there in our own backyard.

Mike Conley

The early to mid-1950s were the most carefree days of my life. Old enough to go places and do things on my own—within reason—I had no worries whatsoever about having a roof over my head, three squares a day to eat, and a loving family. Sociologists would probably classify my family as blue-collar and lower-middle-class, but my friends were all in the same category. If we were poor, we sure didn't know it.

While playing sandlot baseball, riding my bike, holding Monopoly tournaments with my neighborhood pals, or reading my favorite comic strip, *Smilin' Jack*—the fearless aviator that was forever at odds with the hammer-and-sickle pilots of the Red Army—life was good. I loved airplanes, and there was no bigger thrill than to take the bus out to Wold-Chamberlain Field (now the Minneapolis–Saint Paul International Airport) and watch DC-3s and Boeing Stratocruisers bearing the Northwest Airlines logo take off and land.

The Korean War and weekly air-raid drills sparked my early interest in world affairs. Though our news outlets were limited back then, the public libraries were loaded with World War II and aviation books. I remember feeling relieved to learn of the passing of Joseph Stalin, the Soviet dictator, in March 1953, thinking, naively, that the Cold War and threats of an atomic attack would pass away, but alas, that was not to be, as the Red Army in Eastern Europe seemed poised to attack even without Stalin—or so we were told.

Senator Joseph McCarthy demagogued the communist threat to his political advantage. He loudly proclaimed the communists had infiltrated our government and other institutions and led a witch hunt, called McCarthyism, that would ruin many a career before it faltered and led to the senator's downfall.

Fast-forward to the fall of 1957, when, as a ninth grader, I was stunned by the Soviet Union's successful launch of the Sputnik satellite. How could this be? How could they beat us to the punch? They had taken a commanding lead in the new space race, and it was a great concern until we finally launched our own Explorer satellite in January 1958.

Among more mundane things, I received my driver's license in the summer of 1958, prior to starting high school that fall as a sophomore at North High School. It was great to get the family car for a ride with friends, maybe getting everyone to chip in a quarter for gas, which went for about two bits a gallon. I did a lot of odd jobs in the interim and got my first W-2 paying job at age sixteen at the old Rainbow Café, bussing dishes. I thought making seventy-five cents per hour plus tips was a good deal, and I really learned to hustle for those tips. I also remember cashing my check and picking up a new Gant shirt for $5.95 at the Sims Clothing Store next door to the Rainbow.

They were good days and good times, and I didn't mind working for the things I wanted. It was a trait that followed me all the way to my retirement, almost forty years later, in 1998.

Feeling proud: Curt Lange & Mike Conley modeling their first suits – circa 1950s

Classmate Art Jentsch, proudly garbed in his Cub Scout uniform in the early 1950s. **Note:** The large radio console and 45 RPM record player

Summary of the 1950s

In retrospect, the 1950s looks like the last age of innocence in which our government, key institutions, and value systems went largely unchallenged. It featured a quest for bigger, better, faster, and showier things that would gradually erode the frugality, sense of proportion, and generational values of those who had experienced the Great Depression and World War II. The decade's key contributors to the perfect storm are below:

1. **The multidimensional Cold War dominated the geopolitical arena on all major fronts.**

   - The nuclear arms race and delivery system buildups began in earnest.

   - The superpowers contested all grounds and turned brinkmanship into an art form.

- The Korean War, the French defeat at Dien Bien Phu, and other ventures left festering sores.

- Proxy wars and clandestine operations, widely used, were precursors of things to come.

2. **The emergence of the Space Age and its aftershocks.**

- With ICBM capabilities, the next arena of superpower competition turned to outer space.

- The USSR shocked the world with the launch of Sputnik and, later, the first astronaut.

- Stunned, the United States revitalized its educational system and went to work—a long-term win.

- The Space Age and race to the moon would soon be in full swing.

3. **The new age of television, transportation, and technology changed American lifestyles.**

- Television was, for most, the newest medium of information and entertainment.

- Transportation flourished with the Interstate Highway System and advances in air travel.

- Medical advances, such as the polio vaccine, improved mortality and morbidity rates.

- Americans were more connected, informed, and well-traveled than ever before—a new norm.

4. **It was a decade of astonishing global growth and optimism in the United States.**

    - The quest to sate consumer appetites, build homes, and create jobs dominated the decade.

    - The American Dream flourished, but downsides would emerge later.

    - The global population increased over 15 percent against an 18 percent increase in the United States.

    - The strains on Earth's carrying capacity from such growth rates would manifest later.

    - The frugal patterns of the past would soon be replaced with more wasteful practices.

SNAPSHOT: *1950–1960*

	1940	1950	1960	1970	1980	1990	2000
Population in Millions							
World	2,300.0	2,557.6	3,033.2	3,700.6	4,458.4	5,330.9	6,145.0
USA	132.1	152.3	180.7	205.1	227.2	249.6	282.2
US Financials in Billions							
GDP	$98.2	$278.7	$534.3	$1,046.7	$2,791.9	$5,898.8	$10,117.5
Fed. Receipts	6.5	39.4	92.5	192.8	517.1	1,032.0	2,025.2
Fed. Outlays	9.5	42.6	92.2	195.6	590.9	1,253.0	1,789.0
Surplus / (Deficit)	(2.9)	(3.1)	0.3	(2.8)	(73.8)	(221.0)	236.2
Gross Fed. Debt	50.7	256.9	290.5	380.9	909.0	3,206.3	5,628.7
Interest on Debt	0.9	4.8	6.9	14.4	52.5	184.3	223.0
US Domestic Averages							
Wages	$1,725	$3,210	$5,315	$9,400	$19,500	$28,960	$40,343
Cost of new house	3,920	8,450	12,700	23,450	68,700	123,000	134,150
Cost of new car	850	1,510	2,600	3,450	7,200	16,950	24,750

Points of Interest

- Korean War; Cold War escalates—and with it, an arms race with the USSR

- Truman and Eisenhower preside as the last presidents born in the previous century

- Solid economic growth; GDP almost doubles from 1950 to 1960; debt up only 13 percent

- Birth of Interstate Highway System; new television era; jet travel and Sputnik

Snapshot Road Map: *The Snapshot compares key data points from the beginning of one decade to the beginning of the next. Sources are provided under Part II in the endnotes.*

-9-

The 1960s

The "M&M" Boys Are in Town

—Newspaper headline

The 1960s were a tumultuous decade of social unrest and transformation. The contrasts in our social norms, technological progress, and worldviews at the beginning and end of the decade were astonishing. Years of pent-up energy and suppressed grievances erupted into a countercultural revolution that changed our lives and the world we lived in.

The decade started with a symbolic bang as John F. Kennedy became the first president of the United States to be born in the twentieth century. JFK's youth, war record, and charisma energized a younger generation. His administration—the "New Frontier"—was loaded with the best and brightest minds in academia and the business world, and an aura of Camelot was created by the youngest first lady ever, Jacqueline Kennedy. But, like the decade that JFK so aptly represented, his promising light—snuffed out early—was followed by a prolonged period of unrest.

For the class of '61, it was the decade that most shaped our lives and laid the groundwork for our future identities. We entered the decade as juniors in high school, and many of us, by decade's end, had completed our formal education, started families, embarked on lifelong careers, and staked out the trajectory our lives would thereafter take; it was a lot of ground to cover in one decade. In 1961 we turned eighteen and became eligible for the draft, years before it was lifted in favor of an all-volunteer army. The draft was something we took seriously, and it became a lightning rod for the protests against a war that dominated most all of the decade: the Vietnam War.

JFK's term as our nation's youngest president started poorly. He oversaw the humiliating fiasco known as the Bay of Pigs invasion, in which a CIA-sponsored group of Cuban exiles attempted to overthrow Castro's regime, only to be trounced by his forces. By late summer 1961, the world of the 1950s was crumbling. The Soviet Union was clobbering the United States in the space race; Castro's government was firmly entrenched ninety-one nautical miles south of Key West, Florida; trouble was brewing in Vietnam; and the Berlin Wall was being constructed. The wall elevated Cold War tensions, and National Guard units were activated in response to the Berlin crisis. The drums of war were beating.

Amid the turmoil of that hot summer of 1961, the headlines in the Minneapolis *Star* and *Tribune* resonated with a conflict of another kind: the race between Mickey Mantle and Roger Maris to topple the mighty Babe Ruth's season high record of sixty home runs in 1927. The home-run derby reached a crescendo in mid-August as the New York Yankees arrived in Minneapolis to play the major league's newest franchise, the Minnesota Twins. The *Tribune*'s headline read, "The 'M&M' Boys Are in Town." As all eyes focused on this dynamic duo, the Berlin crisis was put on a temporary hold.

In a way, the headline reflected the calm before the storm, an invisible demarcation that separated the carefree "take me out to the ball game" era we were leaving for a new decade of seismic threats and relentless turmoil. In this twilight zone, Mantle and Maris shared equal billing with the momentous events occurring throughout the world. It was a rare inflection point that symbolically separated the old from the new—and more was yet to come.

Though Maris toppled the mighty Babe's record with 61 home runs, the legitimacy of his feat was contested by some because it was accomplished over the span of 162 games versus the 154-game season played in Ruth's record year. The challenge reflected a shifting American culture that was prepared to question the legitimacy of yet another bedrock institution, the sanctity of major-league baseball.

In September 1962, one of the seeds of the later environmental movement germinated. *Silent Spring,* by Rachel Carson, called attention to humans' increasing power to change the natural world—often in destructive ways. Carson brought such matters as the decline of bald eagle populations due to the synthetic pesticide DDT to the public through clear writing and even television appearances. Her work, and that of many others, would bear fruit in new activism and agencies over the next decades.

In October 1962, the Cuban missile crisis brought the world to the brink of a nuclear holocaust as the two superpowers squared off to see who would blink first. After discovering the Soviet Union was in the process of arming Cuba with nuclear weapons that could hit our mainland, the United States placed a naval blockade to prevent a shipment of Soviet weapons from reaching Cuba. No one really knew if the Soviet ships would try to run the blockade, risking a naval battle that could easily escalate into a nuclear war, or turn around. An anxious world breathed a sigh of relief when the latter course was chosen, all part of a behind-the-scenes face-saving deal for Khrushchev that called for the United States to pull its Pershing missiles out of Turkey. We were closer to a nuclear war than ever before or since.

The Vietnam War

Sociologists have long debated the forces behind the countercultural revolution of the 1960s, but few have disputed the dynamic role the Vietnam War played in dividing the nation. Like many military interventions since, it started small, with the deployment of about seven hundred military advisors in 1960 and 1961. Through mission creep and deteriorating conditions, it escalated to more than twelve thousand advisors in 1962, and at the time of JFK's assassination on November 22, 1963, there were about sixteen thousand advisors in South Vietnam. As the military buildup continued, the domino theory—the belief that if South Vietnam fell, other southeastern nations would topple like dominoes—gained prominence as the rationale for American involvement.

On August, 2, 1964, the USS *Maddox,* a navy destroyer on patrol duty off the North Vietnamese coastline, came under attack by three North Vietnamese torpedo boats. Two days later, another attack was reported. The latter was later deemed to be the result of "Tonkin Ghosts," a false reading on the radar images, but the first incident was real. It triggered Congress's passage of the Gulf of Tonkin Resolution on August 10, 1964, authorizing President Lyndon Baines Johnson to take whatever measures necessary to assist Southeast Asian countries jeopardized by communist aggression. The way was now clear for a full-fledged war.

By 1966 more than five hundred thousand American troops had been deployed in Vietnam, and casualties were mounting on both sides. My buddy, Brad St. Mane, was in the thick of the Gulf of Tonkin incident and shared his thoughts on how it felt at the time.

Brad St. Mane

Like many of my friends in the early 1960s, there was a feeling of restlessness while attending the University of Minnesota. Ever mindful of a military obligation to fulfill—either by way of being drafted or enlisting—my choice was the naval reserve. Reporting in for active duty and a trip to the navy's Great Lakes boot camp in January 1963, my orders following boot camp were to ship out on the navy destroyer, the USS *Fechteler* (DD-870), as a quartermaster.

The *Fechteler* was part of the Seventh Fleet and on station in Hong Kong in those fateful moments of early August 1964 when we received the call: "American ship under attack." Within two hours of this notice, the *Fechteler* was underway and bound for the Gulf of Tonkin. It was a madhouse as we scrambled together our crew, made ready to shove off, and actually set out with some of my shipmates still onshore. We left Hong Kong without the aid of a harbor pilot so as to save time, and, if memory serves, it didn't take that many hours before we were able to deploy with our sister ships in the Gulf of Tonkin.

It all happened so fast that I don't think we really appreciated the historical significance of our deployment until it was all over. Within days, we were part of an international incident that subsequently led Congress to pass the Gulf of Tonkin Resolution; the rest is history. We remained on station, patrolling the South China Sea and adjacent areas, until October of 1964.

Mustering out of the Navy in December 1964, it was back to school for me. Like so many others at that time, there was a shared belief that the domino theory was for real and that it was our patriotic duty to serve. As details of the war came out in later years, we began to question its validity. My suspicions and concerns have grown ever since about our involvement in wars and the ease with which we seem to be able to commit our young men and women into military actions; war has to be the very last resort and not an option we commit to early on. But again, in the early 1960s, my sense of accountability to my country and shipmates was heartfelt; serving in the navy most definitely felt like the right thing to do.

By the mid-1960s, the draft was in full swing and college attendance soared as droves of draft-age students opted for a college deferment over a yearlong stint in the jungles of South Vietnam. Within a short period of time, college campuses became ground zero for the protest movements, and a great countercultural revolution was launched.

For the first time ever, the horrors of war crept into the living rooms of American homes through the growing medium of television. We were horrified to watch the fiery suicides of Buddhist monks protesting religious restrictions in Saigon, and by 1965 the networks were rapidly expanding their coverage of the war. It dominated the network news, and over time, the tone of the coverage shifted and reflected a war-weary nation with serious doubts about the war and our national goals.

The credibility of our government was increasingly questioned, and on the evening of March 31, 1968, President Johnson shocked the nation by declaring he would not seek another term as president—an early casualty of the war. Richard M. Nixon won the 1968 election partially because of his promise to end the Vietnam War—a promise he couldn't keep in his first term of office. It would not end until 1975, over a decade after it started—a portent of the drawn-out wars that were to come.

In another part of the world, Israel decisively defeated the armies of Egypt, Syria, and Jordan in the Six-Day War.[1] Israel seized control of the Sinai Peninsula and Gaza Strip from Egypt; the West Bank and East Jerusalem from Jordan; and the Golan Heights from Syria. The die was cast; the Middle East tinderbox would continue to smolder from here on in as a significant threat to world peace.

The Counterculture Revolution

By the mid-1960s, the nation was embroiled in a conflagration of social issues that challenged our norms, values, and institutions. It was an era of intensified social awareness, and college campuses everywhere teemed with activists protesting the status quo. Joan

Baez hauntingly sang of how the "cruel war is raging," and Bob Dylan reminded us that the answer was "blowing in the wind." The Beatles stormed America in 1964 and displaced Elvis Presley as the reigning king of rock. Sean Connery starred in the first of many James Bond movies, *Dr. No,* in 1962.

It was the age of flower children and hippies, and Dr. Timothy Leary admonished us to "tune in and drop out" with a magic elixir known as LSD. It was an age of movements: the sexual revolution, freedom movements, feminist movements, and civil rights movements, to name a few. Draft cards were burned, and radical groups focused on taking ever-more-aggressive actions against the establishment and prevailing institutions. A common phrase at the time was "doing my own thing," and it conveyed the message that we were not bound by the values of our parents or others, free at last to pursue our own destinies—or so we thought.

Massive protests and riots took place throughout the country, often turning ugly as city blocks were burned and looted. Sections of America were placed under martial law, with the National Guard patrolling streets on a periodic basis. The Vietnam War was a festering sore, and the media was there to record it for all in real time and at prime time.

Landmark Political Actions

Vice President Lyndon B. Johnson had been sworn in as our thirty-sixth president aboard *Air Force One* shortly after JFK died from gunshot wounds in Dallas, Texas, on November 22, 1963. LBJ went on to beat Barry Goldwater in the presidential election of 1964 and named his new administration the Great Society. Under his leadership, several game-changing bills were enacted along with a more aggressive approach to government spending that would reshape our institutions for decades to come. They fell into three major categories: civil rights, entitlement programs, and deficit spending on an unprecedented scale.

Civil Rights

The civil rights movement in the 1960s was marked by protests (both violent and nonviolent), boycotts, sit-ins, and marches. Brilliantly led by Martin Luther King Jr. and others, the movement made significant strides. The enactment of three major civil rights bills changed the American landscape and gave teeth to the assertion in our Declaration of Independence that "all men are created equal." They codified the legal underpinnings for ending the blatant discrimination that emerged after the Civil War, but it was only a beginning.

The key bills were the Civil Rights Act of 1964, which banned discrimination in employment practices and public accommodations; the Voting Rights Act of 1965, which restored and protected voting rights; and the Fair Housing Act of 1968, which banned discrimination in the sale or renting of housing. Each was aggressively contested at the time of passage and passively resisted in the decades that followed. Still, these bills codified the legal grounds for changing socioeconomic conditions in America and paved the way for other civil rights issues with respect to immigration policies, women's rights, and the gay rights movements that would gain traction in later years.

Entitlement Programs

Government-sponsored "safety net" programs have been a critical part of our nation's social and financial fabric since enactment of the Social Security Act of 1935. Providing services for tens of millions of Americans, they have been modified and amended along the way, but two events of the 1960s were of particular significance: Medicare and Medicaid were signed into law on July 30, 1965, and the Social Security trust funds were combined into a "unified budget"[2] in 1969, making it easier to comingle these funds with the general operating budget. While the financial impacts of these two initiatives were negligible in the earlier years, they would become exponential over the next several decades. A brief look at our entitlement programs will help clarify the troublesome trajectories now unfolding.

Both Social Security and Medicare are funded on a pay-as-you-go basis. At the time Medicare was passed, in 1965, there were 5.4 active workers for every 1 retiree. Fifty years later, in 2015, the ratio was 3.99 to 1. By 2025, that ratio is expected to decline to 2.97 to 1. What does this mean? The funds generated huge surpluses early on, when the ratio of workers to retirees was high, and the unified budget adopted in 1968 made it easier to raid these trust funds for general operating expenses, leaving IOUs in the form of intragovernmental debt. As the ratio declines, fewer and fewer active workers will be left to pay for more and more retirees, while the IOUs linger, unpaid. In addition, current retirees are living longer and collecting increasingly expensive benefits over a longer period of time. Under current funding arrangements, this unsustainable formula will only worsen over time.

Few perceived this to be a problem in the 1960s, and it demonstrates how good programs with good intentions can go wrong if they are not constantly monitored and upgraded to meet future needs. Through mission creep—a pernicious tendency to extend the mission, scope, benefit levels, and recipients covered beyond a given program's original intent—the changes are made without a corresponding revenue stream to cover the extensions. Faulty assumptions, egregious accounting practices, and waste, fraud, and abuse perpetuate the problem.

Deficit Spending

Prior to the 1960s, the government's deficit spending practices were moderate compared to the staggering numbers we see today. For example, attempts were made to partially fund World War II and the Korean War through war bonds, increased taxes, budget reductions in other spending areas, and so forth. The deficit curve escalated with the Vietnam War, LBJ's War on Poverty programs, and aggressive new government accounting practices. The newly emerging "play now, pay later" culture in America helped pave the way for this dramatic shift.

Consumers were also active in this practice. The explosive growth of credit cards in the 1960s set the stage for a consumer spending revolution. While credit had been available before, it was often installment credit offered by banks or companies focused on financing a specific product—such as an automobile—with a down payment and interest charges built into loans that were amortized and paid off in equal installments, usually of limited size, scope, and duration.

By the mid-1960s, through financial innovation, technology, and changing consumer behaviors, revolving credit hit the streets. American Express, Visa, and Mastercard provided consumers with credit to buy whatever products or services they desired, whenever they desired them, and pay up at leisure. As credit-card usage increased, our buying habits changed. We could go out for dinner, take a trip, or buy furniture when the spirit moved us. Unlike our Depression-era parents, we no longer had to save up for that special dinner or family vacation. We loved the idea of instant gratification, and it has since become a way of life.

Toward the end of the 1960s, roughly 15 percent of all American households had at least one all-purpose credit card. By the end of the century, most American households had several credit cards. The American Dream was increasingly financed on credit, with little concern for rising household debt levels. Deficit spending had become the new norm for both the government and consumers, but, as we would learn later, there is no free lunch.

The Space Age

On May 25, 1961, JFK issued his historic challenge to Congress for the United States to put a man on the moon by the end of the decade. It was a bold move, particularly since the USSR had consistently beaten the United States in earlier space efforts, including the first man to orbit in space, Yuri Gagarin, on April 12, 1961. The race to the moon was on.

The United States made steady progress throughout the 1960s, starting with the Mercury program's single-seat space capsule with various types of rocket boosters. The Gemini space program of 1962–1966 featured a two-seat space capsule that helped NASA learn its craft with respect to orbital maneuvering, space docking, walks in space, equipment testing, and other techniques and technologies needed to land on the moon.

The Apollo program—which developed a three-seat capsule, service module, and lunar lander—started tragically with a space-capsule fire on January 27, 1967, that killed astronauts Virgil "Gus" Grissom, Edward White, and Roger Chaffee. On Christmas Eve 1968, the crew of Apollo 8—Frank Borman, James Lovell, and William Anders—orbited the moon and took the famous *Earthrise* picture that highlighted the fragile nature of Planet Earth in contrast to the dark and hostile environment of outer space.

On July 16, 1969, Apollo 11 astronauts Neil Armstrong, Edwin "Buzz" Aldrin, and Michael Collins strapped down in their Apollo capsule atop the mighty Saturn V rocket booster for the first attempt to land on the moon. The mission received 24/7 coverage, and the world was on pins and needles as Armstrong and Aldrin maneuvered their tiny *Eagle* lunar module for a moon landing. The onboard computers quickly overloaded under the strain of the landing, and Armstrong adroitly landed the tiny craft manually.

It's a small and fragile planet – we'll sink or swim together. Which will it be?

They spent over twenty-one hours on the moon before rejoining the orbiting Apollo spacecraft and returning safely to Earth on July 24. It was a magnificent achievement and fulfilled JFK's remarkable vision in 1961. Sadly, this rate of progress would not continue, but that's another story.

The Computer Age

While the computers on Neil Armstrong's lunar lander were not up to the task, the real story here is the remarkably swift technological progress of the computer in the 1960s and its gradual integration into our culture. Computer technologies had quickly advanced beyond the vacuum-tube computers of the 1950s to integrated circuit—microchip—advances.

Large mainframe computers were improved constantly, with increased power, greater storage capacity, and faster processing speeds. They rapidly became an integral part of corporate America and the Department of Defense, and they offered a quantum leap in processing transactions, designing and modeling new systems and research efforts, and improving productivity at all levels. The sky was the limit, and toward the end of the decade, new microcomputers were introduced. The groundwork for the Digital Age was now firmly in place.

Bye-Bye Boomers—Hello Gen Xers

The baby boomer generation dwarfed its predecessor, the Silent Generation, by a wide margin. By the time it came to an end in 1964, the boomers were over 76 million strong, or roughly 40 percent of America's total population of about 193 million people at that time. Its eighteen-year span—from 1946 to 1964—and its size made it a major social force for change.

Some have divided the boomers into two distinct groups: Phase I, from 1946 to 1955, and Phase II, from 1956 to 1964. Generally speaking, the Phase I cohort has been described as individualistic, free-spirited, experimental, and social cause oriented. The Phase II cohort was, perhaps, less optimistic, more distrustful of government, and generally more cynical. The turbulent 1960s and their aftermath had a profound effect on boomers—in the formative stages of their lives—and shaped their worldview and outlook in later years, as we will discuss later.

By the end of the 1960s, the population of the United States was about 50 percent larger than it had been in 1943. Though we were vaguely aware that class sizes were growing, we had no real idea of how dramatic the increase was and what it would mean for future generations. Our kids—mainly the Gen Xers who followed—would seem few in number compared to the generation they followed.

Amid the population boom and almost unparalleled prosperity that followed the end of World War II, the GDP of the United States grew from about $100 billion in 1940 to over $1 trillion by the end of the 1960s, a tenfold increase in three decades. Was it any wonder that jobs and opportunities were so plentiful?

Mike Conley

Over the span of our lifetimes, every decade has a few seminal events that deeply shape the course of our lives. Taken in its entirety, the 1960s were loaded with more game-changers for me than any others. Within a span of only seven years, I finished high school and college, completed my service in the navy, got married, started a business career that would continue for over thirty years, and transferred to Chicago, the first of many cities and offices in my career.

I took my first classes at the University of Minnesota in fall 1961. With no real idea of what I wanted to do, other than complete school and get a job, I worked throughout school and studied just hard enough to get by. Restless and bored, I dropped out after my sophomore year and joined the navy in search of adventure.

Following boot camp at the Great Lakes in August 1963, I was sent to Pensacola, Florida, for training at what is now called a cryptology school. Code school was challenging, but I really enjoyed the time away from school in Mobile, Alabama, only fifty-nine miles from my base. I was astounded by the culture of the Deep South prior to the enactment of the civil rights legislation, with all its dual facilities: a sharp and scary contrast from the multiethnic environment I was used to in North Minneapolis. I was on base on November 22, 1963, when President Kennedy was assassinated, and like most of the sailors and marines on our base, I was devastated. JFK was the embodiment of youth and vigor, and it was hard to believe he was gone.

I was transferred to a Naval Security Group base near Andrews Air Force Base in the summer of 1964 and spent a good amount of time exploring Washington, DC—an exciting time for anyone interested in history and politics. I also voted in my first presidential election as Lyndon Johnson beat Barry Goldwater, and I found the debates in our barracks to be fun and stimulating. While my hitch in the navy seemed long at the time, I look back at those times now with fond memories and a recognition of how important those formative years were.

Upon my discharge from active duty in June 1965, I enrolled again at the U of M with a double major in political science and education. School seemed to be far more interesting this time, and I found that I actually enjoyed learning. With the help of the GI Bill and part-time work, I was able to graduate in August 1967.

As part of the requirement for a bachelor's degree, I needed two physical education credits. I thought I might as well meet some girls while doing it, and I subsequently enrolled in a ballroom dancing class. It was the best move I ever made, as it was there that I met the love of my life, Sharon Wells, in fall 1966. We hit it off from the get-go, with a few ups and downs along the way, and were married on March 29, 1968. Fifty-two years later, we're still going strong.

The college campus in the mid-1960s was a hotbed of rioting and protests over the Vietnam War, civil rights, and other issues. As a veteran, with my military obligations behind me, I rather enjoyed debating the war with the protesters. At the time, I fully bought into the domino theory. It was not until years later, after reading David Halberstam's book *The Best and the Brightest* (New York: Random House, 1972), that I totally changed my position on the Vietnam War and the futility of wars in general. Halberstam painstakingly explained how, under the Johnson administration, the war in Vietnam gradually escalated into a war they didn't think we could win but, politically, did not want to lose.

The job market in the summer of 1967 was fantastic, and at twenty-four years old, I was ready to go. Though I considered becoming a teacher, I opted instead to get into the business world. I started my career job with Northwestern National Life Insurance Company on October 9, 1967, as a trainee in group insurance sales, selling employee benefit plans to companies through brokers and consultants. Following a one-year training program, I transferred with Sharon to Chicago in fall 1968, shortly after the Democratic National Convention that featured Mayor Richard J. Daly waving his angry fist at rioters.

We rented a place in Des Plaines, Illinois, and I took a commuter train into my office on Madison and LaSalle whenever I could. I also joined the Des Plaines Jaycees after attending an Oktoberfest in our town that they so ably put together, and later was elected president of the chapter. I loved my career, the Jaycees, and life in the Windy City, particularly summer days with the "bleacher bums" at Wrigley Field watching Cubs games. I enjoyed the art of marketing and selling, and I learned much from my boss and lifelong mentor, Don Henyan, about business, life, and living by your code.

It was an exciting decade, and I learned through the school of hard knocks the importance of perseverance, commitment, and sustained effort. Having the good fortune to marry my best friend, Sharon, and to have a significant mentor like Don in my life made it all that much better.

A boot camp picture from my Navy days
– 1963-65

Wedding bells: Sharon & Mike Conley –
March 1968

Summary of the 1960s

The turbulent and transitional 1960s carried us beyond the sleepier 1950s, into a world that more closely resembles what we are part of today. With the Vietnam War as a backdrop, social disorder and open challenges to our norms, authority, and institutions were all part of a greater quest—as a nation and people—for our identity and a brand that defined us. We are still a work in progress. Several game-changing events shaped our pathway to the perfect storm.

1. **The Cold War intensified across all fronts, and the arms race escalated.**

    - The Vietnam War dominated the American landscape—a condition we would repeat.

    - The Berlin Wall was erected, and Armageddon threatened by the Cuban missile crisis.

- Israel won the Six-Day War and became the number-one Arab target thereafter.

- The two superpowers kept relative order, a dynamic no longer existing today.

2. **It was a decade of domestic unrest and landmark legislation.**

   - Assassinations of key leaders, street riots, and draft resistance marked the times.

   - Key legislation—civil rights and Medicare—changed our social landscape forever.

   - TV coverage brought the war and social unrest into our living rooms.

   - Challenges to institutional authority would later become the new norm.

3. **The technological lead of the United States continued unabated and largely unchallenged.**

   - The United States beat the USSR in the race to the moon, a huge win for Western nations.

   - The modern Jet Age came into being and boosted globalization.

   - Computers became entrenched in business and other large institutions.

   - Both superpowers now had the ability to annihilate the other many times over.

4. **The basic constructs of our society, culture, and demographics were rapidly shifting.**

   - The baby boomer generation ended in 1964; Gen X ushered in a new age.

- The global population began a steady upward trend, posing new challenges.

- A new age of credit sparked a "play now, pay later" culture.

- Despite the changes, the American Dream remained a viable reality for most Americans.

SNAPSHOT: *1960–1970*

	1940	1950	1960	1970	1980	1990	2000
Population in Millions							
World	2,300.0	2,557.6	3,033.2	3,700.6	4,458.4	5,330.9	6,145.0
USA	132.1	152.3	180.7	205.1	227.2	249.6	282.2
US Financials in Billions							
GDP	$98.2	$278.7	$534.3	$1,046.7	$2,791.9	$5,898.8	$10,117.5
Fed. Receipts	6.5	39.4	92.5	192.8	517.1	1,032.0	2,025.2
Fed. Outlays	9.5	42.6	92.2	195.6	590.9	1,253.0	1,789.0
Surplus / (Deficit)	(2.9)	(3.1)	0.3	(2.8)	(73.8)	(221.0)	236.2
Gross Fed. Debt	50.7	256.9	290.5	380.9	909.0	3,206.3	5,628.7
Interest on Debt	0.9	4.8	6.9	14.4	52.5	184.3	223.0
US Domestic Averages							
Wages	$1,725	$3,210	$5,315	$9,400	$19,500	$28,960	$40,343
Cost of new house	3,920	8,450	12,700	23,450	68,700	123,000	134,150
Cost of new car	850	1,510	2,600	3,450	7,200	16,950	24,750

Points of Interest

- Vietnam War; Berlin Wall erected; Cuban missile crisis; arms race on

- JFK assassinated in 1963; LBJ and Great Society; Nixon beats Humphrey in 1968

- Civil unrest in USA over war; passage of historic civil rights and Medicare legislation

- USA lands on the moon in 1969 to win the space race against the USSR

Snapshot Road Map: *The Snapshot compares key data points from the beginning of one decade to the beginning of the next. Sources are provided under Part II in the endnotes.*

-10-

The 1970s

"The 'Me' Decade"

—Tom Wolfe

The class of '61 entered the 1970s as twenty-six-year-old adults. With our futures still ahead of us, we staked out our careers and closed out the decade as thirty-six-year-old hopefuls approaching the early thresholds of middle age. The time and energy spent on establishing our beachheads on life in the 1960s had now shifted toward advancing and consolidating our positions. Not yet movers and shakers, we were, nonetheless, starting to make waves.

Our lives took on a more conventional look as our children entered school, our service hitches were behind us, first houses were purchased—many made possible through the GI Bill—and we were up to our ears in debt as we pursued the great American Dream. In a role reversal, a few of us, by decade's end, had even become caretakers for aging parents, a trend that would intensify in the decades to come.

In many respects, the 1970s were a backlash to the chaotic 1960s. In his essay "The 'Me' Decade and the Third Great Awakening," author Tom Wolfe opined that Americans were shifting away from the wars and social movements of the previous decade. Disillusioned and disgusted with the communitarianism of the previous decade, many looked inward for answers—a quest, if you will, to find the "real me." In this milieu of self-analysis and self-development, it was not difficult to stereotype the entire decade as self-involved, but, like all stereotypes, the characterization was not totally accurate.

To be sure, Americans sought self-identity in clothing styles, musical tastes, and behaviors. Bell-bottom jeans, polyester leisure suits, platform shoes, Afro hairstyles, and long and bushy sideburns became popular. Disco music was in, public streaking was a quirky fad, and pet rocks were sold to a public eager to express itself.

We were introduced to *Star Wars, Rocky,* and *The Godfather,* with their endless—but lucrative—sequels. We watched the original *Saturday Night Live* debut on October 11, 1975, and were shocked almost weekly by the pronouncements of Archie Bunker in the hit show *All in the Family.* Sports fans welcomed the return of Muhammad Ali—formerly known as Cassius Clay—to the ring in 1970, after his long banishment from boxing for refusing induction into the army.

In retrospect, it was a watershed decade that set the stage for the remainder of the twentieth century, a geopolitical roller coaster. The Vietnam War ended, but President Nixon opened the gateway to China. The shah of Iran was overthrown, and a new Iraqi regime, under Saddam Hussein, reshaped the Middle East. OPEC and the oil crises shook the global oil markets and economies to the bone, while an energy crisis of another kind, the Three Mile Island meltdown, dampened the development of atomic energy in the United States for decades to come. The terrorist strike at the Munich Olympics introduced a new form of asymmetric warfare, and the two superpowers sought a détente that would quickly end with the USSR's invasion of Afghanistan.

Watergate, and President Nixon's subsequent resignation, dominated the news headlines in the earlier part of the decade just as a new form of economic misery, stagflation—a toxic combination of high inflation, stagnant growth, and high unemployment—dominated the latter part. The United States went off the gold standard, and the petrodollar emerged. Inflationary economic challenges prompted President Nixon to institute price controls, and environmental concerns led to his creation of the Environmental Protection Agency (EPA).

The electronic revolution exploded with the introduction of fiber optics, microwave ovens, VCRs, the Sony Walkman, and consumer video games, and the Apple Computer Company was started in a Los Altos garage in 1977. The supersonic Concorde and wide-bodied Boeing 747 jet changed international air travel, while at ground level, British Rail introduced the high-speed train. American cars reached their largest sizes ever before going smaller at decade's end, and the Big Three automakers lost their dominant grip on the domestic auto market; indeed, Chrysler even went to the government for a bailout, a preview of things to come.

Our futures were inexorably shaped by the volume and frequency of epic events. The forces of change were churning and colliding, creating hybrid challenges never before envisioned. The perfect storm was starting to form, coalescing and taking shape in definable and substantive ways; the pieces were coming together, and the baseline trajectories were being formed. We just didn't know it at the time.

The Perfect Storm Model Applied to the 1970s

The newly emerging forces of the 1970s are too complex and interconnected to describe in the format previously used. Accordingly, we will herein use the perfect storm model—as outlined in chapter 2—as our template for describing events and connecting the dots. As a recap, it organizes the megaforces into quadrants, dubbed the four E-Cells, to identify the pivotal events of the 1970s and beyond.

THE PERFECT STORM

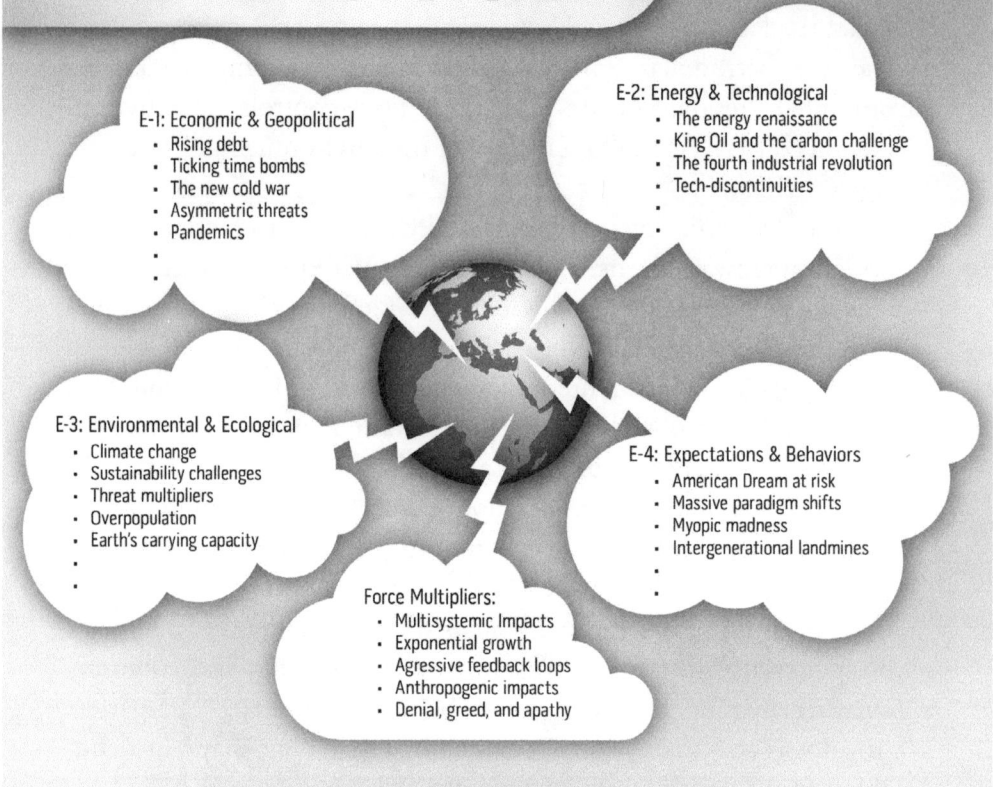

E-1: Economic & Geopolitical
- Rising debt
- Ticking time bombs
- The new cold war
- Asymmetric threats
- Pandemics
- .
- .

E-2: Energy & Technological
- The energy renaissance
- King Oil and the carbon challenge
- The fourth industrial revolution
- Tech-discontinuities
- .

E-3: Environmental & Ecological
- Climate change
- Sustainability challenges
- Threat multipliers
- Overpopulation
- Earth's carrying capacity
- .
- .

E-4: Expectations & Behaviors
- American Dream at risk
- Massive paradigm shifts
- Myopic madness
- Intergenerational landmines
- .
- .

Force Multipliers:
- Multisystemic Impacts
- Exponential growth
- Agressive feedback loops
- Anthropogenic impacts
- Denial, greed, and apathy

E-1: Economic and Geopolitical Forces

In economic terms, the 1970s was the worst decade since the Great Depression. It was marked by a long period of stagflation. Comparatively speaking, the average annual inflation rate from 1900 to 1970 was about 2.5 percent. It soon passed 7 percent and climbed to over 13 percent by December 1979. We were breaking new ground.

Though the economic and financial markets remained tepid as we entered the 1970s, there were economic opportunities for those who could find them. My friend from the class of '61 Bud Schaitberger was one of them.

Bud Schaitberger

Many of the decisions we make in life are reactive; they are in reaction to our personal interests, circumstances, and prevailing conditions. In my earlier years—in junior and senior high school, for instance—I was totally immersed in sports and a very active social life. Hockey was for me both a sport and a next step to my future.

Following high school, I was enrolled in the University of Minnesota and played hockey throughout my freshman year. But, with the draft hanging over my head, a certain restlessness, and the need to work, I enlisted in the navy. I went on active duty in April 1962 and served aboard the aircraft carrier USS *Franklin D. Roosevelt* (CV-42) for two years—much of it in the Mediterranean. I saw the world and gained a broader perspective on life.

I mustered out of the navy in March 1964 and worked and caught up with "old friends" until being recruited to play hockey and enrolling at Cornell University that fall. Being part of the "Big Red" program, working part-time and attending classes until graduating in 1968, it was a busy time. Jeanne and I got married in 1966 and had two children—Christine and Charlie—by 1970. The job market was terrific back then—at least for me—as I had four solid job offers after graduation, before opting to get into the securities business in Minneapolis in 1969.

While the economy was only so-so at that time, there were some great opportunities for firms like mine that specialized in the capital creation markets for start-up businesses. After getting licensed to sell securities, I immersed myself in the "go-go" OTC (over-the-counter) market. It was a dynamic, fast-moving market that appealed to my competitive instincts, but it was not for the faint of heart. We worked and played hard, and we made a lot of money. I was young and, perhaps, overenjoyed the fruits of my labor, living a lifestyle that far exceeded my humbler beginnings. Like so much in life, it was a transition in life that was fraught with a tough learning curve.

By 1973 I could see the writing on the wall. The capital markets were tightening, and selling became a more vigorous and aggressive process. The days of easy money and fast living were taking their toll. I was in the trenches at ground level—a microcosm of what was happening in Wall Street and all the financial markets—and finally decided, enough. Embarking on a new adventure, Jeanne and I opted for a major life change: buying and operating Whitepine Lodge, a bar and resort in Northern Minnesota, in 1973. Living on a lake, managing a seaplane base, socializing and servicing customers and friends with live music and food as we actively managed our business was fun at first, but also very grueling. It became a new life experience for me, with some unantici-pated outcomes, but I guess that's something we can cover at a later time.

As Bud mentioned, the economic times were changing. Despite rising inflation—usually synonymous with a hot economy—the unemployment rate had climbed to 9 percent by May 1975. A "misery index"—combining both the annual inflation rate and the seasonally adjusted unemployment rate—was used to measure stagflation, and the results were ugly. By the time President Jimmy Carter left office, the index had climbed to over 20 percent, and the rate on a thirty-year fixed mortgage had climbed to almost 13 percent. The oil crises of 1973 and 1979—discussed later—pounded the consumer at the pump. The average price of a gallon of gas—unadjusted for inflation—had jumped from $0.36 in 1970 to $1.25 in 1980, an increase of over 300 percent and a precursor of things to come.

The contemporary issues of unemployment, inflation, and rising interest rates and gas prices—so ominously framed in the context of the misery index and stagflation[1]—were the headline stories in the 1970s. But three events of enormous consequence were hardly blips on our radar screens at the time: the exit of the United States from the gold standard, the advent of the petrodollar system, and the Federal Reserve's new "dual mandate" of "promoting maximum employment while stabilizing prices and long-term interest rates." The latter was an egregious example of mission creep with dualistic goals that were often in conflict.

These events were a catalyst for aggressive new fiscal and monetary policies in the United States, the new petrodollar arrangement and its huge geopolitical implications, and the fiat paper currency system that opened the floodgates for printing dollars as needed; all prerequisites for the current ballooning US national debt.

The global order that had existed since the end of World War II was starting to unravel. While the Vietnam War ended for the United States with the signing of the Paris Peace Accords[2] on January 27, 1973, and the superpowers had arrived at a productive détente—signing nuclear arms reduction and other treaties—changes were occurring elsewhere. The big story was Japan's emergence as the world's newest economic powerhouse with national brand recognition for quality products and workmanship. But it was the clandestine meeting in 1972 between President Nixon and Chairman Mao Tsetung of the People's Republic of China that set the stage for the new geopolitical order of the twenty-first century. With a thawing in Sino-American relations, the economic gateways of the world now opened for China. In a stunningly short period of time, China transformed itself from an agrarian and isolated society into a global superpower.

Over three thousand miles west of Beijing, another blockbuster event was unfolding. An Iranian revolution was underway that would ultimately lead to the deposal of the Pahlavi dynasty and the shah of Iran in early 1979. Replaced by a new theocratic-republican government led by supreme leader Ayatollah Khomeini, it became a powerful catalyst for anti-Western sentiment in the Middle East. The

Iran hostage crisis[3] all but cratered President Carter's bid for reelection in 1980. At about the same time, Iraq also found a new leader, Saddam Hussein, a Sunni, and the Iran-Iraq War that followed foreshadowed the great Sunni-Shiite conflicts that still rage across sectors of the globe.

Domestically, a revolution of another kind was taking place in the United States. In a dramatic twist of fate, Watergate[4] triggered a chain reaction that shook the nation and challenged the Constitution. In an astonishing blitzkrieg of events, both President Nixon and Vice President Spiro T. Agnew—the dynamic duo that trounced the Democratic ticket led by George McGovern and Sargent Shriver in the 1972 elections—were thrown out of office. It produced a stunning by-the-numbers outcome that not even the most creative Hollywood writers could have imagined.

Vice President Agnew resigned on October 10, 1973, after pleading no contest to tax evasion charges, and he was quickly replaced by Congressman Gerald R. Ford. Ten months later, on August 8, 1974, President Nixon resigned his office and Ford became president. A few days later, President Ford asked former New York governor Nelson Rockefeller to become his vice president. "Rocky" accepted the offer and was later confirmed. The net effect: three vice presidents and two presidents in less than one year.

While a low point in America's political history, it was also a reminder that America was able to resolve even its worst conflicts in a peaceful and constitutional manner—a lesson to remember as we now confront a politically gridlocked system that seems beyond repair.

E-2.1: Energy Forces

Up until the 1970s, Americans had enjoyed an easy ride with respect to energy. It was cheap, abundant, and accessible, considered by many a given. With the exception of rationing during World War II, gasoline had always been available and inexpensive. Indeed, it literally fueled the American Dream for millions of people moving to the suburbs for that plot of land, house, and car they could call their own.

Two great oil crises in the 1970s changed all that. Stunned, Americans confronted for the first time the harsh reality that cheap and abundant gasoline could no longer be taken for granted. The long gas lines, rationing, skyrocketing pump prices, and "out of gas" signs at local gas stations confirmed their fears. Ironically, though the oil crises of 1973 and 1979 captured all the headlines, a geological event—the peak-oil conundrum—of far greater consequence to an oil-addicted world was all but glossed over.

The Oil Crisis of 1973: In the early afternoon of October 6, 1973, an Arab coalition, led by Egypt and Syria, launched a surprise attack on Israel. Israel quickly regrouped and launched a series of counterattacks, called the Yom Kippur War,[5] that crushed the invading Arab armies and ended victoriously for Israel on October 25. In the interim, President Nixon airlifted weapons to Israel; OPEC, in retaliation, imposed an oil embargo on nations supporting Israel, with a special focus on the United States.

The embargo, imposed in October 1973, lasted until March 1974. OPEC cut production and raised prices, and within three months, oil had climbed from $3 to $12 per barrel, and pump prices, on average, increased from $0.38 to $0.84 per gallon. Prices aside, it was the long waits at the pump and uncertainty over gas supply that most rattled Americans.

This wake-up call generated a number of wide-ranging responses over the next few years, such as price controls, rationing, reduced speed limits, conservation, and fuel-alternative plans. Permanent steps included the creation in 1975 of a strategic petroleum reserve to weather future energy shocks and shortages, the adoption of corporate average fuel economy (CAFE) standards in 1978 to reduce the average fleet gas-consumption level of cars, authorization to proceed with the Trans-Alaska Pipeline System construction project, and the creation of the Department of Energy in 1977. In fact, every presidential administration since has pushed for an energy independence goal of one sort or another.

The Oil Crisis of 1979: Unlike the earlier oil crisis, this one had a less definable beginning and end. It was driven by a combination of a strong global demand for oil and events in the Middle East. Following the Iranian Revolution, the oil production in Iran declined by 4.8 million barrels per day—about 7 percent of the total global production at that time. With a tight supply-and-demand curve, the cutbacks terrified the markets. The price of oil doubled to $39.50 per barrel over twelve months, and gas lines grew long again.

The inflationary impact on the world economy was significant, and more than ever, oil was recognized as a potent new weapon of diplomacy and power. In fact, the Carter Doctrine, enacted shortly thereafter by President Carter, stated that any interference with US oil interests in the Persian Gulf would be considered an attack on America's vital interests—a pronouncement backed by US military power in the Middle East ever since.

Peak Oil: A momentous milestone occurred in the United States in 1970 that went almost totally unnoticed: the production of conventional crude oil in the lower forty-eight states peaked at a level of about 10.2 million barrels of oil per day, and it has been in decline ever since—up to at least the advent of Gulf Coast drilling and shale oil production in more recent years. As the demand for oil increased and domestic oil production declined, the United States was forced to import more and more oil.

Over time, the oil production of several countries went into decline, and the production of exportable oil grew even more concentrated in fewer countries—many of them OPEC nations. The immutable laws of geology and supply and demand, it seems, could not be glossed over, and the issue would escalate into a geopolitical hot potato with every passing decade, a significant contributing force to the perfect storm.

The Three Mile Island Debacle: An energy crisis of another kind was triggered at 4:00 a.m. on March 28, 1979, at the Three Mile Island nuclear power plant in Pennsylvania. It started innocently enough with a failing feedwater pump in a secondary nonnuclear cooling system, and it quickly escalated into what could have been a major nuclear meltdown. The fallout, though contained, had a devastating ripple effect on the development of nuclear energy in the United States throughout the remainder of the century and beyond.

Fourteen years and almost $1 billion later, the nuclear reactor cleanup job was at last completed. The general public was absolutely terrified of another accident, and the Three Mile Island disaster became a rallying point for the antinuclear movement. Not a single new nuclear power plant would be built in the United States until the next century. With nuclear power production limited, coal remained the predominant baseload fuel for electrical power for many decades. And this, of course, led later to serious environmental concerns, something not at the forefront of public opinion prior to the 1970s.

E-2.2: Technological Forces

With little stretch of the imagination, the 1970s—with the advent of integrated circuits—could be dubbed the decade of modern computing. The Intel 4004 microchip, introduced in November 1971, with thousands of interconnected transistors embedded on a small silicon chip, revolutionized computing. The microprocessor allowed computing to be done in a device of reasonable size, cost, and efficiency. With each new generation of microchips—like the 286, 386, 486, the Pentium chip, and beyond—the ability to push more power through thinner wires to exponentially more transistors in smaller spaces, using less energy and producing less heat, created an explosion in computer advances and computing power.

Intel cofounder Gordon Moore suggested in 1965 a trajectory for computing power and costs that became a given. Dubbed "Moore's Law," it stated that computing power will double every two years, and the cost of processing will decrease. To the surprise of skeptics, it has held true in the many decades since, and many still wonder how long it can continue.

With the introduction of the Apple II, Commodore, and Atari computers, these embryonic devices were starting to become a household item. Video games moved into arcades and sports bars.

On the mainframe end, new Cray supercomputers were phased into major research, defense, and academic facilities.

The space-age technologies that led to our moon landing began taking a turn in the earlier part of the decade. With the splashdown of Apollo 17 on December 16, 1972, the Apollo moon program unofficially ended. The space race was over, and the United States and Soviet Union initiated a collaborative program known as the Apollo-Soyuz Test Project. On July 15, 1975, American astronaut Thomas Stafford docked with the Soyuz capsule and shook hands with cosmonaut Alexei Leonov. An era of space cooperation had begun that still exists today, although in practice it is often spotty. The Voyager deep-space exploratory program launched in 1977 reflected a new shift toward long-term exploratory efforts.

The new technologies of the 1970s introduced fiber optics, commercially produced microwave ovens, VCRs, answering machines, eight-inch floppy disks, the laser printer, CAT scans, and the first MRI images. Genetic engineering was still in its infancy.

E-3: Environmental and Ecological Forces

On June 22, 1969, the Cuyahoga River on the southern shores of Lake Erie caught fire. The oil, chemicals, and debris floating in the water fueled the blaze, and the absurdity of a burning river created national attention. Coupled with other anthropogenic insults, a large-scale movement—and concomitant political will—developed to clean up our environmental act. The stage was set for an aggressive agenda in the 1970s.

On the first day of 1970, President Nixon signed into law the National Environmental Policy Act of 1970. NEPA, as it was called, required that all major federal actions with significant environmental repercussions include an environmental impact analysis. It was the first of many laws that would establish and codify the legal framework that exists today. While global warming was not yet on our radar screens, stewardship of our national resources had become a focal point of our national policy efforts. The first Earth Day took place on April 22, 1970. Further action followed:

- The EPA and NOAA were created in 1970.

- The Clean Air Act of 1970 was enacted to control air pollution.

- The Water Quality Improvement Act of 1970 oversaw water quality standards.

- The Endangered Species Act of 1973 protected imperiled species from extinction.

- The Safe Drinking Water Act of 1974 was passed to safeguard public water supplies.

- The Federal Land Policy and Management Act of 1976 preserved national resources and land usage.

- The Toxic Substance Control Act of 1976 protected human health and the environment.

These examples suggest the diversity of the legislative and policy efforts designed to address the environmental challenges that had slowly crept into the picture. They created a strong environmental policy base that exists today, though it is regularly challenged by special interest groups all the way up to the Supreme Court.

E-4: Expectations, Behaviors, and Attitudes

The class of '61 was too busy raising young families to recognize the many sociological macroshifts that were changing the country and, with it, the behaviors and expectations of its citizenry. Our kids were dubbed the "latchkey generation," many of whom returned from school to an empty house with both parents at work. The Xers were fewer in number and sandwiched in between two massive demographic cohorts, the baby boomers and Millennials. They are considered by some to be the least parented and nurtured of all generations. Their parents were getting married later in life, divorcing at a higher rate, having fewer children, and working more to make ends meet in a costlier inflationary economy.

The Xers were also the first generation to grow up in a post-integration world. The seeds had been planted for the characteristics that would be attributed to them as they aged: entrepreneurial, savvy, technologically oriented, and loners, they were distrustful of institutions. They were also products of a changing demographic that made them more at ease with racial and ethnic diversity.

Meanwhile, global and domestic economies and the world's population were rapidly growing. The GDP of the United States almost tripled, from about $1.1 trillion in 1970 to $2.8 trillion in 1980. The global population grew almost 20 percent in the 1970s to reach a new threshold of over 4.4 billion people in 1980.

With the end of the Vietnam War, anti-war protests eventually subsided, but the feminist and other movements gained traction. The landmark *Roe v. Wade* Supreme Court decision changed the social landscape, and feminist leaders such as Gloria Steinem, Betty Ford, Audre Lorde, Bella Abzug, and others led the charge for women's equality. Helen Reddy's hit "I Am Woman" became almost a theme song for the movement. The passage of the Twenty-Sixth Amendment, lowering the voting age from twenty-one to eighteen, opened the political arena to new—and previously unheard—voices. The decade saw the founding of a number of movements that would gain traction and recalibrate the norms in America.

Though the word *me* is often ascribed to the decade, it is not totally accurate. Some, like my friend Brad St. Mane from the class of '61, were already making a difference.

Brad St. Mane

My wife, Zoe, was intensely interested in alternative educational systems, as was I. When our son, Brad Jr., was only a tot, we became interested in pursuing a Montessori education for him. We were not totally pleased with what was available. So, along with other like-minded people, we had a vision of a school and staff that worked together, sharing, discussing, and working out problems in a positive climate. We had a broader vision of providing a multidimensional learning experience for our son and others, one that would blend together traditional learning experiences with a social and moral development curriculum that would employ a variety of new initiatives.

The problem was, this sort of school did not exist for kids beyond age six, at least in the area in which we lived. Rather than grouse about current arrangements, a few families got together and created—in 1973—the first Montessori elementary classroom. It subsequently evolved into Lake Country School. It was tough sledding in the early stages, as we were challenged to secure funding, teachers, students, a facility, and more, but it became for us a cause greater than ourselves. We ultimately prevailed, and the end result was most gratifying.

Author's Note: Brad was reticent about his role in this effort, so I did a little digging on my own: Under Brad's leadership, the Lake Country School has flourished since its inception in 1976. Brad was a significant driving force behind the school and the founding president of the board of directors from 1976 to 1979. In the book *Creating a Real*

School: Lake Country School Montessori Learning Environments 1976–1996 (Minneapolis: Nodin Press, 2016), authors Larry and Pat Schaefer, with Lori Sturdevant, describe Brad as having "not only strong executive and management abilities, but also finely tuned senses of order and of how communities function. He is inspired to take risks and make things work. Brad has a highly practical intelligence and imagination, and he is deeply human hearted. He knows well what it means to be an ally and a friend."

As but one metric of its success, a guesstimate of the number of students completing their schooling at Lake Country School since 1976 would be about fifteen hundred. The program is still going strong as of this writing and is a tremendous reflection of the efforts made by Brad, Zoe, and other committed families to make some positive things happen for children and the families they would later raise—a great legacy.

Brad was old-school in his effort, almost reminiscent of the manner in which the Greatest Generation stepped up to the plate to deal with problems in a hands-on manner. As the class of '61 matured and took positions where they could take a leadership role in the community, a few—like Brad—jumped into the arena and made a huge difference.

Mike Conley

In addition to the birth of our two daughters, Kristen in 1971 and Heather in 1975, we lived in five different houses in four cities within a span of a little over seven years. Transfers were common back then, and it was considered unwise to turn down an opportunity for promotion. Our stints in Chicago, Detroit, San Francisco, and back to Minneapolis gave me a boots-on-ground feel for different markets and how they operated.

My transfer back to Minneapolis in 1979 was the most significant career move, as it involved a shift from direct sales to management. Being in the trenches for so many years, I'd had a ringside seat to how distribution channels worked. As a newly minted regional vice president of national sales, I was also blessed to be back with my mentor, Don Henyan. On a steep learning curve and nowhere near as good as I thought I was, I had a voracious appetite to learn more about the business world and how it operated at a higher level, and Don was a great teacher.

I learned from him the value of being able to sell an idea—not just to a local insurance broker but also within our home office structure and at the board level. He taught me how to create and sustain a market, how to differentiate a product or service with value-added features others didn't think about, and how to think beyond a sale and, in effect, "sell the sizzle, and not just the steak." Above all, he was a man of integrity who believed your word was your bond and that keeping promises was a bedrock belief you never violated.

The school of hard knocks was also a part of my education. During the Recession of 1974, I learned in Michigan—a market dominated by auto manufacturers and suppliers—how important the economy was to my business and why I needed to stay abreast of local and national trends and events. I also learned later how, with a stroke of a pen, a regulator, politician, or bureaucrat could put you out of business. Bottom line: we ignore the "external" environmental issues that impact our business at our own peril.

I was an early-morning guy and would routinely get into the office around 5:30 a.m.—no traffic, phones, or drop-in calls to distract me, but quiet time to strategize and plan for the day. I was always more comfortable and confident being as prepared as I could be with an understanding of the dynamics surrounding any business situation that I was in. The street smarts I picked up as a kid in North Minneapolis didn't hurt either. Sixty-plus-hour work weeks were more the rule than the exception, but I tried to attend Kristen and Heather's events as much as possible. Sharon had to be the greatest mom ever and always had my back, regardless of the situation.

In retrospect, there's not much I would've changed, but I can say this with certainty: success in anything we do— business or otherwise—is greatly enhanced by having a great spouse and family; a solid employer, company, or product; a willingness to learn with a resiliency to change; and great mentors—such as I had in Don. I was fortunate to have all of the above going for me, more or less, at the same time.

Mike Conley with his mentor, Don Henyan

Summary of the 1970s

It was as an astonishing decade of grassroots changes: the world's population grew by almost 20 percent, and the American GDP almost *tripled* in one decade, to $2.8 trillion. The building blocks and trajectories of the perfect storm were rapidly forming—we just didn't know it. The top five longer-term contributors to the perfect storm were as follows:

1. **The global financial systems were reshaped in ways that would feed the perfect storm.**

    • The gold-backed currency system was scrapped in favor of a paper-backed fiat currency.

    • The new petrodollar system helped enhance the dollar's world reserve currency status.

    • Both offered access to cheap capital, putting new monetary and fiscal policies on steroids.

2. **The geopolitical landscape was recalibrated in several significant ways.**

    • The Vietnam War ended, and early-stage struggles to control the Pacific Rim began.

    • The stage for Middle East unrest and future Sunni-Shiite conflicts was set.

    • Nixon's trip to China started the long process of China's emergence as a new superpower.

3. **Domestic events set the stage for future political and social divisiveness in the United States.**

    • The Watergate scandal and Nixon's impeachment and resignations challenged our Constitution.

- Passage of Twenty-Sixth Amendment opened voting to eighteen-year-olds and new voter blocs.

- Roe v. Wade and feminist movements changed domestic political and social paradigms.

4. **King Oil emerged, and new technologies changed the playing field.**
   - Two oil crises exposed the vulnerability of cheap energy, a key enhancer of the American Dream.

   - Production of crude oil peaked in the United States in the mid-1970s while demand increased.

   - The modern Computer Age flourished, with growth in breadth, depth, and digital access.

5. **Environmental concerns and actions—precursors to climate change—emerged.**
   - Initial environmental actions focused on clean air, water, natural resources, and wildlife.

   - Significant protective legislative actions were enacted, including the creation of the EPA.

   - *The above building blocks would improve focus on climate change in future years.

SNAPSHOT: *1970–1980*

	1940	1950	1960	1970	1980	1990	2000
Population in Millions							
World	2,300.0	2,557.6	3,033.2	3,700.6	4,458.4	5,330.9	6,145.0
USA	132.1	152.3	180.7	205.1	227.2	249.6	282.2
US Financials in Billions							
GDP	$98.2	$278.7	$534.3	$1,046.7	$2,791.9	$5,898.8	$10,117.5
Fed. Receipts	6.5	39.4	92.5	192.8	517.1	1,032.0	2,025.2
Fed. Outlays	9.5	42.6	92.2	195.6	590.9	1,253.0	1,789.0
Surplus / (Deficit)	(2.9)	(3.1)	0.3	(2.8)	(73.8)	(221.0)	236.2
Gross Fed. Debt	50.7	256.9	290.5	380.9	909.0	3,206.3	5,628.7
Interest on Debt	0.9	4.8	6.9	14.4	52.5	184.3	223.0
US Domestic Averages							
Wages	$1,725	$3,210	$5,315	$9,400	$19,500	$28,960	$40,343
Cost of new house	3,920	8,450	12,700	23,450	68,700	123,000	134,150
Cost of new car	850	1,510	2,600	3,450	7,200	16,950	24,750

Points of Interest

- Vietnam War ends; OPEC oil crises; USA exits gold standard; new petrodollar system

- GDP almost triples; national debt more than doubles; inflation intensifies

- Watergate ousts Nixon; Ford and Carter presidencies follow

- Voting age reduced from twenty-one to eighteen; birth of Apple, Microsoft, and the 747 jetliner

Snapshot Road Map: *The Snapshot compares key data points from the beginning of one decade to the beginning of the next. Sources are provided under Part II in the endnotes.*

-11-

The 1980s

"Mr. Gorbachev, tear down this wall."

—President Ronald Reagan

By 10:30 p.m. on the evening of November 9, 1989, thousands of East Berliners had congregated at the Bornholmer Strasse for the opening of the Berlin Wall—a historic turning point in the Cold War.

For almost twenty-eight years, the Berlin Wall, separating East and West Berlin, had visibly divided and vividly contrasted the two competing systems: communism under the USSR and democracy under the anticommunist Western coalition led by the United States. Its sixty-six miles of concrete walls—almost twelve feet high and adorned with more than three hundred watchtowers—were constant flash points of Cold War tension.

On June 26, 1963, President John F. Kennedy defiantly proclaimed in his famous "Ich bin ein Berliner" speech to almost a half million Berliners that we had their backs. Twenty-four years later, on June 12, 1987, President Ronald Reagan stood before the

Brandenburg gate in Berlin and challenged Soviet leader Mikhail Gorbachev with the words, "Mr. Gorbachev, tear down this wall!" The die was cast; the wall would soon come down, sparking a momentous chain reaction that would lead to the fall of the Soviet Union and the end of the Cold War. A young KGB operative by the name of Vladimir Putin, stationed in Dresden in 1989, was crestfallen at the news, but that story would play out later.

The decade started poorly, with a global recession and inflation rates that soared to 13.5 percent before coming down. Former movie star Ronald Reagan served as US president for most of the 1980s. Globalization had gotten legs, and world tensions were on the rise. Leveraged buyouts and corporate raiders—the new gladiators of Wall Street—epitomized the go-go business tempo of the time. A new cable network, CNN, kept us apprised 24/7 of the breaking economic and global news. Household computers were growing in number, but the fledgling internet was still primarily the domain of students, techies, and the military.

Many in the class of '61 were preoccupied with the mundane challenges of daily life as we entered the ranks of the middle-aged at the start of the decade. While a good number of us had settled on a career and company and were busy working our way up the ranks—confident in the American Dream, as many of us were better educated and had a higher earnings potential than our parents—others, such as Andrea Hricko Hjelm, were pursuing their American Dream through their entrepreneurial activities. Andrea was always a hard worker, and the results attest to her work ethic and good character.

Andrea Hricko Hjelm

Andrea Hricko Hjelm is a living embodiment of the American Dream, and she did it the old-fashioned way; she earned it.

Brought up to believe it was her responsibility to make what she would of life, she took ownership in the process early on. As the first in her family to graduate from college, Andrea noted, "There was never any question that we were going to go to college." Inspired by her Depression-era parents, Andrea became a lifelong advocate for a good education.

Among other things, Andrea learned to multitask with the best of them. For example, she had the rare distinction of being a cheerleader and homecoming queen twice in three years, The first, at North High School, and then later at the University of Minnesota. The latter involved a brutal schedule of cheerleading practices and games, participating at events on behalf of the U of M, working part-time jobs throughout school, and still graduating in four years with a BS degree in education, and a minor in journalism.

In 1965, Andrea married Ken Hjelm, a West Point grad with an MS degree from MIT. They toured the world together due to his work, and Andrea pursued her postgrad studies in mass communication at the University of the Philippines. Following Ken's service, she modeled in Boston, and in the Minneapolis market she staged major fashion shows.

The entrepreneurial side of Andrea emerged with her purchase of Moore Creative Talent Inc. in 1981. While still raising her family, Jon and Alycya—and later five grandkids—Andrea found the time to build a premier modeling and talent agency. The business grew through hard work, tenacity, and working smart, though, in the early years, she sometimes worked without pay. She said, "You did what you had to do," and that speaks to Andrea's grit and determination.

When asked about her business success, Andrea said she "pays close attention to detail, watches expenses carefully, and shies away from any debt. My dad was a 'cash-only' guy, and I guess I learned from him." Andrea credits her staff as "smart people working hard" and still gives freely of her time to mentor people. She coauthored a book in 1976 titled *The Person You Are*—a how-to book about business etiquette and conduct in a challenging environment—something she knows quite a bit about.

While learning through the school of hard knocks, Andrea is blessed with a natural grace and ability to make hard things look easy as well as an engaging personality that recognizes the value of networking and the importance of honoring her commitments.

Andrea and Ken are also generous givers of their time, talent, and treasure, and many have benefited from their generosity. Andrea is a tireless advocate and fundraiser for several nonprofit causes—many with a strong educational focus—and the University of Minnesota, and her beloved Gophers, have particularly benefited from Andrea's giving spirit.

Her commitment to family, community, and friends is part of her DNA. Her marriage of over fifty-four years, raising a family, building a business, living in the same beautiful home on an urban lake for over forty years, and not forgetting her roots and friends from North High School are all examples of Andrea's love, loyalty, and commitment to her values. Andrea is a living example of the American Dream, and we are all the better for it.

A number of the forces in play during the 1980s would hasten our journey toward the perfect storm. It was a complex decade, and we will turn once again to the perfect storm model to frame the issues and connect the dots in a meaningful way.

E-1: Economic and Geopolitical Forces

The Economic Arena

In many respects, the new decade was a bleak continuation of the previous one. Inflation soared to over 13.5 percent in 1980, and the unemployment rate peaked at 10.8 percent before subsiding. The global economy was on the ropes, and stagflation ran rampant in the United States. Federal Reserve Chairman Paul Volcker courageously attacked inflation with tight monetary policies that rocked the economy. As an example, the prime rate peaked at over 21 percent before subsiding.

By 1983 Volcker's policies were taking hold and the economy was rebounding. President Reagan's supply-side economic policies and tax cuts were having a stimulative effect. In this milieu, the federal deficits also climbed, and our gross federal debt increased from over $909 billion in 1980 to over $2.8 trillion by the end of the decade, a threefold increase.

Another casualty of the 1980s downturn was the savings and loan (S&L) crisis.[1] A combination of sky-high interest rates, inadequate capital, deregulation, lax oversight, and speculative investment strategies combined to create an institutional financial crisis of a magnitude not experienced since the Great Depression. Between 1986 and 1995, more than a thousand S&Ls went under, and by the end of the carnage, the federal bailout had cost taxpayers something north of $130 billion.

A great innovation of the 1980s, one that would permanently change the country's financial landscape and turn tens of millions of Americans into "market watchers," was the birth of the 401(k) plan. Like many great movements, it started out small—almost as an afterthought—but gained traction and grew into an economic behemoth and financial lifeline for a high percentage of retirees. It was drawn from provisions in the Revenue Act of 1978 and codified by the IRS into the rules for a 401(k) plan in 1981.

Under the old retirement models, called defined "benefit" plans, employers or plan sponsors assumed the plan's financial risk by guaranteeing a defined benefit that was payable monthly to their retirees. By contrast, 401(k) plans, using a defined "contribution" model, limited total benefit payouts to only what was contributed into the plan plus or minus investment earnings and expenses. Ergo, the benefits available depended on the performance of an individual's investment portfolio in the stock market. In effect, it shifted the benefit risk from the employer or plan sponsor to the employee.

Many plan participants felt flush with money; their plan assets were often huge in comparison to their weekly paychecks. Some used their 401(k) plans as a rainy-day piggy bank and prematurely drew out money—at a huge penalty—only to discover later that their accounts were underfunded and unable to meet their retirement needs.

With their own skin in the game and their retirement plans dependent on how well the market performed, vast numbers of Americans suddenly became market watchers. Market downturns— like the crash of 2008—would have a devastating impact on the financial stability of mainstream American households as well as the growing disconnect between Wall Street and Main Street.

The economic ripples of the 1980s forecast the economic tsunamis to come. The enormous power of the Federal Reserve under a forceful chairman like Paul Volcker was fully confirmed. Reagan's deficit spending and supply-side economic policies also demonstrated the short-term economic surge of such policies; the longer-term consequences on our debt-ridden balance sheets would not be felt until years later.

The Geopolitical Arena

It was a decade of globalization, with seismic forces that changed the global power structures for decades to come. The USSR was in its last full decade of existence, the Cold War was on its last legs, and a new era of destabilization in the Middle East was about to unfold. China was on the rise, and the Sino-American relationship was gaining traction. Terrorism was escalating, and OPEC oil was changing the world's power dynamic.

Globalization took firm root in the 1980s across a wide spectrum of economic, cultural, and political fronts. Countries were moving away from protectionist trade policies toward more open, free-market economies with a flurry of new trade agreements and alliance. National economies were increasingly connected in a broader framework of global economic integration.

As one metric of economic globalization, the balance-of-payments (BOP) position of the United States—as reflected in its import-export balances from 1980 to 1989—reveals a sizeable shift in our trade imbalance position that still exists today. The BOP figures for 1970 and 2015, shown in chart 11.1, highlight the dramatic shifts that have taken place. Oil imports and trade with China were important factors.

Chart 11.1: USA Trade in Goods and Services—BOP Basis

Value in Millions of Dollars			
Year	USA Exports:	USA Imports:	BOP Position:
1970	$56,640	$54,386	$+2,254
1980	$271,834	$291,241	$−19,407
1989	$487,003	$580,144	$−93,141
2015	$2,261,163	$2,761,525	$−500,361

Source: US Census Bureau; Economic Indicator Division, June 3, 2016

Mike Conley

In the summer of 1986, my company gave me a leave of absence to attend the Stanford Executive Program. If memory serves, there were about 180 participants—an equal split of executives from major American and foreign countries—in attendance. Following the classes during the day, we met nightly in small study groups to go over the business case studies for the following day. It became quickly apparent to me how much the foreign executives knew about the international market—particularly the American political system and economy—and how little I knew about foreign markets. Clearly, globalization and international trade were an everyday part of their work lives, but this was not so much the case for the American executives. It was an eye-opener, and from that point on I became more of a student of the international markets, currency exchange dynamics, continuous quality-improvement methods—a biggie with the Japanese executives in attendance—and the global economy.

The Soviet-American Cold War Shift

President Reagan moved into the White House in 1981 with one major foreign policy goal in mind: win the Cold War and defeat communism. The "Reagan Doctrine," as it became known, featured a massive military buildup, opposition to communism on all fronts with a "we win, you lose" philosophy, and an economic revival. Reagan dubbed the USSR the "evil empire," and there was never any ambiguity over his position; tensions between the two adversaries escalated.

In the meantime, things were not going well in the USSR. Their war against rebel forces in Afghanistan lasted throughout most of the decade and was a military and economic drain that was made worse by the falling price of the oil they exported. The economic strain of maintaining any semblance of military parity with the United States had become problematic. President Reagan's proposed Strategic Defense Initiative in March 1983—dubbed "Star Wars"—was designed to intercept Soviet ICBMs and overwhelmingly tip the nuclear scales in America's favor. Its astronomical costs would have been well beyond the USSR's financial capacity.

In 1985 Mikhail Gorbachev ascended to power as the new Soviet leader. He recognized the USSR's predicament and quickly embarked on a move to restructure the system known as *perestroika* and to liberalize the economy and political arenas via *glasnost*. Reagan, in turn, saw in Gorbachev a partner he could work with. The two leaders had a series of successful summit meetings following their introductory meeting in Reykjavík in October 1986, and by the end of the decade, the adversarial relationship—and Cold War—that had dominated the geopolitical landscape for forty-five years was about to end.

The Iran-Iraq War

Saddam Hussein's Ba'athist (Sunni) party ruled the Iraqi Shiite majority population in a secular setting with an iron fist. Wary of Iran's new religious leader, Ayatollah Khomeini, Hussein was concerned that Iran's Islamic revolutionary government would incite Iraq's Shiite majority to rebel against his regime. His desire to be the dominant force in the Middle East set the stage for an almost decade-long war with Iran.

Sensing a weakness in his Shiite adversary, Hussein invaded Iran on September 22, 1980. After initial Iraqi gains, the battle turned into a long war of attrition—reminiscent of World War I—that didn't end until August 1988. Sunni governments in the Middle East lined up with Hussein, and proxy forces lined up with countries that most reflected their religious beliefs. Even the United States— still smarting from the Iran hostage crisis and the fall of its ally, the shah of Iran—was tacitly supportive, at least initially.

While the war ended in a stalemate, it left behind a thick residue of resentments, distrust, and razor-sharp flash points that haunt us today. Two in particular are worth noting: First, with the end of hostilities, Hussein was left with a large and powerful army and air force ready to be deployed elsewhere; the preconditions for the invasion of Kuwait and the Gulf War that followed were now in place. Second, the war sharpened the chasm between Shiites and Sunnis and the respective countries and regimes each represented. The rift widened and has become a lightning rod for religious wars and terrorism now embroiling the Middle East.

Sino-American Relations

In its first two decades of existence, the People's Republic of China looked upon the United States as an imperialistic enemy. The feeling was reinforced by their adversarial positions in the Korean War and over Taiwan. With President Nixon's visit to China in 1972 and Mao's wariness of China's former ally, the USSR, the new ties culminated in the establishment of formal diplomatic relationships on January 1, 1979.

In a major breakthrough, the United States pledged in 1982 to limit arms sales to Taiwan, and China affirmed that a *peaceful* reunification with Taiwan was its formal policy. With the Taiwan question off the table, both countries started to forge closer economic ties. By the end of the decade, the United States had become one of China's largest trading partners.

The People's Republic of China undertook a number of reforms to open up and modernize its economy with a heavy focus on international trade, but not all went smoothly. In June 1989, a massive student protest in Tiananmen Square was met with tanks and gunfire. Nonetheless, China made tremendous strides in the 1980s and established a solid foundation for becoming the world's second superpower within two decades.

Asymmetric Warfare and Terrorism

In asymmetric warfare, a weaker nation or group uses unconventional weapons and/or tactics against a vastly superior enemy force. It can take many forms, ranging from guerrilla warfare and terrorism to high-tech cyberattacks on the energy grids or financial institutions of a developed nation. Henry Kissinger once said, "The guerrilla wins if he does not lose; the conventional army loses if it does not win." The successful guerrilla tactics used by the Vietcong in Vietnam are a classic example of asymmetric tactics used effectively against an opponent with superior power.

The Afghan War between the mujahideen rebel forces and the Soviet Union was another example. In this war, the United States supplied the rebel forces with Stinger missiles, hand-portable surface-to-air missiles used to knock down Soviet Union aircraft through our proxy—the rebels—without the United States ever firing a shot. Another example of an asymmetric proxy force is the support provided by Iran and Syria to Hezbollah[2] in its attacks against Israel.

Asymmetric warfare was expanded in the 1980s to include hijacking, kidnapping, and a growing use of suicide bombers. In October 1983, a suicide bomber attack against US Marine barracks in Lebanon killed 241 marines and wounded more than 100 more. In 1988, Pan Am flight 103 was blown out of the skies over Lockerbie, Scotland, by Libyan-supported terrorists. With a rich supply of displaced, battle-hardened troops from Afghanistan, Iran, and the Middle East to draw from, it was not hard to predict—even then—that this wasn't going to end well. Many of the asymmetric tactics employed today were developed and fine-tuned in the 1980s.

E-2: Energy and Technological Forces

Energy Forces

Compared to the sharp volatility of the oil markets in the 1970s, the 1980s were relatively calm; but looks can be deceiving. A closer look at the energy data foretold a deepening problem for the United States and others. Simply put, we were consuming more oil and producing less oil domestically—and the gap was widening.

Our love affair with automobiles fueled our addiction to oil. As a nation with less than 5 percent of the world's population in the 1980s, we produced less than 12 percent of the world's oil but consumed almost 27 percent. With the production of crude oil in the United States peaking in 1970 and dropping by almost 22 percent by 1989, our dependence on oil imports to sate our unquenchable oil thirsts climbed.

Domestic production numbers in the lower forty-eight states were even more dismal. The Trans-Alaska Pipeline System was fully operational by the early 1980s and produced a steady 1.8 million barrels per day—about 25 percent of America's domestic production—throughout the decade. (Alaskan oil production would start to decline in the 1990s.) The trajectories were ominous, and energy independence would become an issue of growing concern in the United States for years to come. Chart 11.2 illustrates the problem.

Chart 11.2: Oil Production and Consumption 1970–1989

Oil Production			Oil Consumption		
MB/D—million barrels per day			MB/D—million barrels per day		
Year	Global	USA	% of Total	Year	USA	% of Total Production
1970	48.06	9.64	20.1%	1970	14.70	30.05%
1980	62.95	8.60	13.7%	1980	17.06	27.10%
1989	64.04	7.61	11.8%	1989	16.99	26.53%

Source: Supporting data sets from Lester R. Brown, *World on the Edge: How to Prevent Environmental and Economic Collapse* (New York: W.W. Norton, 2010)

While the domestic oil crises of the 1970s were instigated by OPEC and the world oil markets, America's declining domestic production and growing reliance on foreign oil in the 1980s changed the global oil picture. Though oil prices were relatively stable in the 1980s, the control and production of oil would become a powerful bargaining chip in later decades.

America's electrical baseload power mix—the energy that creates electricity—was also changing in the 1980s. That mix would change even more in later decades to reflect new environmental and resource constraints. Chart 11.3 illustrates the baseload energy sources, as a percentage of the total, used to produce electricity in the 1980s.

Chart 11.3: US Electricity Generation Fuel Sources

Year	Coal	Petrol	Nat. Gas	Nuclear	Hydro	Renewable	Other
1980	50.7%	10.7%	15.1%	11.0%	12.2%	0.2%	0.1%
1989	53.4%	5.5%	11.9%	17.8%	9.2%	0.6%	1.6%

Source: Energy Information Administration, *Monthly Energy Review April 2016*

There are several key takeaways from this chart to keep in mind:

- Coal, as a baseload energy source, reached its peak of 53.4 percent in 1989. That percentage dropped to 33.2 percent by 2015.

- Petroleum, as a baseload fuel, dropped by almost half in the 1980s, reflecting the oil shortages and dramatic price increases of the 1970s.

- Nuclear power, as a baseload fuel, increased by almost 60 percent by decade's end. The number of nuclear reactors peaked at 112 in 1990. Three Mile Island and the Chernobyl nuclear accident of April 26, 1986, deterred the construction of new nuclear power plants in the decades that followed.

- Natural gas dropped from a 15.1 percent to 11.9 percent share in the 1980s, a trend that would reverse itself in the next century as new shale oil technologies and environmental concerns came into being. The use of natural gas as a baseload fuel was almost equal to that of coal in 2015, with a 32.7 percent share, and surpassed coal in 2016.

- Renewable energy was an insignificant factor in the 1980s; the boom would come later.

The Technological Juggernaut

Technological developments flourished on all fronts in the 1980s. From the launch of the space shuttle *Columbia,* the first of several spacecraft providing round-trip spaceflights, to the microscopic new world of genetic engineering, technology was on the move. The digital technology advances of the 1980s had an enormous impact on our daily lives.

The building blocks of the "connected" world we live in today came together in the 1980s. The technological trifecta of hardware, software, and networking infrastructures were developing and being commercialized, and computers were becoming smaller, cheaper, more powerful, and easier to operate. The computer revolution was rapidly branching out from large mainframe computers in corporate or academic settings to a distributed and connected set of computers linked to workstations and eventually to our homes.

The IBM 5150 personal computer was introduced in 1981, and the Apple Macintosh in 1984. Microsoft Windows 1.0, launched in 1985, enabled users to "point and click" in an integrated operating system that tied computer hardware to programs and printers. The advance toward a worldwide network (internet system) was jump-started in 1983 with the official adoption of the TCP/IP standards: transmission-control protocol (TCP) defined how packets of data moved back and forth between computers, and the internet protocol (IP) set up an internet addressing system. Breakthrough strides brought us to the cusp of a worldwide network by decade's end.

The technology blitz extended well beyond the computer realm. The Walkman became a "must" for every teenager; video cassette recorders (VCRs), camcorders, game consoles, and compact discs (CDs)—all part of our home "media centers"—kept us entertained and occupied for hours. Cable TV was a standard feature in many households by the end of the 1980s, and more affluent techies were early buyers of Motorola's 8000X mobile phone in 1983. The fax machine was an integral part of every office, and smart systems and advanced digital technology were used increasingly in every sector, from air traffic control and utilities to financial services. Cyberespionage and identity theft threats were not yet on our radar screens, but the doors were left ajar for the unwanted intrusions that would explode in the decades to come.

E-3: Environmental and Ecological Forces

Environmental initiatives in the 1980s began to gradually shift focus from the protection of natural resources—water, land, and air—to a broader construct that included global warming. Warnings from leading climate scientists, such as Stephen Schneider and James Hansen, drew attention to the correlation between the buildup of greenhouse gases and rising temperatures. The "greenhouse effect"—the theory that an umbrella of greenhouse gases would trap heat and warm the planet—was reinforced by a rise in global mean temperatures and a growing compilation of core ice samples and other data.

Our awakenings to the threat of global warming remained bumpy and gradual. For most of the decade, they were confined to the scientific community—or, more specifically, the arcane realm of climate science. But, as evidence mounted and the scientific community became more engaged, it busted out of this exclusive milieu and became part of the international policy-making agenda. Climate change began to attract the attention of powerful vested interests, particularly in the fossil-fuel sectors, and the fuse was lit for a contentious clash between climate-change believers and those contesting its legitimacy and/or the costs and benefits of acting on it.

Two groundbreaking events in the late 1980s brought the international community together to legitimize the growing threats of climate change and the efficacy of a global response to a climate-sized challenge: the first was the creation of the IPCC, and the second was the global agreement to address ozone depletion called the Montreal Protocol.

The International Panel on Climate Change

With strong leadership from the United States, this formal body was established under the auspices of the United Nations in 1988 to track and report on climate change and its social and economic implications. The IPCC was made up of thousands of international scientists and other experts charged with reporting regularly on the status of climate change. Their assessment reports were to be well vetted by a consensus agreement from the participating countries. Though challenged, the IPCC has been generally accepted as the prominent international authority on climate change.

The IPCC and its work will be discussed in future chapters. Every report since its inception has confirmed that climate change is happening, it is advancing at an accelerated pace, and it is, to a large extent, fueled by anthropogenic activities. For now, the important thing to know is that the IPCC framework established in the 1980s was based on growing concern that the world was warming.

The Montreal Protocol

Our planet has a razor-thin stratospheric layer of ozone that shields us and other living organisms from the toxic ultraviolet (UV) radiation from the sun. Scientists voiced their concerns in the 1970s that Earth's protective ozone umbrella was being destroyed by the release of CFCs—such as the refrigerant Freon—and the complex process it triggered. Their fears were confirmed in 1985 when satellites revealed a giant hole in the ozone shield above Antarctica as well as diminished ozone density in the Arctic regions.

Alarmed, the international community made a concerted effort to develop the Montreal Protocol, a global plan of action to eradicate ozone depletion. It was ratified by 196 nations and went into effect on January 1, 1989. Though ozone depletion levels worsened before they got better, they did improve in the twenty-first century, and the prognosis now looks very good. Two important lessons learned from the Montreal Protocol were that even something as humongous as a global atmospheric problem can be effectively addressed when the world mobilizes around a common challenge, and that challenges of this magnitude—with long timeframes—are not amenable to quick fixes and are best addressed sooner rather than later. Perhaps the greatest environmental contributions of the 1980s were the institution of credible international mechanisms for addressing the threats and demonstrating the efficacy of well-executed, determined global efforts.

E-4: Expectations and Behaviors

For many in our class of '61, the rapid-fire events of the 1980s were difficult to process and digest. Globalization, new technologies, changing power structures, confusing economic disconnects, and mysterious new developments like global warming and the HIV/AIDS epidemic were topics we left for academics and policy wonks to resolve. The totality of these events most certainly influenced our expectations and behaviors. Connecting the dots was not always easy, and rapid technological advances reduced the response time left for pondering and making decisions. The pace of living accelerated, our interconnections with others intensified, and the American Dream seemed slightly more elusive than before.

Charlie Darth pursued the American Dream through his career experiences, many of them in the public eye, during the turbulent 1970s and 1980s. In later years, he turned these experiences into meaningful efforts to help others in the nonprofit and educational arenas.

Charlie Darth

Charlie Darth's first foray into politics and the public eye did not end with his stint as vice president of the class of '61; in fact, it was only a beginning.

He parlayed his strong interest in economics, business, and public policy into a multifaceted career in city government, college academia, and the nonprofit arena. It was his pathway to the American Dream, and he pursued it with hard work, discipline, and tenacity. With a BA and Master's degree in business administration and finance from Mankato State in hand, Charlie embarked on a new career. Before doing so, however, he made what was probably the greatest career move of his life; he married his college sweetheart, Jan. And now, over fifty-two years later, with two kids, Hunter and Nicole, and five grandchildren, Jan and Charlie are still going strong.

Charlie's first career, almost twenty-five years in public service, started in 1969 when he joined the City of Brooklyn Park, now the sixth-largest city in Minnesota. He later became its director of finance and intergovernmental relations. Often in the public eye, he served in several city administrations, including that of a future governor, the Honorable Jesse Ventura. Charlie understood and adroitly worked through the complex contours of the political, public policy, and economic arenas in which he worked, a major win for the citizens of Brooklyn Park.

He started his second career in 1993 by sharing his experiences with the students of North Hennepin Community College as a business instructor. He worked tirelessly to get his students, young and older, prepared for a rapidly changing job market, and his practical firsthand knowledge of the business arena was of great value for many of them.

An activist, he joined the board of the nonprofit Housing Alternatives Development Company (HADC). Specializing in facilities for seniors, HADC appealed to his sense of community, and his expertise in strategic planning and finance were of particular value. Paul Abzug, President and CEO of HADC, said, "I relied heavily on Charlie as a barometer for guidance in strategic and financial direction and was always certain of Charlie's steadfast moral compass and leadership as a director of HADC."

Charlie remained a director of HADC for many years after retiring from the college in 2008. He has also served with other nonprofits, and both he and Jan are active in their church and with their family. Humble and unpretentious, they are living examples of "walking the talk."

A life well lived: with his old-school work ethic, grit, integrity, reliability, and respect for and commitment to others, Charlie has made his mark. His hope now is that those who follow him will have access to that same American Dream, with ample opportunities to be who they can be.

Despite a plethora of technological advances in the American worksite, global competitors were making huge inroads into the market share of our domestic companies. For example, the Big Three automakers were losing ground to foreign competitors as consumers focused more on the quality of the products they were buying. In 1982 Thomas J. Peters and Robert H. Waterman Jr. wrote the bestselling book *In Search of Excellence: Lessons from America's Best-Run Companies* (London: Profile Books, 1982). It quickly became required reading for every corporate employee, as it explored the art and science of effective management. Coupled with a new movement called Total Quality Management, American companies began an all-out effort to enhance the quality of their products and services and, in the process, recapture market share from the quality giants in Japan and elsewhere.

With new technologies and media options, our recreational choices also changed. Home video game systems offered youngsters an alternative to playing baseball down at the local park. Many adults were enthralled by the new electronic gadgetry in their homes, and others enjoyed the challenge of the Rubik's Cube or the hot new board game called Trivial Pursuit. Oprah Winfrey and Barbara Walters represented the rise of women in the media, and Walter Cronkite, perhaps the most trusted news anchor ever, retired in the early 1980s. More than 122 million Americans watched the final episode of *M*A*S*H* in 1983. Amid these changes, a new generational cohort, the Millennials, entered the scene; digital games would be to them what Tinkertoys and Lincoln Logs were to the class of '61.

On a less pleasant note, the death of Hollywood star Rock Hudson in 1985 from a mysterious illness known as AIDS (acquired immunodeficiency syndrome), shook the world and called attention to a disease that was afflicting the gay community and others. It terrified the public and conjured up, perhaps, the feeling of what leprosy must have seemed like in earlier times. It was the start of a world health problem that exists to this day, though our knowledge of and treatment for the disease—while expensive—has improved dramatically.

It was a decade of tremendous technological, geopolitical, and economic change, leaving the world a little smaller and certainly more interconnected. It was a springboard for the internet explosion that would close out the final decade of the old millennium and usher in the twenty-first century ten years later.

Mike Conley

I was filled with deep concern as I watched the stock market crash and burn on October 19, 1987. In an event called Black Monday, the Dow lost 22.6 percent of its value in one day, equivalent to a drop of almost sixty-five hundred points or so in today's market. The Federal Reserve quickly slashed short-term interest rates to prevent a recession and banking crisis, and the market stabilized not long after. It was a powerful reminder of how fast things could go south.

My concerns were compounded by the serious losses we were taking on our group health insurance business line in 1987. The knowledge that I would be taking over the entire group operation within a few months—with bottom line responsibility and care for our national operations and the thousands of people depending on my leadership—added to the tension. I was blessed with a top-notch team of senior officers and managers and a solid company that didn't panic in tough times, but it was still a scary situation.

I learned to believe that "this too shall pass," and it did. In retrospect, my climb up the corporate ladder in the 1980s had prepared me for these challenges, but crisis management, though energizing, is never a lot of fun. It has given me a deep appreciation for the struggles that many companies and good people go through in trying times. At least we didn't have to worry about cyberattacks and a host of new threats that have arisen since, such as the 9/11 attack, the market crash of 2008, and the new trade war with China.

On a more personal note, things were also changing on the home front. My oldest daughter, Kristen, started college in 1989 at the University of Wisconsin, and my youngest daughter, Heather, would soon be getting her driver's license. I could see, with more than a little nostalgia, a significant shift in the family dynamics of yesteryear. It is something we all go through, and it made me wish, occasionally, that I had spent more time at home; it was one of many trade-offs many of us make in life to balance a career with a family.

A ton of other changes and challenges would rock my world in the years to come, but I came to believe that though I couldn't change the direction of the wind, I could adjust my sails to weather the storms.

Summary of the 1980s

Globalization and technology were among the great game-changers, but the perfect storm was gaining traction on several fronts.

1. **Several economic milestones were bellwethers for the economic tsunamis of the future.**

    -   New Federal Reserve, deficit spending, and supply-side economic policies were introduced.

    -   The S&L industry collapse exposed dangers of deregulation, lax oversight, and hubris.

    -   The 401(k) plan revolutionized the pension market but shifted retirement risks to workers.

2. **Globalization and seismic geopolitical power shifts intensified the perfect storm risk.**

    -   Free trade and open markets surged: US trade balances suffered as other nations gained.

    -   Greater interconnectivity propelled growth but increased economic and health exposure to global risks.

- Terrorism and asymmetric warfare were firmly introduced into the power equation.

3. **Environmental concerns began to shift noticeably more toward global warming.**
   - The United Nations sponsored new infrastructure to monitor and report on global warming.
   - The Montreal Protocol to combat ozone depletion validated the global efforts.
   - The idea of global warming began to attract greater public attention.

4. **The strategic importance of King Oil—and OPEC—became dangerous new trip wires.**
   - Peak oil, increased oil usage, and declining production in the United States became a costly problem.
   - The economics of oil necessitated a greater military presence in the Middle East.
   - OPEC dominance of the global oil markets changed power structures and alliances.

5. **New digital technologies and greater connectivity sparked new norms and expectations.**
   - Greater connectivity changed the way we receive and process information.
   - The go-go milieu affected work routines, job security, and worker bonds.
   - The babies of the new Millennial generation arrived.
   - The die was cast—we just didn't know it.

SNAPSHOT: *1980–1990*

	1940	1950	1960	1970	1980	1990	2000
Population in Millions							
World	2,300.0	2,557.6	3,033.2	3,700.6	4,458.4	5,330.9	6,145.0
USA	132.1	152.3	180.7	205.1	227.2	249.6	282.2
US Financials in Billions							
GDP	$98.2	$278.7	$534.3	$1,046.7	$2,791.9	$5,898.8	$10,117.5
Fed. Receipts	6.5	39.4	92.5	192.8	517.1	1,032.0	2,025.2
Fed. Outlays	9.5	42.6	92.2	195.6	590.9	1,253.0	1,789.0
Surplus / (Deficit)	(2.9)	(3.1)	0.3	(2.8)	(73.8)	(221.0)	236.2
Gross Fed. Debt	50.7	256.9	290.5	380.9	909.0	3,206.3	5,628.7
Interest on Debt	0.9	4.8	6.9	14.4	52.5	184.3	223.0
US Domestic Averages							
Wages	$1,725	$3,210	$5,315	$9,400	$19,500	$28,960	$40,343
Cost of new house	3,920	8,450	12,700	23,450	68,700	123,000	134,150
Cost of new car	850	1,510	2,600	3,450	7,200	16,950	24,750

Points of Interest

- Berlin Wall is torn down; USSR is on the brink of collapse in the Reagan/Bush decade

- GDP more than doubles, but national debt—and interest on it—more than triples

- Birth of cable networks such as CNN, Fox, and others gain traction

- Chernobyl, Challenger disaster, and AIDS virus shake the world

Snapshot Road Map: *The Snapshot compares key data points from the beginning of one decade to the beginning of the next. Sources are provided under Part II in the endnotes.*

-12-

The 1990s

The Last "Best" Decade?

The last decade of the twentieth century was an extravaganza befitting the conclusion of the millennium. A transitional decade, it represented an inflection point of closures and new beginnings. In retrospect, many saw it as our last "best" decade. The future looked bright, and the hard work of the past half century seemed to be paying off—but things are not always as they seem to be. The glitter and glow of the 1990s—like a dramatic burst of a supernova—concealed the aftershocks of many of our so-called successes, time bombs that would erupt with a vengeance in the new millennium.

The class of '61 entered the decade as forty-six-year-olds approaching the mid to upper limits of their respective careers and closed with retirement as more than a casual afterthought. Indeed, some of us had entered the retiree ranks by decade's end. Most of us were now empty-nesters, despite intermittent visits from our Gen-X children between jobs, marriages, or whatever, and our attentions were increasingly redirected toward care for our aging parents. Wedged between these two generational cohorts, we struggled with the added responsibilities.

In this last decade of both the century and the millennium, there were prognostications galore about a future that started with a *2* and a past that was still fresh in our minds. We would also see some darker sides of events we'd once viewed as accomplishments.

The digital revolution, for instance, had concealed the Y2K threat that brought the century to a climatic close. The internet explosion of the 90s was laced with trip wires for cyberwars less than two decades later. The booming dot-com bubble would quickly burst in the new millennium. The Cold War that had once so dominated the world ended in a whimper with the collapse of the Soviet Union in 1991 while planting the seeds for a new cold conflict.

For the class of '61, the daily grind overshadowed how quickly the years were slipping by. Looking beyond the events of the day and grasping their longer-term significance was all but impossible. However, had we looked back to the changes that had occurred since we graduated, we would have been astonished.

Chart 12.1: Trendlines: 1961–2000

Event Category	1961	2000	Magnitude of Change
Global population[i]	3.1B	6.1B	Almost doubled
GDP in USA[ii]	$547.6B	$10,148.2B	Almost twentyfold increase
Gross federal debt[iii]	$292.6B	$5,628.7B	Almost twentyfold increase
Debt as % of GDP[iii]	53.4	55.5	Constant
Average wage[iv]	$5,315	$40,343	Almost eightfold increase
Average cost of new car[iv]	$2,850	$24,750	Almost nine-fold increase
Average cost of new house[iv]	$12,500	$134,150	About elevenfold increase
Gallon of gas[iv]	$0.27	$1.26	About fivefold increase
Buying power of $100 dollars in 1961[v]	$100	$17.36	Decrease of over 80%

(i) US Census Bureau, International Database, (ii) OMB: Fiscal 2017 Historical Tables, Table 10.1, (iii) OMB: Fiscal 2017 Historical Tables, Table 7.1, (iv) thepeoplehistory.com–Official Site: Years 1961 and 2000, (v) usinflationcalculator.com

Since our graduation, the world population had doubled and the American economy had increased almost twentyfold. While the debt-to-GDP ratio had remained fairly constant, it would climb dramatically in the new millennium. And, though wages had not kept pace with inflation, our access to easy credit and the growing move toward two wage earners per household accelerated consumer spending. It was an explosive decade of transition and transformation, and we now turn to the perfect storm model for a deeper look into the last best decade.

E-1: Economic and Geopolitical Forces

Economically, the 1990s started poorly and ended as one of the strongest decades ever. The aftershocks from the Black Monday Wall Street crash, collapse of the S&L industry, concerns over growing budget deficits, and inflationary ripples of the 1980s spilled into the new decade with a recession that lasted from July 1990 to March 1991.

Politically, though the United States led an international coalition that trounced and pushed the armies of Saddam Hussein out of Kuwait, President George H. Bush lost his presidential reelection bid to William Jefferson Clinton. After a rocky start, inability to pass a significant new health reform program (an omen of things to come), and a government shutdown in 1995, President Clinton and House Speaker Newt Gingrich found a way to work together in the second half of the decade, and a number of significant domestic initiatives were enacted.

The second half of the decade differed dramatically from the first. Our average GDP growth rate climbed into the 4.3 percent range—numbers we just don't see anymore. It was the age of a new economy, as the United States shifted away from a manufacturing to a more service-based economy. The internet explosion triggered a dot-com boom that turbocharged the economy until it burst at the start of the new millennium, as bubbles always do.

The internet was changing things at warp speed. With processing areas ripe for computerization, the United States made tremendous new productivity gains. While exciting, the explosion also highlighted our vulnerability to the Y2K bug, a fear that due to a bug in data formatting and storage, IT systems would be unable to distinguish the year 2000 from the year 1900; crash programmers and corporate staff worked overtime to ensure that the threat never materialized.

The 401(k) boom skyrocketed in the 1990s, and stock market results were watched more closely than ever before by rank-and-file Americans. As one measure of growth, a comparative look at the Dow Jones averages in chart 12.2 reflects the bust and boom economy of the 90s:

Chart 12.2: Dow Jones Averages

Timeframe	1990	1995	1999
Year-end open:	2,749	3,834	9,184
Year-end close:	2,629	5,117	11,453
Net change:	−4.4%	+33.4%	+24.7%

Source: DJI Average Historical Data – Yahoo Finance

Despite the modest recession of the early 1990s, the market—as reflected in the Dow Jones average—grew fourfold in only a decade. It prompted Fed Chairman Alan Greenspan to use the term "irrational exuberance" in 1996 to describe the market. From Wall Street to Main Street, we were on a roll. The median household income had grown by about 10 percent, and the federal government actually generated a budget surplus by the end of the decade, something unlikely to ever happen again.

In this flurry of growth, a number of game-changing legislative actions helped reshape the economy, including changes in financial structures, the financing of social welfare plans, and a bias for international trade arrangements. Ironically, many of these actions would become powder kegs for the contentious political dialogue that exists today. Three acts, in particular, are worth noting for their impact on our nation:

1) Financial Services Modernization Act of 1999: This act repealed the Glass-Steagall Act of 1933 that separated the various areas of financial services. It opened the floodgates for comingling the activities of banking, securities, and insurance services, and it created a market ripe for the fallout that so often accompanies rapid deregulation. (Parenthetically, it also paved the way for the Commodity Futures Modernization Act of 2000 that many believe opened the door for the shadow banking and derivative transaction markets that played such an egregious role in the market meltdown of 2008.)

2) Welfare Reform Act of 1996: Known officially as the Personal Responsibility and Work Opportunity Reconciliation Act of 1996, this bipartisan plan dramatically changed the welfare system. It required work in exchange for time-limited assistance and restructured the federal-state relationship with respect to providing welfare benefits linked to a set of performance metrics, a requirement for maintaining the programs.

3) NAFTA: The North American Free Trade Agreement that went into effect on January 1, 1994, was controversial from the start. Designed to eliminate trade and investment barriers between the United States, Canada, and Mexico, it became a lightning rod for pitting the advantages of globalization against nationalistic goals most favored by labor.

Three game-changing geopolitical events in the 1990s set the stage for the new millennium: the fall of the Soviet Union and end of the Cold War, the Gulf War and terrorism, and the restructuring of Europe and Asia.

The Fall of the USSR

On December 26, 1991, the Soviet Union was officially dissolved. Its incremental unraveling can be traced back to events such as the fall of the Berlin Wall, the costly war in Afghanistan, an inability to maintain military parity with the United States, and the gradual collapse of several communist regimes in Eastern Europe.

In the summer of 1991, hardliners of the old communist order, sensing its end, staged a coup that failed. While diminishing the power of Mikhail Gorbachev, it propelled Boris Yeltsin into a position of power. Belarus and the Ukraine declared their independence from the USSR, and things began to quickly unravel. The hammer and sickle flew over the Kremlin for the last time on Christmas Day of 1991. Gorbachev resigned, and Yeltsin became the president of the new Russian state.

As this shocking reality set in, the disposition of the arsenal scattered throughout the Soviet Union was of great concern to the world. The United States became a major funder of the costs of consolidating and dismantling the nuclear, biological, and chemical weapons scattered throughout the former USSR. In good faith, the Ukraine and others turned their nuclear weapons over to Russia for assurances that its natural gas and other resources would flow freely in return, a decision that many Ukrainians would later come to regret.

With the fall of the Soviet Union, the Cold War, by default, was over. It left an enormous power vacuum in which the former Soviet republics, client states of the old USSR, and global power circles all over the world sought new partnerships, military ties, and economic alliances. The North Atlantic Treaty Organization (NATO) expanded its membership eastward to include some of the former Eastern Bloc nations that once formed the buffer zone between the West and the USSR.

While welcomed by many, it was a bitter pill for the old communist hierarchy to swallow. The loss of their superpower status and territory left many of them bitter and resentful, ripe for the messages of an obscure but rising young leader with a dream of restoring Russia to past glories.

There was little Vladimir Putin could do to change the situation in the years immediately following the fall of the USSR, but Russia still possessed the world's second-largest nuclear arsenal with ICBM delivery systems, and hence, they were a superpower in at least a military sense. Their vast reserves of oil, gas, and other resources enhanced their position. Still, their glory days were over, and Khrushchev's threat to "bury" the West was no longer in the cards.

Opportunities to bring Russia into the fold as an equal partner were squandered, and it would again emerge as a formidable player—a reflection of the fluid nature of geopolitical history. Power structures, empires, and world currencies come and go, and nothing in history suggests that the United States will remain a superpower in perpetuity; it is something that has to be constantly worked on and earned.

The Gulf War and Terrorism

The bloody Iran-Iraq War, fought between September 1980 and August 1988, was a conflict between two despotic regimes and part of a greater Sunni and Shiite struggle. It sparked fears of further violence in the Middle East, and the Saudi and Kuwaiti governments, fearing Iran, provided Iraq with significant financial support. The war ended in a stalemate.

With no clear-cut winners, and Iraq still possessing the fourth-largest army in the world, Saddam Hussein turned his eyes to the south and invaded Kuwait on August 2, 1990. In less than forty-eight hours, Kuwait was declared Iraq's nineteenth province. Hussein then repositioned his armies on the Saudi border, raising grave concerns that he would attack Saudi Arabia and target its major oil fields. Any threat to the Saudi oil fields—the world's largest producers—was deemed a dire threat to global security.

President Bush announced that Hussein's invasion "would not stand" and amassed an international coalition force to oust his armies from Kuwait. Despite UN resolutions, threats, and blustering, Hussein failed to evacuate. On February 24, 1991, an American-led coalition launched a ground attack—code-named Operation Desert Storm—and the Iraqi army was thoroughly defeated in short order.

The allied forces did not cross the Iraqi border in pursuit of Hussein. His decimated armies quickly regrouped and soon thereafter repressed a Kurdish uprising in the north and a Shiite movement in the south. As a condition of peace, the allies established a no-fly zone that Iraq chafed over; the so-called peace was not so peaceful.

In the aftermath, the US military maintained a powerful presence in the Middle East, something Arab hardliners and terrorist groups saw as a new form of Western occupation. The volume and intensity of terroristic attacks escalated, beginning a chain reaction of events that would erupt in the new millennium, including the 9/11 attack, the second Gulf War in Iraq and Afghanistan, the Arab Spring uprisings, the growth of ISIS, ongoing Sunni-Shiite conflicts, and uneasiness in Israel. Isaac Newton was right: where's there's an action, there is also a reaction.

The Restructuring of Europe

Within a span of only a decade, the nations of Europe forged together to create a giant community of nations called the European Union. The fall of the Soviet Union changed international dynamics as the Eastern Bloc nations, once part of the Warsaw Pact—the USSR's counterforce to NATO—were freed to develop their own political and economic systems. Western European nations, in the meantime, were thriving and quick to see new trade opportunities. They looked at the trade rules and regulations, currencies, cultures, and other barriers that impeded their ability to fully leverage and capitalize on a greater European community as a market. The reunification of Germany had sparked a host of initiatives that eased trade barriers and restrictions between the European nations; the doors were opening for a broad community of European nations operating together.

The Birth of the European Union (EU): While the European community had been working toward a single market for decades, the 1992 Treaty of Maastricht officially opened the doors of the new European Union on November 1, 1993. The founding nations of Europe were now bound together toward a uniform platform of governance; economic, financial, and social integration; and, of course, greater security under the covenants of NATO.

Their quest to facilitate the movement of people, goods, services, and capital between EU nations was highly successful. As a unified bloc, the EU had a twenty-eight-nation membership base of more than five hundred million people with an aggregated GDP roughly equal to that of the United States by 2017. The euro is now one of the strongest currencies in the world.

NATO Expansion: NATO was formally established on April 1, 1949. The original twelve nations inking the treaty, including the United States, had incorporated under article 5 of its charter a provision that "an attack on one member is an attack on all." It was clearly meant to deter attacks from the Soviet Union.

With the end of the Cold War in 1991 and the dissolution of the Warsaw Pact, the old power structure crumbled. By the end of the first decade in the new millennium, twenty-eight nations had enrolled as members of NATO, many of them former Warsaw Pact members. The old Russian Bolsheviks watched with alarm as their former buffer states changed sides and the West encroached ever closer to their motherland. The seeds of a new cold war were being sown, particularly after the Republics of Georgia and the Ukraine flirted with NATO membership.

The Pacific Rim in Transition

This vast geographic expanse includes nations and islands bordering on or islanded within the Pacific Ocean. China, Japan, Australia, and South Korea are among the larger nations within this parameter. In 1967, the governments of Indonesia, Malaysia, the Philippines, Singapore, and Thailand founded the Association of Southeast Asian Nations (ASEAN).[1]

A comparison of the two major economic powers in this region over the period from 1990 to 2010 illustrates how significantly the balance of power has shifted in the Pacific Rim from Japan to China.

Chart 12.3: Nominal GDP

–in Billions of US Dollars–			
Country	1990	2000	2010
Japan	3,032	4,669	5,449
China	390	1,198	5,950

Source: Data taken from composite economic reports.

The Japanese economy, about eight times larger than China's in 1990, was surpassed by China around 2010. By 2015 China's economy was almost three times the size of Japan's. The 1990s were known as the Lost Decade[2] for Japan, and indeed, the country's economy continued to stagnate into the new millennium. China's emergence as a superpower, as well as South Korea's strong standing in the Pacific Rim, took root in the 1990s.

The Asian financial crisis of 1997–1998 was particularly devastating for Indonesia, Thailand, and the Philippines. Japan was already in an economic abyss, but China, while feeling its effects, fared better than other Asian nations. The causes of the Pacific Rim crash resembled the bursting asset bubble that would trigger the Great Recession in 2008: an overheated market, subprime lending, speculative borrowing, currency exchange issues, and other risks. Without doubt, the 1990s represented a major inflection point in the coming transition to new global power structures not only in the Pacific Rim but also in Europe and the Middle East.

E-2: Energy and Technological Forces

The 1990s were made to order for a dramatic surge in energy consumption. The key driving forces were all in place, including huge growth in population, rising rates of per-capita energy consumption, a growing global economy, and relatively low energy costs.

Despite the economic bumps previously mentioned, the overall global economy was good. The dot-com surge in the United States alone produced an average GDP growth rate exceeding 4 percent in the latter half of the decade. As one measure of the economic-energy correlation, the total energy consumption level in the United States jumped from 84.3 quads of energy in 1990 to 98.5 quads in 2000—a remarkable increase of over 16 percent in just one decade. (See chapter 3 for a description of energy metrics.)

Oil—the mother's milk of economic growth—was favorably priced throughout the decade and averaged around $23 per barrel for most of the decade, even though global demand grew by almost 20 percent from 63.5 million barrels per day in 1990 to 75.5 in 1999.

Despite stable prices amid a remarkable ramp-up in consumption, oil would soon become an Achilles' heel for not only the United States but also the world. At its peak, the United States, with only 4 percent of the world's population, consumed about 25 percent of its oil. As our oil consumption increased and production dropped, we turned increasingly to foreign markets for oil to sustain our economic growth. Chart 12.4 sketches America's growing dependence on foreign oil.

Chart 12.4: US Oil Use 1990–2000

–In Millions of Barrels Per Day of Oil–			
	1990	2000	Change
Domestic oil consumption*	17.0	19.7	+15.8%
Domestic oil production*	9.6	8.7	−9.4%
Oil import (estimates)	7.0	10.2	+45.7%

* Source: EIA Monthly Energy Review, April 2014, Table 3.1. Imports are estimated.

The chart reveals three troubling trajectories of the 1990s: domestic oil consumption increased by 15.8 percent, domestic oil production dropped by 9.4 percent, and the United States increased its foreign oil imports by over 45 percent to make good on the shortfall.

By decade's end, OPEC was in the driver's seat, and the United States was paying dearly for its addiction to oil. The annual drain on our economy from importing 10 million barrels per day of oil at $23 per barrel is about $84 billion. At $100 per barrel, that number climbs to about $365 billion per annum. In our consumer-based economy, the shifting of these discretionary dollars from domestic consumption to foreign coffers for oil purchases would become an increasingly serious problem.

On a different front, the technological blitzkrieg of the 1990s changed our world, and it all happened so fast. The Hubble Space Telescope launched to explore deep space from space; construction began on the International Space Station in a joint operating agreement with several nations; the Global Positioning System (GPS), now widely used everywhere, launched; and micromapping of human DNA commenced through the Human Genome Project. The impact on humankind has been incalculable, but nothing has affected more people more quickly than the growth and commercialization of the internet and World Wide Web.

Their explosive growth within a span of only a decade defies description. In short order, the manner in which we worked, played, communicated, processed information, and engaged in commerce at all levels changed or was in the process of changing. The dot-com revolution connected computers and people to a worldwide network, thanks to many developments, including

- increased speed and decreased cost of computing power,

- continuous improvements in data storage and retrieval capacity,

- software applications growing in scope and becoming more user-friendly,

- improvements in networking and connectivity at all levels, and

- better performance in sensors and devices that respond to various inputs.

The World Wide Web was officially introduced in the early 1990s; its fifty or so web servers around the world in January 1993 increased to more than five hundred by October of that same year. By decade's end, there were more than seventeen million websites in operation. Meanwhile, operating systems, such as Windows 95 (introduced in 1995), became more user-friendly, and the growth in household computers increased as well. Between 1990 and 1997, home ownership of computers is estimated to have increased from 15 percent to 35 percent; computers quickly changed from a "luxury" to "necessity" status.

Corporate America and entrepreneurs were quick to recognize the potential of this digital arena; new e-commerce marketing initiatives and distribution opportunities gained traction. Traditional brick-and-mortar retailers and print media, among others, would soon be struggling to protect market share and remain relevant.

In an explosion of new "dot-com" start-ups, venture capitalists spent fortunes on companies that had never made a profit or sale, betting that they would revolutionize the marketplace. The market caps of a start-up company sometimes exceeded those of long-proven legacy companies. That bubble would burst early in the following decade.

Through the Y2K issue and the birth of the internet and World Wide Web, we got our first real look at how dependent we had become on this new cyber world—and how vulnerable we were to system threats. In retrospect, the Y2K scare seems minuscule compared to later cyberthreats.

E-3: Environmental and Ecological Forces

The 1990s marked a turning point in our approach to environmental and ecological issues. Global warming and climate change joined issues like clean water, clean air, and waste management and quickly gained traction.

Scientists and others were increasingly concerned about a growing body of research suggesting the intensification of global warming. In the late 1980s, the Montreal Protocol—focused on the ozone depletion threat—had demonstrated the efficacy of pulling together the international community to address a global atmospheric threat, providing a model for a systematic effort to address global warming.

This recognition became a reality in the 1990s with the adoption of the United Nations Framework Convention on Climate Change (UNFCCC). The UNFCCC became operational on March 21, 1994, with the objective of stabilizing GHG concentrations in the atmosphere at a level that would prevent dangerous anthropogenic interference with the climate system. Ratified by 197 nations, including the United States, it provided a nonbinding framework and a recognized international authority for monitoring and reporting on climate change. At last, there was an institutionalized global structure and process for addressing climate change.

As part of that process, The UNFCCC organized an annual Conference of the Parties (COP) forum, and each successive meeting was numbered. Its job was to provide annual assessments and develop agreements or protocols for addressing climate-change-related issues. The Paris Agreement—discussed later—was a product of COP-21.

The IPCC, established in 1988 to prepare a report on climate change in 1990, has provided periodic assessments ever since. IPCC assessments are developed by an international group of climate scientists and other specialists and then exhaustively vetted. Though fiercely debated and often challenged, their painstaking work and the gravitas they provide as an international authority on climate change is well accepted by almost all scientific bodies and countries. Over time, these assessments have become increasingly assertive in reporting that climate change is a progressively growing threat, it is highly shaped by anthropogenic forces, and it is growing at a more rapid pace than previously thought.

The Kyoto Protocol, the first major international product of the UNFCCC, was adopted in Kyoto in 1997. It provided an international framework for addressing greenhouse gas emissions and was signed by President Clinton in 1998. When it finally took effect in 2005, the US Senate refused to ratify it, and the United States never became a partner in this international venture. As the world's largest emitter of greenhouse gases in the 1990s, we dealt a major blow to the international community with this rejection. Domestic opponents of the protocol rejected it out of fear the United States would be targeted and the economic costs of compliance prohibitive. The protocol was thought to be flawed in its exemption of China, India, and other developing nations from emissions controls; it was too much for many Americans to swallow.

In retrospect, the 1990s will stand out as the decade in which the international challenge of climate change was identified and widely accepted as a growing threat, and in which a formal set of internationally agreed-upon structures and protocols were established to address climate change in a systematic way.

E-4: Expectations and Behavioral Forces

As the class of '61 entered the last decade of the millennium, our world was about to change in ways we couldn't imagine. The two defining events of the 1990s, arguably, were the end of the Cold War and the birth of the World Wide Web. The former had been an everyday threat since our childhood, and the latter would change major aspects of our lives and the way we lived them. Worldwide connectivity would influence our worldviews, expectations, and behaviors, and we struggled to understand it. The speed of change would once again exceed our ability to assimilate and adapt accordingly.

We marveled at how our children seemed to intuitively adapt to internet technologies and the plethora of new electronic devices, games, and gadgetry that seemed to crop up at warp speed. Though many of us owned home computers, we struggled with change as our children embraced it.

Without doubt, our expectations and behaviors were shaped by these developments. Still, many of us entered the new millennium a quart or two low on the resiliency needed to complete the transition. Clearly, we had a lot to learn. Some, like Mike Bernick, embraced the learning process.

Mike Bernick

My life changed in the mid-1990s when I decided to go back to school and renew my teaching certificate. As part of that requirement, I was required to take a human relations course. It was a game-changer for me.

I'm not sure if it was the course itself, the instructor, or if it was just a time in my life that I was open to new ideas; whatever it was, it awakened a new energy in me to learn more about the geopolitical world we live in and what, in effect, makes it tick. It was one of those great "aha" moments in life that has turned me into a lifelong learner.

For openers, it made me realize how uninvolved I was outside of my own small universe. Raising a great family was such a crucial part of that existence for so many years that I tended to gloss over many of the pressing world events that were transpiring around me. For whatever reason, that course triggered in me a voracious appetite to learn more.

In my personal journey of discovery, it became obvious to me how willing we are to accept news events at face value without digging into their accuracy and the underlying forces and motivations behind them. I became more energized, and, like a detective looking for clues, I started to dig deeper into the current events unfolding before my very eyes. And, as I dug into these issues, my concerns—and curiosity—grew. My quest to learn was turbocharged by two significant events:

First, the 9/11 attack—and its aftermath—was troubling. To this day, I don't believe we have an accurate picture of what really happened. I've read and cross-checked several references and reports that don't jibe with many of the official government accounts, and this bothers me. My search into these—and other similar issues—has been long, deep, wide, and ongoing.

The second event is the awesome power of the internet and my ability to quickly access the information I want to review. The accessibility makes it easier to dig deeper into the complex issues of our time. I often supplement this information with books that I heavily mark up as reference points. While disturbing at times, it's satisfying to discover the interconnectivity of all the moving parts—an awareness that had previously eluded me.

At this stage of my life, I want to learn more. Maybe it's the old-school teacher in me, but I enjoy researching and assembling the data I collect into a logical story. As one example, I've done a considerable amount of research on Venezuela and have packaged it all under the heading of "Logic Takes a Vacation." One of my bigger challenges is to find good avenues for disseminating this information. For now, let's just consider this and other stories I've done as "works in progress."

In a culture that has become increasingly enamored with sound-bites, celebrity, social media, advocacy journalism, and broadcasting that best reflects our beliefs, our desire to delve deeper into the issues to formulate our own conclusions would become more the exception than the rule in the new millennium. Mike Bernick's self-study approach is well worth considering.

Our behaviors and expectations were also changing in other ways. Birth rates were down, and divorce rates were up; marriage rates were lower and the average age of marriages higher. With both parents working, part of the child-raising process was outsourced to a caring adult or daycare center. Gender roles were changing as more women climbed the corporate ladder—albeit more slowly than desired—and engaged in more jobs that were once the domain of men. The multicultural movement broke many of the barriers that existed only a few decades back, but we still had (and have) a long way to go.

As we watched the intensity and tempo of life ramp up, we found ourselves more often than not in the twilight zone. Far less resilient to change than those following us, we looked for ways to ride it out until we reached retirement—not that far off as the decade came to a close.

Little did we know that the 1990s would represent the last full decade that analog systems dominated the landscape, that big book-stores with coffee shops would thrive, that newspapers and traditional broadcast media outlets would dominate our information-gathering processes, and that the big-box stores and retail malls that epitomized our marketing and distribution channels for decades would exist as they had in the "good old days." Before moving on to the new millennium in the next chapter, a few closing reflections on the 1990s—the last best decade—are in order.

Mike Conley

The 1990s were fascinating times. As head of our Employee Benefit operation, selling benefit plans nationwide, and a member of our senior executive team, I was heavily involved in new activities, like lobbying in Washington on healthcare-related issues; setting up a new worksite marketing operation to seamlessly offer a portfolio of our company products and services—employee benefits, 401(k) plans, counseling services, etc.—to our employer customers; and working with business analysts, trade organizations, rating agencies, and the Wall Street crowd.

It was gratifying to watch our business grow, but working with Wall Street—with its myopic focus on quarterly earnings and not strategic opportunities—got to be a drag. While I loved my job and the people I worked with, I had a plan B in mind to become financially able to retire at age fifty-five. I spent the last half year of my career working on an orderly transition—not hard to do in a great company with great people.

As part of that process, I talked to retired executives and read a lot about the transitional dynamics of retirement. We often validate ourselves through our careers, but I never wanted to do this. With my identity detached from my career, I found it amusing to see how, when I became a lame duck, the phone didn't ring as often, and folks didn't laugh as loud at my jokes. I was ready to move on when I retired on June 30, 1998, and I've had no regrets since.

In fact, I took my first flying lesson the day after I retired and pursued it with a passion. I bought a plane and got my private pilot and instrument rating as soon as possible. It was a dream come true, and it was not unusual for me to go flying several times a week. I was also interested in giving something back for all that I had received, and Sharon and I set up the Conley Family Foundation to engage in planned giving in a meaningful way.

Working with wonderful nonprofit organizations has been most rewarding, and I was honored to serve as chairman of the board of Hazelden shortly after retiring. I looked at it as being in the "miracle" business because of the life-transforming nature of the recovery it brought to the folks we served, something I knew from personal experiences.

On the home front, my dad died in 1998, but we gained a great new son-in-law when Todd Hoatson married Kristen. Heather was busy in school, and Sharon and I immersed ourselves in building our foundation. I also traveled regularly to New York as an outside director on the ReliaStar of New York Board—a board I was on while employed at ReliaStar.

I look back on the 1990s with wonderful memories and feelings of gratitude. I didn't know it at the time, but the new doors and opportunities that were opening a crack would soon lead to things that I could never have imagined. But that's a story for the next chapter and the new millennium.

Summary of the 1990s

It was a decade of closures and new beginnings. The Cold War had ended, but the seeds of a new one were sown. The internet connected the world but opened the door to cyber shenanigans. Global warming concerns were rising. Key contributors to the perfect storm included the following:

1. **The abrupt end to the Cold War created a geopolitical power vacuum.**

    - The fall of the USSR and dissolution of the Warsaw Pact were never accepted by Russia.

    - The Gulf War, an increase in terrorist activity, and strife in the Middle East followed.

    - Europe restructured as the new EU; in the Pacific Rim, China emerged as a more powerful player.

2. **The strong global economy concealed a few ticking time bombs.**

    - The quest for free-trade alliances created an economic bonanza, but it would turn ugly in later years.

    - The dot-com bubble expanded in the United States, setting up the next decade's problems with speculation and a herd mentality—fueled by the 401(k) boom.

- The United States enjoyed its last balanced budgets; debt would fuel growth thereafter.

3. **Technology and the internet explosion changed the world and the way that we lived.**

   - The speed of global connectivity intensified; cybersecurity was not on the radar screen.

   - Business and marketing models began to change, but many could not adapt.

   - Advances in medical science further increased life expectancy.

4. **Global warming was increasingly recognized as a world threat.**

   - Global actions resulting in the Kyoto Protocol attested to the concerns—recognizing that climate change is real, largely anthropogenic, and intensifying.

   - A backlash followed as vested interests dug in to preserve the status quo.

5. **Longer-term energy issues—mainly the oil markets—were coming to a head.**

   - The shortfall between US domestic oil production and consumption widened.

   - OPEC oil producers gained tremendous leverage and changed dynamics in the Middle East.

   - Global consumption patterns climbed as China and others rapidly grew.

SNAPSHOT: *1990–2000*

	1940	1950	1960	1970	1980	1990	2000
Population in Millions							
World	2,300.0	2,557.6	3,033.2	3,700.6	4,458.4	5,330.9	6,145.0
USA	132.1	152.3	180.7	205.1	227.2	249.6	282.2
US Financials in Billions							
GDP	$98.2	$278.7	$534.3	$1,046.7	$2,791.9	$5,898.8	$10,117.5
Fed. Receipts	6.5	39.4	92.5	192.8	517.1	1,032.0	2,025.2
Fed. Outlays	9.5	42.6	92.2	195.6	590.9	1,253.0	1,789.0
Surplus / (Deficit)	(2.9)	(3.1)	0.3	(2.8)	(73.8)	(221.0)	236.2
Gross Fed. Debt	50.7	256.9	290.5	380.9	909.0	3,206.3	5,628.7
Interest on Debt	0.9	4.8	6.9	14.4	52.5	184.3	223.0
US Domestic Averages							
Wages	$1,725	$3,210	$5,315	$9,400	$19,500	$28,960	$40,343
Cost of new house	3,920	8,450	12,700	23,450	68,700	123,000	134,150
Cost of new car	850	1,510	2,600	3,450	7,200	16,950	24,750

Points of Interest

- USSR falls; end of Cold War; Gulf War in 1991; spread of terrorism

- World population doubles between 1960 and 2000

- GDP in USA doubles, but Fed. debt grows by 75 percent under Bush and Clinton

- Birth of the internet; the Y2K threat is mitigated

Snapshot Road Map: *The Snapshot compares key data points from the beginning of one decade to the beginning of the next. Sources are provided under Part II in the endnotes.*

-13-

The New Millennium: 2000–2009

*What's intoxicating on the way up
can be devastating on the way down.*

On January 1, 2000, many awoke to the new millennium breathing a sigh of relief that the dreaded Y2K threat had not materialized. Weeks later, a computer-related problem of another type—the bursting of the dot-com bubble—would send the NASDAQ plummeting, a harbinger of things to come. The IOUs from the previous century were about to come due; the proverbial chickens were coming home to roost, and we were about to embark on the ride of our lives.

For members of the class of '61, now fifty-six-year-old life-hardened veterans, the specter of retirement loomed large; indeed, some had already entered the ranks. Our net worth was heavily tied to our 401(k) plans and the rising value of our houses. Both strongholds would be ravaged by the market meltdown in 2008, leaving many fearful they might outlive their savings.

Few could have imagined on that New Year's Day 2000 the many game-changing events that would so unravel their lives by the end of the decade. On the morning of September 11, 2001, we watched in horror as a handful of terrorists brought down the Twin Towers in New York City, an event that would lead to America's longest war. A few years later, we watched the subprime mortgage fiasco escalate into the worst global economic meltdown since the Great Depression of the 1930s. Soaring oil prices threatened our economy, and climate-change tremors increased in frequency and intensity. Our story begins with the 9/11 terrorist attack, our new Pearl Harbor, if you will.

E-1: Economic and Geopolitical Forces

Geopolitical Forces

The first of four hijacked planes, American Airlines Flight 11, crashed into the North Tower of the World Trade Center at 8:46 a.m. on the morning of September 11, 2001. Shortly after, United Airlines Flight 175 crashed into the South Tower. In less than two hours, both 110-story towers collapsed, with a huge loss of lives. Meanwhile, a third plane, American Airlines Flight 77, crashed into the Pentagon, and a fourth, United Airlines Flight 93, was brought down by heroic passengers before the hijackers could redirect the plane to their Washington, DC, target.

The world was stunned by the audacity of this al-Qaeda-led attack on the most powerful nation on Earth. Within days, the United States declared war on terrorism and advised other nations that they were either with us or against us. On October 7, 2001, under the code name Operation Enduring Freedom, the United States launched its first military attack against the Taliban and al-Qaeda targets in Afghanistan. In the meantime, a war of words began between Iraqi leader Saddam Hussein and the Western powers. Many believed that Hussein had or would soon possess weapons of mass destruction, and others believed he had a hand in the 9/11 attack. They were wrong on both counts.

On March 20, 2003, an American-led coalition launched a "shock and awe" bombing campaign prior to the invasion of Iraq.

Under the code name Operation Iraqi Freedom, Hussein's forces were decisively defeated in a matter of weeks. Though militarily successful, the Bush administration quickly learned two things: Iraq did not possess weapons of mass destruction, and occupying Iraq would be infinitely more difficult than winning the actual war.

The occupation of Iraq went bad from the get-go and left the United States deeply enmeshed in the quagmires of Iraq and Afghanistan. The mismanaged occupation led to sectarian violence between the Shias and the Sunnis and an ongoing insurgency against occupation forces. The tenets of General Colin Powell's "Powell Doctrine"—that war, as a last resort, should have a clear-cut mission and objectives, be fought with overwhelming force, and have within it an exit strategy—were all but forgotten.

The financing of the war was also unclear. Using off-the-books accounting gimmicks, such as "emergency funding" that did not count against the Pentagon's budget, as well as private contractors and other schemes, the wars were essentially financed on credit. Proposed funding from our partners or from Iraqi oil revenues never materialized. The estimated cost of the wars varies widely, but it is likely in the $3–5 trillion range by now and still climbing; exact numbers have never been given.

As a sign of our growing addiction to debt, two tax-reduction bills were passed in 2001 and 2003 respectively. The latter, passed *after* the start of the Iraq War, added to and accelerated the level of debt. Previous wars had been partially funded with war bonds, higher taxes, and reductions in nonessential spending, but not this time.

With the United States heavily engaged in the Middle East and fighting well-financed terrorist groups, other sectors of the globe were changing. Russia was regrouping under Putin's leadership and gradually reasserting itself on the global stage. With archrival Saddam Hussein out of the picture, Iran was stirring the pot in the Middle East through its proxy Hezbollah. Latin America was all but forgotten, and China was quietly working to become the world's newest superpower.

China's model of expansion in the twenty-first century is worth noting. The first thing to know is that China thinks and acts strategically, developing and executing its five-year plans with care and determination. This model featured an economic, not military, focus and looked something like this: First, China engaged with countries without preconditions, such as human rights or power alignments. It could then offer new partners protection from outside threats, such as UN sanctions, via its veto power on the UN Security Council. It would then provide capital and technological assistance to develop infrastructure, including roads and ports. It would then lock in access to the host country's natural resources, extract them, and manufacture end products to be sold back as finished goods to the host country and others.

China invested heavily in other countries, including the United States. For instance, prior to the 2008 economic collapse, China held over $1.2 trillion in US reserve currency and well over $500 billion in US treasury securities. China was a lead partner in developing the Shanghai Cooperative Organization (SCO),[1] a Eurasian alliance that includes several oil-rich and strategically located nations that have become a growing counterbalance to traditional Western powers.

In summary, the geopolitical landscape had rapidly changed. With the United States heavily engaged in Iraq and Afghanistan, China was emerging as the world's newest superpower, and Russia, North Korea, Iran, and others were in a resurgent mode.

Economic Forces

In the autumn of 2008, the worst economic meltdown since the Great Depression erupted with a fury and speed that stunned the world. Its causes are complex and involve a number of financial concepts that are not easy to understand. Without getting too deep into the weeds, the real story rests in the chain reaction of events that triggered the great meltdown.

While the meltdown was immediately attributed to the subprime mortgage crisis and a bursting housing bubble, its destructive seeds had been planted long before the actual event. Chart 13.1:

Anatomy of an Economic Meltdown illustrates the chain reaction of the disaster and its aftermath. In a chronological order, it played out something like this:

1. Sloppy fiscal and monetary policies coupled with relaxed regulatory oversight, a quest for easy money, and excess liquidity set the stage years before the actual crash.

2. The contagion of deficit spending spread across all levels of government, corporate America, and individual households.

3. Institutional and regulatory oversight became lax, fostering an institutional spread of egregious, anything-goes practices.

4. The financial markets created exotic derivative-based financial instruments[2]—dubbed "financial weapons of mass destruction" by Warren Buffet—to foster indiscriminate growth.

5. The concept of moral hazards—a mentality that fostered the paradigm of privatizing profits and socializing risks—became prevalent, mainly for banks deemed "too big to fail."

6. The herd mentality that helped create bubbles went far beyond the norms of rational risk taking. The market was overleveraged and overpriced; something had to give.

7. The bubble burst when subprime lending practices and a weakened housing market could no longer be sustained. Imploding under its own weight, it quickly escalated into a full-scale global collapse. Cascading events shook the world to the bone, and draconian measures were taken to stem the tide.

Parenthetically, many of the egregious practices that led to the 2008 meltdown are now being repeated, and the risks are amplifying. Have we not learned anything?

In the run-up to the crash, the economy was overheating. One sector in particular, the highly leveraged intermediaries in the so-called shadow banking system—an eclectic collection of investment banks, hedge funds, private equity firms, and others— used an exotic mix of financial instruments and counterparties to generate capital, increase leverage, build customer bases, and spread out risk exposure. One of the more egregious transactions involved purchasing and packaging subprime loans that were then securitized and sold to the public. A subprime loan is one that exceeds normal underwriting risks and requires higher risk charges. Third party mortgage originators would often write them and transfer the loans to banks and others. With no skin in the game, many originators found these loans to be highly profitable; the greater the risk, the higher their loan-origination fees.

The banks and others assuming the loan risks would then "package" them into a securitized, mortgage-backed asset portfolio that the hedge funds and others were happy to purchase and sell. A typical package was loaded with subprime loans and laced with a smattering of triple-A-rated loan tranches for greater respectability. In turn, rating agencies would often incorrectly rate them as a far-higher-grade asset than was justified.

At a grassroots level, many new subprime homeowners bought houses they could ill afford. Leveraged to the hilt, and using their house as collateral for borrowing more money, they quickly found themselves in a bind that could only be sustained if the housing market continued to climb. At about the time that the housing market started to crater and housing values fell, interest rates on adjustable-rate mortgages rose. Many homeowners found themselves in a position of negative equity, in which they owed far more on their house than it was worth. Default rates on these loans started to climb, and foreclosures were right around the corner.

Chart 13.1: Anatomy of an Economic Meltdown"

The economic meltdown of 2008 and the financial carnage that followed were preceded by a toxic trifecta of substandard policies, practices, and oversight. They contributed to and triggered a chain reaction of events that led to the Great Recession, which in turn almost cratered the global economy. This chart illustrates how the economic meltdown unfolded.

1. Warning Signals

Alarms that were ignored

- Excess liquidity and a housing bubble
- Economic growth by debt and excessive leveraging
- Wide use of exotic financial instruments
- Moral hazard risks, lax oversight; a disregard for basics

2. Subprime Fiasco

Risky practices that triggered the fall

- Shift of risk from loan originators to loan holders
- Rapid growth of poor loan underwriting practices
- Securitization of loans into highly rated packages sold to financial markets

5. The Meltdown

World markets imploded

- Stock markets crashed on a worldwide scale
- Major financial institutions fell as markets deteriorated
- World banking systems were on verge of collapse
- Global crisis of confidence
- Massive government intervention worldwide to restore financial order

6. Teetering on the Brink

The world economy entered a life-or-death struggle

- Economy became *the* issue in 2008 presidential election
- Draconian government steps taken to quell the disaster
- Outcome unknown, as no one knew where the bottom was
- Violent market fluctuations on a daily basis
- Widening global downturn

3. The Crisis Spread

From Main Street to Wall Street and the world markets

- Housing bubble burst and foreclosure rates climbed
- Highly leveraged securitized loans buckled; defaults climbed
- World banks and financial institutions felt the pinch
- Deleveraging and sell-offs to meet debt obligations intensified

4. The Bailouts Began

Feds reacted; primed the liquidity pump, but ...

- Credit and liquidity dried up; world economies now at risk
- Massive bailout efforts started; major institutions fell
- Problems intensified as Feds failed to halt the credit crisis
- Financial institutions were greatly weakened

7. From Wall Street to Main Street & Beyond

The financial crisis turned into a global recession

- Home values, 401(k) plans, and net worth fell to new lows
- Consumers were tapped out, and spending dried up
- Key economic indicators plunged
- Business and consumer confidence were shattered as markets and currencies fell
- Global recession was now in progress; unemployment rose

8. Aftershocks & New Realities

Things will never be the same again

- Global balance sheets weakened
- Massive central bank stimulus taken
- Financial reforms instituted
- Tepid and costly recovery
- Red ink: mounting debt weakened ability to meet next crisis

By the summer of 2007, the housing bubble was in trouble. The ripple effects reached the securitized subprime loan market. As it unraveled, weary investors began exiting these once-lucrative hedge fund packages. The hedge funds—with leverage ratios of 30:1 and more—soon encountered severe cash-flow problems to cover the payouts. To meet investor calls, they sold off many of their other highly rated assets, flooding the market with more selling than buying volume, which only exacerbated the problem. Though the broader markets were still chugging away, conditions below the waterline were rapidly deteriorating.

With the Bear Stearns collapse in early 2008 and a number of large hedge funds in deep trouble, the warning lights were flashing. Escalating oil prices, which peaked at over $147 per barrel in July, added to the misery. Consumer confidence plummeted, and the discretionary dollars normally available to support our consumer-based economy were now being spent at the gas pump and not at local stores. With new housing construction and purchases of durable and household goods rapidly dropping, the crisis escalated.

In retrospect, the market crash was inevitable, but its scope, speed, and intensity were stunning. Conditions continued to deteriorate throughout the summer and came to a head in early September, when major institutions started to fall like tenpins. Within weeks, the world was on the brink of a total economic meltdown.

In short order, old-line institutions were permanently changed, merged, or put out of business. Lehman Brothers filed for bankruptcy. Merrill Lynch was bailed out and purchased by Bank of America. American International Group (AIG)—the giant American insurance company—on the brink of going under from its toxic derivative exposure, was bailed out by the federal government. Two major players in the subprime fiasco—both government-sponsored institutions—Fannie Mae and Freddy Mac, were put into conservatorship. Even the mighty Goldman Sachs and Morgan Stanley were forced to convert their charters from investment banks to bank holding companies to gain readier access to capital. Liquidity everywhere had all but dried up.

Foreign banks—and countries—with close ties to financial sectors and/or export sales to the United States were almost immediately affected, with many teetering on the brink of disaster. The global stock markets went into a tailspin, and the US markets alone were off 40 percent from their highs of one year earlier. On the week of October 6, the Dow and S&P 500 fell −22 percent and −18.2 percent, respectively, wiping out over $7 trillion of market value in that one week alone. A global meltdown seemed imminent.

Wall Street suffered, but Main Street fared even worse. Unlike the major banks that received huge cash infusions to stay alive, average Americans received no bailouts. In a flash, 401(k) plans lost up to half or more of their value, and housing values plummeted along with the net worth of almost every American household. Consumer spending and access to credit dried up; credit cards were quickly maxed out, and large-scale job layoffs became the new norm. The stock market continued to plunge, reaching a low in March 2009; the total decline was about 54 percent from the market high in October 2007.

The Federal Reserve and Treasury Department teamed up to provide massive bailout packages for distressed institutions and pump liquidity into the system. For example, the Troubled Asset Relief Program (TARP), was authorized to buy up to $700 billion in toxic assets from troubled financial institutions. European and other governments arranged similar programs. The quantitative easing process (covered in chapters 3 and 10) was underway.

In early 2009, the newly elected Obama administration put together a $787 billion stimulus package that was quickly approved by Congress. General Motors and the Chrysler Corporation were early beneficiaries of the program. By late 2009, it was estimated that over $4 trillion had been pumped into the economy by a worried government to "save the system." After debt repayments, the net total was estimated to be in the range of "only" $1.2 trillion. The federal spigots would remain open into the next decade—as we shall soon see.

The bailouts, reduced tax revenues, and off-balance-sheet financing of the wars in Iraq and Afghanistan took a toll on our balance sheets. As an aggregated measure of its impact, a quick review of the numbers in 2000, 2005, and 2009 is revealing.

Chart 13.2: US Government Deficits and Debt

Year	Receipts	Outlays	Surplus/ Deficits	Gross Debt	% of GDP
2000	$2,025.2	$1,789.0	+$236.2	$5,628,700	55.6%
2005	$2,153.6	$2,472.0	−$318.3	$7,905,300	61.6%
2009	$2,105.0	$3,517.7	−$1,412.7	$11,875,851	82.3%

—Current Dollars in Billions—

Source: OMB: President's Budget—FY 2020

As illustrated, the federal deficits and accumulated debt were within a respectable range in the early part of the decade. By decade's end, the surplus of 2000 turned into a deficit in which the United States was borrowing about forty cents on every dollar it was spending. The gross national debt—public and intergovernmental borrowing—climbed to about $11.9 trillion in 2009, equal to about 82.3 percent of our GDP at that time.

While the debt-to-GDP ratio improved following the recession, the aggregated debt and carrying charges on that debt continued to mount. With more than ten thousand baby boomers per day due to retire in 2011, the Social Security and Medicare benefits they would soon be collecting were, for the most part, unfunded liabilities the government would pay on for decades to come. The future was murky, and the mounting debt would climb and crowd out other expenditures in the future; we were in serious trouble. In was in this environment that Karen Holtmeier, of the class of '61, would start her new business in 2008.

Karen (Bachman) Holtmeier

Karen Holtmeier became the CEO and President of her company, Medical Weight Management Centers Inc. in 2008—at the height of the Great Recession—and weathered that storm through grit, sweat equity, and determination, all reflective of an entrepreneurial spirit that has often taken her outside of her comfort zone and into uncharted waters.

With a strong faith and a friendly, easygoing manner that has endeared her to friends and associates throughout her career, Karen is one of those remarkable women that has raised a family—two sons and three grandchildren—while pursuing her education, professional career, and an eclectic assortment of other interests. Like other self-made pursuers of the American Dream, Karen had her share of challenges along the way with twists, turns, and "aha" moments that changed and energized her life, eventually directing her toward a career she had never dreamed possible in her earlier years.

Her trek toward a Master's degree in Public Health from the University of Minnesota in 1987 and, indeed, her career as a nutritionist, consultant, researcher, and guest lecturer evolved over time. Her early discovery that she liked and was good at chemistry and science—biochemistry in particular—was a game-changing "aha" moment for her. It shaped her career and led to various internships and work experiences that honed her focus on nutrition and its impact on our overall health and quality of life.

Through her work with a prominent endocrinologist, Karen became an early believer in the value of low-carb diets. Though not in the mainstream of the low-fat, high-carb diets so in vogue at the time, she did not shy away from her convictions. She became a tireless advocate and disciple of lower-carb diets and often spoke of them at industry forums, medical school classrooms, and other settings. The low-carb approach has now become a prevailing doctrine, and Karen was certainly an important part of that effort.

By 2008, Karen was ready for command—with a well-rounded nutritional background in a corporate wellness setting as Director of Nutrition for the Minnesota Beef Council and as a boots-on-ground clinical counselor working directly with patients at various organizations.

Like many professionals, Karen has a multitude of interests. She started running marathons at age thirty-five—finishing at least ten, by her count—and is into long-distance biking, Pilates, aerobics, and long walks. She is a volunteer in her church, loves international travel, and has an innate curiosity that has made her an incurable lifelong learner. Karen has achieved her piece of the American Dream through hard work, a belief in herself, and a passion for her causes. In doing so, she has counseled, touched, and improved the lives of more people than she can probably imagine, and it's no stretch to say that we are all the better for her contributions and efforts.

E-2: Energy and Technological Forces

Energy Forces

Rising oil prices and other challenges in the first half of the decade came to a head in the summer of 2008. The festering oil crises sparked a wake-up call: that cheap and abundant oil were no longer assured. Oil quickly became the eight-hundred-pound gorilla that could no longer be ignored.

In 2008 the United States, a country with 4 percent of the world's population and about 3 percent of the world's proven crude oil reserves, consumed over 20 percent of the world's oil. As domestic production declined, we became more reliant on foreign oil to sustain our economy. We were on schedule to "export" over a half-trillion dollars of our nation's wealth for the foreign oil we needed to keep our economy afloat.

Oil-exporting nations were straining to meet the demands of a thirstier world. Developing nations were consuming more oil to support their growing economies, and China's thirst was noteworthy. The immutable laws of geology, stating that we have only a finite amount of oil and not one drop more, were being challenged. The world was consuming oil at a rate far exceeding the amount of new oil coming online.

The oil markets were nervous. The mere hint of a supply shortage would set the oil futures market soaring, and the rising oil prices would quickly translate into an increase in pump prices. By spring 2008, the price of oil was over four times higher than it was at the beginning of the decade, and pump prices of $4–5 per gallon were common. It was a tremendous drag on household incomes and a direct hit to our domestic economy. The sharp and sustained increase in gasoline prices was a precursor to an economic downturn. Oil was at an all-time high of $147.30 per barrel in July 2008, just as the greatest economic meltdown since the Great Depression was about to be triggered. A coincidence?

While the laws of geology weighed heavily on the oil crisis, it was the aboveground, non-geologic factors—geopolitical and market conditions, cost of drilling and exploration, supply-and-demand disturbance, terrorist attacks, etc.—that triggered the pricing spikes. The declining value of the US dollar also meant that it required more dollars to purchase a barrel of oil, and the world, tied to the petrodollar system, felt the impact in the form of the higher prices they had to pay OPEC. In effect, we were exporting inflation.

The fears were well grounded. With no alternative energy systems of scalable size to replace the oil that fueled the transportation systems of the world, the future looked dim. Efforts to produce more oil from unconventional sources, such as tar sands, deep-water drilling, and shale, were costly and not of sufficient scale to replace the conventional crude oil reserves extracted the old-fashioned way. New drilling technologies, including horizontal drilling and fracking, were not yet fully commercialized, and demand-reduction efforts and renewable energy were only starting to gain traction. The sale of fuel-efficient hybrid cars was making a difference, but America's love affair with SUVs and pickup trucks gave them the lion's share of new vehicle sales.

Ironically, it was the Great Recession that finally broke the back of rising oil prices. As the global economy sputtered and the demand for oil abruptly fell, oil prices fell over 78 percent to a low of $32 per barrel by the end of the year. Oil companies shifted into a survival mode, and oil exploration efforts were cut back dramatically. While expedient, it also meant that new oil would be in short supply years later.

The changes were swift and dramatic, and they reshaped the dynamics of the global oil markets for years to come. It also gave us a sobering look at what the energy markets of the future might look like if we failed to change our ways. We would leave the decade with a deeper understanding: that energy—in all forms—could no longer be treated as a given.

Technological Forces

It was a decade of technological wizardry on many fronts. For example, the Human Genome Project, completed in 2003, sparked a plethora of medical breakthroughs. The MQ-1 Predator drone, launching a missile on an unmanned vehicle in 2002, ushered in a new era of drone warfare that would change battlefields for decades to come. But of all the decade's technological advances, none would so profoundly transform the lives of so many so quickly and profoundly than the digital trifecta of the internet, social media, and mobile connectivity. The speed of changes in how people and businesses connected and communicated were breathtaking. The marketing, distribution, and development of products and services erupted with an explosion of new opportunities while harshly challenging the business models of legacy companies tied to old technologies.

The internet, increasingly a primary news source, challenged the networks and print media in ways never imagined. Publishers and bookstores watched their revenues decline as Amazon combined convenience and a vast inventory to claim an increasing market share—and gain unheard-of buying leverage—while also navigating the new technological territory of e-books. Ordinary citizens had growing access to new avenues of self-expression through emerging social media networks. Advances in one area spurred growth in others.

As one measure of growth, there were approximately 16 million internet users, about 0.4 percent of the global population in 1995. By the end of 2000, there were more than 361 million users, and by the end of the decade, there were more than 1.8 billion global users, representing about 26 percent of the world's population. Within half a dozen years, we saw the debut of LinkedIn, in 2002; Myspace, in 2003; Facebook, in 2004; YouTube, in 2005; and Twitter, in 2006. Google, Amazon, and eBay were already making their mark.

With the introduction of the iPhone in 2007, social media and websites went mobile. The Apple App Store was an instant hit. Barack Obama became the first presidential candidate to understand and use the social media in his campaign efforts. Years later, Donald Trump would use Twitter as a major medium for communicating his messages.

Understandably, legacy marketers using old technologies were rattled, and older generations struggled to keep up. Though business models were updated, e-marketers clearly had the upper hand over brick-and-mortar competitors. The pace of technological change was increasingly outpacing our ability to assimilate it into our normal routines.

In his superb book *Thank You for Being Late: An Optimist's Guide to Thriving in the Age of Accelerations* (New York: Farrar, Straus and Giroux, 2016), Thomas L. Friedman describes 2007 as a vintage year for great technologies. He opines on the "new set of capabilities to connect, collaborate, and create throughout every aspect of life, commerce, and government" and notes:

> "Indeed, there is a mismatch between the change in the pace of change and our ability to develop the learning systems, training systems, management systems, social safety nets, and government regulations that would enable citizens to get the most out of these accelerations and cushion their worst impacts. This mismatch, as we will see, is at the center of much of the turmoil roiling politics and society in both developed and developing countries today. It now constitutes probably the most important governance challenge across the globe."

Like so many wonderful inventions, the internet and social media had dark sides that would emerge later. The use of data to misinform, manipulate, defraud, influence elections, and peddle pornography were some of the nastier byproducts of these marvelous new technologies.

E-3: Environmental and Ecological Forces

Climate Change

The new millennium brought with it a growing awareness of global warming—a term that would gradually morph into *climate change*. The threat had finally escaped the territory of nerdy scientists and academicians and became a mainstream issue. As it gained traction, vested interests, threatened by the change in the status quo, ramped up their efforts to discredit the alarms.

The stakes were high. While many viewed climate change as an existential threat to the planet and future generations, others saw it as a pretext for government intervention that would stifle economic growth. In what was shaping up to be a classic battle between science and ideology, the public was starting to believe that global

The Class of 1961 in the New Millennium

The Four Amigos: Charlie Darth, Bud Schaitberger, Mike Conley, and Brad St. Mane, September 2003.

Congressman Jim Ramstad and Mike Conley, following congressional testimony leading to the subsequent passage of the Mental Health Parity and Addiction Equity Act of 2008 co-sponsored by Congressman Ramstad.

Andrea Hricko Hjelm while serving as president of the U of M Alumni Association in 2004.

Minneapolis Senior Aquatennial Ambassadors Karen Holtmeier and Dr. Michael Espeland, attending a St. Paul Winter Carnival Coronation event in 2020.

Art and Colleen Jentsch enjoying their life in retirement.

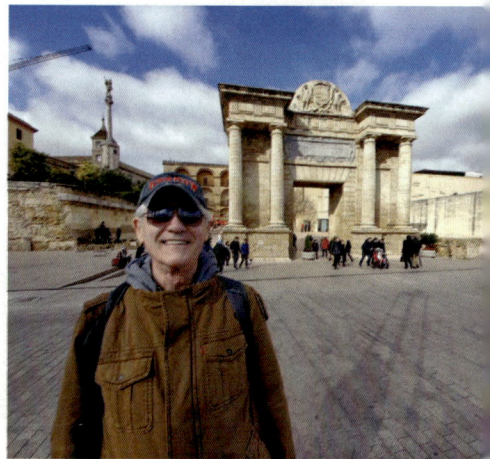

Mike Berneck taking in the sites in Cordoba, Spain, in January 2020.

Conley Family Foundation board meeting—circa 2005. *Left to right:* Brant Kairies, Mike Conley, Steve Kairies, Sharon Conley, Charlie Darth, Bud Schaitberger, Brad St. Mane.

Conley Family Foundation Board in 2019. *Left to right*: Sharon Conley, Mike Conley, Karen Holtmeier, Charlie Darth, Curt Lange.

Flying with my best friend, Sharon Conley, in my Piper Archer III—circa 2006.

Family—what it is all about: Grandkids, Sammy & Keri Hoatson; Mike & Sharon; Todd Hoatson, son-in-law, & daughter, Kristen; and Matt Hoiland, son-in-law, & daughter Heather.

temperatures were rising. There was far less certainty, however, as to what was causing it. The scientific community, however, was rapidly coalescing around a belief that climate change really was happening, it was heavily shaped by anthropogenic causes, and the frequency and intensity of its trajectories were accelerating.

Opponents suggested it was all part of a natural, cyclical phenomenon and often attacked or questioned scientists and their motives. They opined that the scientific community was heavily divided—which it wasn't—and that we should all take a deep breath and wait until "all the science was in" before jumping to hasty conclusions. It was similar to the tobacco industry's playbook of yesteryear, warning the public not to treat the threat of tobacco as a foregone conclusion until we had "all of the data."

In the meantime, the world was moving ahead with climate-change initiatives, and the Kyoto Protocol became effective on February 16, 2005. The United States had bailed out earlier, claiming that the protocol was flawed and unfair to the United States, and an economic liability if we chose to participate in it. China gained the dubious distinction of becoming the world's greatest emitter of greenhouse gases by decade's end, replacing the United States as the world's number-one polluter.

As the controversy raged, a rush of scientific data corroborated the growing threat. The data collected, vetted, and published by the UN organizations was even more conclusive, and it was starting to bear fruit. The IPCC's Third Assessment Report, completed in 2001, garnered a great deal of media attention and concluded that observed warming was "likely" (greater than a 66 percent probability, based on expert opinion) caused by human activity. The IPCC's Fourth Assessment Report, in 2007, was even more definitive. It concluded that the average global warming over the past fifty years was "very likely" (greater than a 90 percent probability, based on expert judgement) due to human activities.

The reports were widely covered and discussed by the media, public, and policymakers. To some extent, they played off Al Gore's documentary film *An Inconvenient Truth,* released in 2006. A box-office hit, it was widely credited for raising public awareness and energizing the environmental community at a grassroots level. Conversely, the counterforces were also digging in with well-financed efforts to discredit the scientific community and the so-called liberal media that was perpetuating a hoax.

A number of different climate consensus studies have corroborated the widely cited consensus that 97 percent of the climate scientists surveyed viewed climate change as a real threat. Interestingly, the media's attempt to give equal time to both sides left an impression that the scientific community was heavily divided— which was clearly not the case. If anything, the nonbelievers were given a disproportionately high level of media attention in relationship to the scientific minorities they represented.

By 2009, three significant things had happened: The global economic meltdown diverted attention away from climate change, and opponents suggested that initiatives for climate change were job killers. The scientific process preceding the climate-change meeting in Copenhagen in 2009 was corrupted in a couple of areas and provided ammunition for those labeling the entire process surrounding climate change as junk science. And the combination of these two factors caused a slight shift away from the general public's belief in climate change—but only a temporary one.

With the election of President Obama, climate change became a top priority. Progress would continue to be incremental, but the activities of this decade provided a solid launchpad for the quantum leaps that would be made in the following decade.

Ecological Forces

In a titanic struggle pitting the demands of a growing global population with rising expectations against our planet's finite capacity to support the growing demands of life as we know it today, the contest continues to tighten.

With a global population that had doubled to more than six billion people over the previous four decades, the strains on our ecological systems were noticeable. Global access to fresh-water had become problematic, with about one-third of the world suffering from some scarcity of fresh-water. Land-management practices had also deteriorated as deforestation and land desertification levels ticked upward. The world's rainforests—those precious life-giving carbon sinks that stabilize our atmosphere—were rapidly disappearing.

The challenge of feeding a growing population was becoming costlier, and underdeveloped countries were particularly hard hit. As an example, in 2007 estimated household food budgets dwarfed other expenditures—representing highs of as much as 73 percent of a household budget in Nigeria, 65 percent in Vietnam, and 50 percent in Indonesia. The use of American-grown corn to make ethanol fuels for our cars did not play well in a world starving for food exports from the United States. Wasteful and pollutive behaviors had become a new global norm, and conditions would worsen as we plunged deeper into the new millennium. The world's environmental and ecological footprints were taking a more noticeable toll.

E-4: Expectations and Behaviors

By the end of the decade, we could see that what was so intoxicating on the way up was even more devastating on the way down. For many, the American Dream was no longer the reality in which they lived. Younger generations now questioned what was once a given, that their living standards would be better than those of their parents. An optimistic vision of upward mobility was now tinged with nagging doubts, reinforced by the carnage of the Great Recession.

In retrospect, the expectations and behaviors shaping the American Dream were always in a state of transition, too imperceptible to notice, but changing nonetheless. A look back at those beliefs since the end of World War II will help readers appreciate just how much things had really changed.

The American Dream was built on cheap energy, abundant resources, a spirit of optimism, and a belief in unlimited opportunities for those willing to work for it. Every successive generation believed it would live better than the previous one. We experienced continuous growth and thrived on the upward mobility reflected in our new suburban homes with a car or maybe two in every garage. We were mobile and delighted in the weekend visits to our lake homes or overseas travel in low-cost jetliners.

We marveled at our ability to grow, farm, mine, fish, and produce prodigious amounts of everything through energy systems we took for granted. New technologies were forever improving productivity and making life easier for us. Accessible and affordable educational opportunities were within easy reach, and solid career opportunities were usually there for the taking. Upward mobility was almost a given, and our voracious appetites for consumption and instant gratification helped feed those mighty wheels of growth. Sadly, the debt we took on to sustain it seemed like an acceptable price to pay.

There were negative side effects, to be sure, but we were able to overlook them. The collateral damage of our throwaway culture was not yet noticeable. The waste, pollution, and growing debt at all levels were passed on to future generations with nary a thought.

It all worked until it didn't. By the turn of the century, the aftershocks were noticeable. The dream enablers—cheap energy, abundant resources, and unlimited opportunities—were starting to disappear. College costs were rising, and student-loan debts were climbing. Rising oil prices and visible signs of climate change were becoming more manifest. Good jobs were harder to find, and seas of red ink seemed to engulf us. Though we clung to the notion of the American Dream, it was not the dream we had once known.

The Great Recession of 2008 brought many issues to a head. The bubble had burst; the emperor had no clothes. We were abruptly exposed to the house of cards once mistaken for a solid foundation. Within weeks, the nest eggs we had so painstakingly accumulated over the years—the value of our houses and 401(k) plans—violently collapsed. Our paper fortunes had evaporated, and our household debt seemed overwhelming in proportion to our capacity to pay it off.

The American Dream was looking more like an equal-opportunity nightmare for all generations. For many in the class of

'61—sixty-five years old at the time of the meltdown—the dreams of golden retirement years were often replaced with the fear of outliving our savings. Older baby boomers did the math and found their decimated 401(k) accounts would not support their dream of an earlier retirement; the necessity of working a few more years—for those still fortunate to have a job—was becoming the new reality. The Gen Xers, ensconced in their middle-management jobs and a pile of debt, were laid off in large numbers, the prospect of returning to an equivalent job anything but certain. The so-called good life many enjoyed before the crash was gone in a flash.

The Millennials, many of them newly minted college graduates in the early stages of a career they thought would fulfill their American Dream, were often the first to get laid off and last to get rehired. Deep in debt with college loans they could not pay off with jobs they couldn't find, many took refuge in their parents' basements or spare rooms. For many, the American Dream was something that happened in a different time and place, and, like their Gen-X friends, many doubted the entitlement benefits enjoyed by their elders would be available for them—at least in their present form.

Millennials' attitudes, behaviors, and expectations were shaped by this experience, and it would profoundly affect the way they perceived and approached the future. College debt and the lack of a good job would keep many from ever buying a house, and the thought of deliberately taking on long-term debt seemed appalling. A car was no longer a must, especially if public transportation was available near the apartments they rented.

Their job preferences were also changing, with less emphasis on career advancement and more on job fulfillment in relation to all other aspects of their lives. The need for health insurance—usually through employers—also created a "job-lock" that had not existed before. Corporate loyalty became a thing of the past, as many remembered just how loyal companies had been to employees when times got rough.

In summary, the seismic events of the new millennium and its toxic aftershocks were game-changers of the first magnitude. Our culture, values, expectations, behaviors, views of the American

Dream, and cherished assumptions were, and will be, challenged for a long time to come. Indeed, it could be considered our entry into this new paradigm shift that we still don't understand. The next decade would reinforce that notion.

Mike Conley

The events of the first decade of this new millennium reshaped my life, my worldview, and the course I would follow thereafter.

The 9/11 terrorist attack, the great economic meltdown of 2008, and the dramatic changes in energy that sent oil prices soaring to over $147 per barrel were only part of it. There were changes happening on a more personal level that played off these external events.

The whole concept of the perfect storm, reinforced by these dramatic events, began to take shape, and the imperative to do something about it was reinforced by the births of my granddaughter, Keri, in 2005, and grandson, Sammy, in 2007. This was no longer an abstract concept you write books about; it was about them and the future we were leaving them. The more I thought about it, the more concerned I became. Their futures were at stake, and I could only wonder: What kind of mess were we leaving them, and what could we do about it?

The confluence of these events and a natural curiosity led me on my quest to learn all I could about the perfect storm and ways that I could get the message out to others. This was a decade of discovery for me, and I chronicle part of that journey in chapter 17.

My lifestyle was also shaped by two other events: First, I developed arthritis in the back and had to discontinue golf and running. This opened a new door, however, to a passion for long-distance biking. I loved the freedom of long rides and the time it gave me to reflect and enjoy the beauty of nature, and it most definitely contributed to a better aging process. Second, I sold my plane and discontinued my private flying activities later in the decade, mostly because of the CO_2 I was putting into the air for my grandkids to deal with. It left me with more time to face the perfect storm in a practical way, particularly with the Conley Family Foundation and finding ways to direct our efforts toward these issues.

I learned some invaluable life lessons that I will share here with you. First, in life, doors close and windows open. With an open mind and a little resiliency, new avenues will open that might never have been imagined before. Second, with the passing of my ninety-seven-year-old mother in 2007 and births of our grandchildren, I could feel the grand cycle of life turning and the need to make the most of whatever time I was allotted on this planet.

It solidified a belief that we all have an intergenerational responsibility to do whatever we can do to make this a better planet for those following us. It took me into new arenas I never would have imagined at the start of this decade, and I'll talk more about them in the next chapter.

Summary of the 2000s

The decade started with a bursting dot-com market bubble and the 9/11 attacks and beginning of America's longest war. It ended with the greatest recession since the Great Depression. Key fuelers of the perfect storm quickly gaining traction include the following:

1. **The terrorist attack on 9/11 abruptly changed the geopolitical landscape.**

   - The United States struck back in the Afghan, Iraqi, and antiterror wars that dominated the decade and beyond.

   - Destabilization in the Middle East spread as Sunni-Shiite conflicts proliferated.

   - Russia reemerged, and China's economy boomed: new challenges to American hegemony.

2. **The Great Recession of 2008 was an economic meltdown of global proportions.**

   - Major systemic failures triggered the greatest economic meltdown since the Depression.

   - Draconian measures to resolve it weakened our ability to fend off the next crisis.

   - Global and domestic debt—as a catalyst for growth—climbed recklessly, creating a looming threat.

3. **The global addiction to King Oil spiked while new smart technologies soared.**

   - Oil prices peaked at $147 per barrel in 2008 before collapsing six months later.

   - The destabilized energy markets floundered, posing a huge question for the future.

   - New smartphones and technologies changed economic and social landscapes forever.

4. **Threats of climate change and ecological destruction became mainstream issues.**

   - The Kyoto Protocol was ratified as hard data, sense of urgency, and global concerns grew.

   - Stresses on Earth's carrying capacity grew as population doubled over fifty years.

   - Global drawdown of scarce resources intensified, threatening future generations.

5. **The American Dream began to be challenged—globally.**

   - The dream enablers—cheap energy and abundant resources and opportunities—started to erode.

   - The Great Recession dampened hopes as household wealth was decimated and debt climbed.

   - Doubts emerged that youngsters would live better than their parents, including access to the same Social Security benefits.

SNAPSHOT: *2000–2010*

	2000	2010	2018
Population in Millions			
World	6,145.0	6,958.2	7,632.8
USA	282.2	309.3	327.2
US Financials in Billions			
GDP	$10,117.5	$14,838.9	$20,235.9
Fed. Receipts	2,025.2	2,162.7	3,329.9
Fed. Outlays	1,789.0	3,457.1	4,109.0
Surplus / (Deficit)	236.2	(1,294.4)	(779.1)
Gross Fed. Debt	5,628.7	13,528.8	21,462.3
Interest on Debt	223.0	196.2	325.0
US Domestic Averages			
Wages	$40,343	$39,856	$46,464
Cost of new house	134,150	232,800	318,500
Cost of new car	24,750		

Points of Interest

- 9/11 attack; terrorism; Iraqi and Afghanistan wars; climate change

- Great Recession, market collapse and global meltdown in 2008

- Stagnant federal revenues with debts and deficits that more than doubled

- Massive bailouts follow in Bush and Obama administrations; interest rates fall

Snapshot Road Map: *The Snapshot compares key data points from the beginning of one decade to the beginning of the next. Sources are provided under Part II in the endnotes.*

-14-

The 2010s

The Chickens Come Home to Roost.

The class of '61 entered the second decade of the new millennium as sixty-six-year-old senior citizens. Most of us were retired and collecting Social Security, Medicare, and any private retirement benefits we had accumulated. As, perhaps, a sign of our advancing years, President Obama, the thirteenth president of our lifetimes, had been born *after* we had graduated from high school. Authority figures, such as doctors and cops, began looking a little too young for the responsibilities they held. Conversations with our peers increasingly revolved around grandkids, the medications we were taking, or the all-too-many funerals we were attending. Good grief! We really were getting old.

The baby boomers who followed us would soon be collecting on those wonderful entitlement promises of yesteryear—a burden that future generations would be saddled with on our behalf. Sadly, we would also leave them with IOUs of another kind, the residue from our wasteful practices of the past: depletion of fresh-water, oil, and minerals; a planet straining to meet the demands of a growing global population; and the escalating ravages of climate change. The chickens were finally coming home to roost.

As we entered the new decade, still reeling from the Great Recession, our nation was still at war, and the global economy was swimming in red ink. The Middle East was chaotic, and a new threat, ISIS, was about to get off the ground. Russia was flexing its muscles, and North Korea and Iran were pushing hard to join the world's exclusive nuclear club. China was rapidly emerging as the world's newest superpower.

The tempo of change intensified with a blast of feedback loops and a gridlocked political system incapable of addressing the growing threats, many of them edging us closer to irrevocable tipping points. Amid a rush of new technologies, overconsumption of scarce resources, and the cacophony of growing threats, the storm forces were building. We turn now to our perfect storm model for a deeper look into their progressive development and the price we would increasingly pay for past transgressions.

E-1: Economic and Geopolitical Forces

Economic Forces

The economic tremors of the Great Recession rippled into the new decade. Consumer confidence was still shaken, and published unemployment rates hovered around 10 percent—though the real rates were higher. Main Street America was strapped with a glut of empty, foreclosed houses, and stunned 401(k) holders were still grasping for a safety line.

The optimism that had started to emerge on Wall Street after the market low of March 2009 had not yet caught up with the bunker mentality of Main Street. Laid-off breadwinners returned to jobs that were not equivalent to their previous jobs in wages or stature. Families drove their used cars longer and saved more for the rainy days they felt were around the corner. Companies struggled to repair their decimated balance sheets and scaled back in response to a consumer base still hesitant to purchase their products and services.

While significant efforts were made to prevent a relapse through massive deficit spending and Fed monetary policies on steroids, the long-term debt taken on to do so would hamper the economy later in the decade. Chart 14.1 illustrates the explosive growth in deficits and the cumulative debt between 2010 and 2018. The deficits, on average, climbed over $1.2 trillion per annum between 2010 and 2012 before dropping to an average of $606 billion between 2013 and 2018. Prideful politicians could boast of "reducing" deficits by a half in this period while failing to mention we were still spending over a half-trillion dollars more per year than we were taking in. The cumulative debt and interest paid on it will be a huge drag in the coming years, but we are doing little about it.

Chart 14.1: Federal Government Debt and Deficits

—In Rounded Billions of Dollars—						
Fiscal Year Ending	Receipts	Outlays	Annual Deficit	Gross Fed. Debt	GDP	Net Interest Paid on Debt
2010	2,163	3,457	−1,294	13,529	14,839	196
2011	2,304	3,603	−1,300	14,764	15,404	230
2012	2,450	3.527	−1,077	16,051	16,057	220
2013	2,775	3,455	−680	16,719	16,604	221
2014	3,022	3,506	−485	17,794	17,333	229
2015	3,250	3,692	−442	18,120	18,090	223
2016	3,268	3,853	−585	19,539	18,551	240
2017	3,316	3,982	−665	20,206	19,272	263
2018	3,330	4,109	−779	21,462	20,236	325

Source: OMB: President's Budget FY 2020. Historical Tables.

Fearful of an economic relapse, our Federal Reserve kept the monetary spigots open by increasing money supply, lowering interest rates, and increasing the velocity—movement—of money via quantitative easing (QE; see chapter 3). As QE in 2010 and 2012 pumped vast amounts of new money into the economy, the Fed's balance sheet skyrocketed.

The QE process, used heavily in 2008–2009 to purchase toxic assets and provide bailouts for banks and others "too big to fail," was followed by QE-2 in 2010 and again in September 2012 with QE-3. The 2012 effort was aimed at buying up to $85 billion per month in open-ended assets. By the middle of the decade, the Fed started to taper down its monthly purchases, with mixed results. The Fed's ultimate goal of divesting of these assets will be a daunting task, given its bulging balance sheet of roughly $4 trillion in 2014. This process will rattle markets as vast amounts of money trade hands.

Now, here's the rub: the stock market loves low interest rates and reacts negatively to any suggestion of a rate hike. The long-term consequences of the Fed's earlier efforts to save the economy could come back to haunt us. Two areas in particular are worth noting: First, the Fed's ability to stave off the next major downturn has been weakened by its earlier actions, leaving less room for maneuver in the next downturn. Second, the low interest rate environment created by the Fed has driven weary investors in search of higher returns toward the stock market. The fear of leaving something on the table has caused many investors to ignore fundamentals and follow the herd, a sure prescription for creating an asset bubble. Buyers beware! All bubbles eventually burst.

In addition to these revved-up fiscal and monetary policies, another economic game-changer, the Affordable Care Act (ACA), was signed into law on March 23, 2010. Its intent was to make affordable health insurance available to tens of millions of uninsured Americans, regardless of income or health status. The ACA changed the dynamics of the healthcare market and greatly expanded the Medicaid program. While the outcome is uncertain, the ripple effects of anything representing healthcare, at almost 18 percent of the GDP, are huge.

The political polarization surrounding the ACA spilled over to other crucial areas, including defense spending, national debt, and futile attempts to address the entitlement system reforms needed to sustain the programs. Congress and the White House were gridlocked in a pattern of brinkmanship and the fear of taking a tough vote on a contentious series of issues. Relying heavily on continuing resolutions—a stopgap measure used by Congress to fund the government for a final resolution later—the government achieved procrastination, not progress.

Despite bumps in the road, the resilient American economy steadily improved. By the time Donald J. Trump was sworn in as our forty-fifth president in January 2017, the stock market was flourishing, and unemployment rates were under 5 percent. The global economy also picked up steam in the second half of the decade, despite mixed results internationally. Falling commodity prices, volatility in the financial and currency-exchange markets, and persistent job creation challenges and unemployment issues continued to plague a number of nations. Falling oil prices and sanctions put a heavy hit on Russia; Japan stagnated in a deflationary economy; India was on the rise; and Brazil and Venezuela were floundering.

China was clearly the superstar, with India and other developing nations closing ranks. With a population roughly four times larger than the United States and a GDP growth rate about three times greater, China was on track to surpass the United States as the world's largest economy within a few years. In terms of the relative GDP purchasing power,[1] the IMF claimed that China had already overtaken the United States by the middle part of the decade.

The EU, as a whole, was underperforming. Exhausted from previous efforts to stave off an economic meltdown and plagued by the plight of the so-called PIGS—the troubled economies of Portugal, Italy, Greece, and Spain—its overall growth rate was marginal. Greece, in particular, was on the brink of a complete sovereign debt default that threatened the unity of the EU.

In 2015, the European Central Bank—overseeing the eurozone monetary system—embarked on a QE *Programme* of its own by acquiring up to 40 billion euros a month in a wide universe of assets through 2017 and beyond. While it made progress, the EU's momentum was interrupted on June 23, 2016, when the "Brexit" referendum on the exit of the United Kingdom from the union passed by a close 52–48 percent vote. A shock to the world, it would involve a long and difficult disengagement process for the British Commonwealth, loaded with land mines and unintended consequences; the end is nowhere in sight as of this writing.

The global economy is now so deeply intertwined that when powerful nations sneeze, others catch a cold. The interrelationship between economics and geopolitical power structures brings us to the next major force in play.

Geopolitical Forces

Less than two decades after the fall of the Soviet Union and end of the Cold War in 1991, a new cold war emerged. Unlike the first Cold War, with its clearly defined sides and focus on ideology, Cold War II will be contested around access to scarce resources, control of global markets, technological superiority, strategic alignments and alliances, trade agreements, and competition over the international levers of power.

Cold War II will take place in a globalized economy, around the rising expectations of a growing population competing for scarce resources. Its tone and tempo will be influenced by nationalistic movements, an escalation in regional and religious wars, and a dramatic growth in asymmetric warfare. In this calculus, conventional military superiority alone will not guarantee success. Recent American retrenchment has further destabilized the situation.

As nations struggle to navigate these shifting paradigms, the relative balance of power will continue to shift. The United States is no longer the dominant superpower it once was. China's emergence as an economic powerhouse, Russia's reentry into the international scene, growing threats of nuclear proliferation, ramped-up asymmetric attacks, and the drain of continuous military deployments have weakened our position. Domestically, America's dysfunctional political system and skyrocketing national debt have crimped our capacity to act unilaterally on major global issues.

In this new milieu, the old Cold War playbook is obsolete. The notion of unilateral action and winning only at the expense of others is obsolete. Misguided actions—devoid of nuance—by a super-power in this interconnected world will invite multiple responses and unintended consequences in other areas. Failure to recognize these shifting tides will hasten the arrival of the perfect storm.

The margins for error are small, and the need for predictability cannot be overstated. Until recently, the United States represented a constant that helped anchor a turbulent world and global economy. But now, the world is struggling to understand the new playing field, as the United States has exited the Trans-Pacific Partnership treaty and the Paris Agreement on climate change, decertified the Iranian nuclear treaty, scrapped NAFTA, and left other agreements and alliances. The global trend toward nationalism, trade wars, and new threads of deglobalization is fraught with worldwide threats.

The Middle East: On December 17, 2010, a Tunisian street vendor named Mohamed Bouazizi set himself on fire over the humiliation and harassment he suffered from his local government. It sparked a riot that led to the Tunisian Revolution and later esca-lated into grassroot protests throughout the Middle East. Dubbed the Arab Spring, it was a rebellion against oppressive regimes and the socioeconomic orders they represented.

In short order, several regimes, including those in Egypt and Libya, were toppled or disrupted. Almost every Middle Eastern country was threatened by massive protests and a proliferation of political dissidents and new splinter groups. The repercussions were profound: it sparked a civil war in Syria; destabilized the existing, uneasy Islamist and secular divisions; widened the Sunni-Shiite rift into a wider regional civil war; and generated new economic uncertainties and thus fewer job opportunities for a growing base of youthful citizens. The uprisings continued throughout the decade.

In this maelstrom of violence, the last convoy of American combat troops left Iraq in December 2011. The destabilized regime of Prime Minister Nuri Kamal al-Maliki continued to fight off a simmering Sunni insurgency that destabilized the region. The Syrian civil war erupted that same year against the regime of Bashar al-Assad, whose regime, with its close ties to Iran, Hezbollah, and Russia, became a focal point of a conflict that polarized the region with an array of proxy forces engaged in the conflict. It would also be the breeding ground for a deadly new enemy.

By 2013, a splinter group of al-Qaeda had morphed into what became known as ISIS or ISIL, the Islamic State in Iraq and the Levant. In 2014 ISIS announced the creation of a caliphate (Islamic state) that erased all state borders and declared itself the authority over the world's estimated 1.5 billion Muslims. In blitzkrieg attacks, it erupted from its base in Syria and overtook a number of key Iraqi cities. Coupling Sharia Law with modern social media tools to recruit and promote their religious fundamentalism, it formed a destabilizing force.

In 2016 a coalition of forces began to dislodge ISIS from its strongholds, and in October 2017, its self-proclaimed capital, Raqqa, Syria, was retaken. While no longer holding any meaningful territory in the Middle East, its efforts appear to be shifting toward the building of terrorist cells all over the world, a force that will be difficult to eradicate and a significant threat for many years to come.

The Middle East today is in shambles. Shiite Iran is emerging, and antagonism between Iran and Saudi Arabia is escalating. The US Fifth Fleet is now a semi-permanent fixture in this area, and Afghanistan has the dubious distinction of hosting the longest American war in history. In this tinderbox, proxy wars between major powers are drawn into the conflagration. The Iranian nuclear treaty, Iran's support of Hezbollah and Syria, the unsettled Kurdish question, and hatred toward Israel will be focal points of future conflicts in that region and beyond.

Russia: Following the fall of the USSR in 1991 and Vladimir Putin's gradual rise to power at the turn of the new millennium, the Russian Federation began to regroup. While unable to cope with NATO's encroachment in Eastern Europe or the withdrawal of the United States from the Anti-Ballistic Missile Treaty, signed in 1972, Putin began to flex his muscles as rising oil prices and his consolidation of power took hold. By 2012 Putin was reaching out to his former client states of Iran and Syria. A reinvigorated Russia became a major power broker in the Middle East, and tensions between

Washington and Moscow worsened. Attempts to reset the relationship failed.

In 2014 an activist Russia contested the replacement of Ukrainian President Viktor Yanukovych's administration with a pro-Western government, and, in short order, skirmishes with Russian troops on the eastern Ukrainian border ramped up. In March 2014, a military force of "unidentified" soldiers occupied the Crimea, and Putin was soon in control of Russia's only viable warm-water port and gateway to the Mediterranean and open waters beyond.

In retaliation, a number of sanctions were levied against Russia. Coupled with falling oil prices, it sent Russia's economy into a steep decline. Putin's popularity remained strong, and his appeal to nationalistic feelings continued to be powerful. Putin began to reinvent Russia—not as the world superpower it once was but rather as a major global player and power broker. With its modern military, nuclear weapons, oil reserves, natural resources, and advanced cyberwarfare capabilities, Russia was creating a new geopolitical ball game.

As relations with the United States and European powers deteriorated, Putin pivoted to Asia, the Middle East, and a host of oil-producing nations unhappy with the West. He established new ties with China, and both nations are founding members of the Shanghai Cooperative Organization (SCO), a counterbalance to NATO.

Russia bolstered its ties to Syria and Iran with air support for the Assad regime and the sale and installation of its potent S-300 surface-to-air missile system[2] to Iran to fend off air attacks by Israel and other powers. Putin has courted Turkey with hopes of weakening Turkish ties with Western powers, and it is not inconceivable that Turkey will someday relinquish its NATO ties for the SCO or some other Eurasian alliance.

As one of the world's largest exporters of oil and natural gas, Russia has used its state oil company, Rosneft, to make inroads in Venezuela, Cuba, Vietnam, Egypt, Iran, and other countries with deteriorating relationships with the United States, and it has courted

OPEC to reduce its oil exports to stabilize prices and increase leverage.

Major investigations by the United States revealed Russian interference in the 2016 presidential elections, which caused relations with Russia to degrade further. Looking ahead, it seems clear that Russia has reemerged as a major player on the global scene, and that as relationships with the West sour, Russia will ramp up its old Eurasian vision and pivot to Asia for greater trade, economic, and military relationships and the leverage they entail.

China: Under the leadership of Xi Jinping—China's most powerful leader since Mao Tse-tung—since 2013, China has fully emerged as the most dynamic nation of the twenty-first century and the world's newest superpower. Its growth reflects Xi's "dream of national rejuvenation," a vision and plan ratified and enshrined in the constitution at the historic Nineteenth National Congress of the Communist Party of China in Beijing in October 2017, where Xi was formally elevated to the same status as Mao Tse-tung and Deng Xiaoping—a sign of his unchallenged stature.

Xi recognized that the internal security of China depended upon its continued economic growth and stability, which, in turn, required a strong international presence with secure access to global markets and resources. Xi has internally consolidated the Communist Party of China, the driving force behind his vision, while expanding its efforts outwardly. China's strategic outlook and disciplined adherence to its five-year plan are formidable components in this equation.

Economically, China's economy has grown at an astonishing average per-annum rate of nearly 10 percent since 1980. Still strong, it has slipped in recent years, but its heavy investment in infrastructure, education, high-tech R&D efforts, and a huge account-balance surplus to fuel long-term strategic plans will fortify future growth. Efforts are now underway to rebalance its economy toward greater consumer spending and upgraded living standards as the migration from a rural, agrarian-based society to large-scale urbanization continues.

China's low-key foreign policy posture of the past has become more muscular. While avoiding direct confrontations, China continues to systematically build the platforms of global leadership needed for a more forceful worldwide posture. These platforms include a powerful industrial and infrastructure base, growing military capabilities, expanded global alliances, and a willingness to fill the power vacuums left by the United States' retrenchment on several multinational arrangements.

China's "One Belt, One Road" (OBOR)[3] strategy focuses on building connectivity and cooperation with other nations, particularly in the Eurasian and African arenas, through China-centered global trading networks. China uses its vast capital resources and international banking and trade alliances to invest in other nations' infrastructure projects: roads, ports, airports, power grids, and resource-development projects. In return, China gets access to the raw materials it needs to provide finished goods for purchase in the host countries and others. OBOR's economic arrangements are more binding, perhaps, than military alliances, and while still a work in progress, it has shown great promise.

China has also ramped up its military and space-age capabilities in dramatic fashion. It is building a "blue-water" navy that can extend sea power beyond its coastal waters, as well as a new, modernized army and air force with a growing capacity for cyber and space warfare. With an antisatellite capability, it has the ability to disrupt our previous space-age edge, and its anti-ship missile systems could pose a significant threat to our Seventh Fleet in the Pacific. Its nuclear and ICBM delivery systems with MIRV (multiple independently targeted reentry vehicle) warheads give it a strategic military capability that dwarfs those of most other nations.

China's expansion of its territorial reach and underseas mining in the East and South China Seas through the expansion of its exclusive economic zones (EEZs)[4] could be problematic. That said, China still seems to prefer soft-power solutions that rely more on economic than military clout. In this regard, the IMF's recent approval of the renminbi, or yuan, as an international reserve currency has strengthened China's currency position against the dollar. Its OBOR investments are usually transacted in yuan rather than dollars, and its leading role in the Asian Infrastructure Investment Bank (AIIB)[5] is a powerful magnet for Asia-Pacific countries in need of capital.

While the geopolitical shifts in the Middle East, Russia, and China are game-changers, regional flash points in nuclear-armed nations—including India, Pakistan, and North Korea—could ignite a broader nuclear conflagration. Two significant threats of note are nuclear proliferation and asymmetric warfare, with an emphasis on cyberwarfare and terrorism. Both threats can be disproportionately high in comparison to the size and economic strength of the country, rogue regime, or terrorist groups creating them.

Nuclear Proliferation: The nuclear Non-Proliferation Treaty went into effect in 1970, with 190 nations subscribing to it. It called for nations with nuclear weapons to work on disarmament, nations without nuclear weapons *not* to acquire them, and allowances for all nations to have access to peaceful nuclear technology. The five founding nations were the United States, USSR, China, France, and United Kingdom. Newer known members of the world's "nuke club" include Israel, Pakistan, India, and North Korea, with several others considering it or having advanced bomb-making capability, as do Iran, South Africa, and others.

North Korea withdrew from the treaty in 2003 and continued its efforts to build a nuclear weapon. On October 9, 2006, it conducted its first nuclear test and has completed several tests since, despite UN sanctions and international condemnation. In 2009 it launched a satellite and has aggressively pursued a long-range ICBM delivery system. While a major showdown with North Korea is a high-probability threat, other potential nuke-related threats include converting an atomic device into an electromagnetic-pulse (EMP) weapon, which could release an enormous burst of electromagnetic energy in a power surge that could destroy virtually all electrical devices and grids, crippling communications and infrastructure over a vast area. In another scenario, North Korea or even a well-financed terrorist group with access to weapons-grade plutonium could detonate a dirty bomb that would render a port or city a radioactive wasteland for decades. Nuclear proliferation poses the greatest existential threat to humankind at this time, and the number of nuclear players is growing.

Asymmetric Warfare and Cyberattacks: As a recap, in asymmetric warfare, a weaker combatant employs unconventional strategies or tactics against a stronger combatant. While guerrilla and terrorist attacks have been deadly effective, the most effective and economically disruptive attacks to come will be digital. The United States, with its digitally connected infrastructure, is vulnerable to cyberattacks. Assaults on corporate giants and financial institutions have resulted in the loss of sensitive data on tens of millions of Americans at a crack, and the problem is global. Data and identity theft, cyberespionage, data-ransom schemes, and more are now pervasive threats throughout the world, complicated further by state-sponsored assaults. There are no rules of engagement on this new global battlefield. The barriers to entry are low, and the fact that serious—even catastrophic—damage can be inflicted on so many by so few is chilling.

While digital forensics are improving, the task of identifying the sources of cyberattacks is daunting. The frequency, scale, and sophistication of the attacks, as well as the severity of impact, continue to escalate. Cyberattacks have taken on many forms, including denial of service, data and supply-chain disruptions, cyberespionage, and penetration of seemingly secure sites, such as those of the Department of Defense and the National Security Agency.

For example, a sophisticated hacker group known as the Shadow Brokers is alleged to have penetrated and extracted the National Security Agency's most secret "toolbox" of software codes, used to break into high-security data repositories of countries and companies throughout the world. Shortly after the alleged thefts in 2017, the world was barraged with major disruptions in critical public and private sector operations. Millions of computers were rendered inoperative and held for ransom.

Threat levels will worsen as cyberwarfare escalates into attacks that shut down or disrupt an electrical grid or power facility; air traffic control systems; or financial, utility, and national security systems. The targets of opportunity are everywhere. It is truly an existential threat and a clear example of how new technologies can easily surpass our ability to assimilate or defend against them.

E-2: Energy and Technology

Energy Forces

In the second decade of the twenty-first century, an exciting new energy renaissance emerged. To appreciate its magnitude, we must first understand the forces driving it, which include climate change and the quest to reduce carbon emissions, technological advances that are revolutionizing the energy arena, and market-driven forces within the public and private sectors. Combined, they will transform the global energy landscape and spark a strategic redirection of national energy policies, business models, infrastructures, economies, and consumer and household behaviors; a work in progress.

Environmental concerns were early drivers of the clean-energy policies, and later, as the threat of global warming and climate change became evident, efforts to reduce GHG emissions through clean energy and other measures were ramped up at a global level. The Paris Agreement, in 2015, strengthened the political will of nations to reduce carbon footprints and reconfigure power-generation, grid, and transportation systems to achieve desired policy targets. At state and local levels, the quest has led to a number of new initiatives. At least twenty-nine US states have adopted some form of renewable portfolio standards that call for utilities to generate a specified amount of power from renewable energy sources by a specified date. Dates and percentages vary by state, but it is not unusual to see a mandate for a 25 percent mix of renewable energy for electrical power generation by 2025. The mandates usually come with tax incentives or other inducements for achieving goals or penalties for falling short.

By 2017 the GHG-reduction targets established by the Paris Agreement began translating into mandated target dates in which countries would discontinue the production of new gasoline- or diesel-powered cars. While target dates for these zero-emission vehicles vary from 2025 to 2040, the goal is stimulating the mix of new electrical and hydrogen fuel-cell vehicles as well as the infrastructure needed to maintain them. As China, India, and several European countries, among other nations, phase in these mandates, and as price points and infrastructure improve, the energy renaissance will rapidly advance. New technologies also support the energy renaissance as energy storage, renewable energy sources, smart grids, distributed-power models, high-speed rail, fracking and horizontal drilling technologies, and so on change the power mix.

The oil and natural gas industries and global markets in which they operate changed in almost a fortnight. With a significant reserve of shale oil and new fracking, drilling, and refining technologies to extract and produce oil and natural gas, the United States grew less reliant on foreign oil and even became an exporter of liquified natural gas and light crude oil. The ramifications for OPEC, Russia, and other net-oil-exporting nations are significant. Within the United States, the heavy new flow of cheaper natural gas has prompted many utilities to convert coal-powered plants to natural gas—better for the environment, but not so good for the coal industry. Nuclear power generation has held steady.

New technologies are also being employed to improve power plant efficiency, modernize the grid systems that deliver electrical power, and direct power to end users with two-way smart systems. New renewable energy tech and demand-reduction efforts offering greater efficiencies are rapidly improving price points, energy storage capacities, and the ability to produce and use energy locally in a distributed manner.

With mandates to spark growth, new technologies and infrastructures, and a receptive marketplace, energy producers and collateral energy-intensive businesses are gradually recalibrating their business models to this new energy environment. Auto companies, for instance, are developing new lines of electric and hybrid vehicles, and service stations are starting to offer battery-recharging stations to accommodate a growing fleet of electrical cars.

A reality check is due, however. Despite its solid launch, the energy renaissance is still in its early stages. It takes decades to transition to a new energy system, and fossil fuels will play a leading role in all global energy power structures for some time to come. A quick look at our legacy fuel systems in this decade is revealing.

It has been a turbulent decade for the global oil markets. Volatile pricing and the vicissitudes of supply and demand have been exacerbated by the US shale oil revolution. As the economy stagnated and global demand leveled somewhat, oil inventories grew and created a glut of oil on the world markets. Oil prices fell, and the oil producers of the world reeled. Countries and oil companies alike were threatened. The Saudis, with the clout to manipulate prices, decided to let the market play out; this strategy allowed them to maintain market share while driving out marginal players and US shale oil producers. While the verdict is not in, it is interesting that Saudi Aramco went public for the first time in late 2019 to raise capital.

While consumers, lulled into a false sense of security, once again bought SUVs and light trucks at a record clip, the immutable laws of geology and the supply-and-demand curve will ultimately prevail, setting us up for another time of reckoning. We are racing against time, hoping that new fuel systems will be functional and at sufficient scale to replace oil and other fossil-fuel systems in a timely manner. The economic alternative is almost too ugly to imagine. While the energy renaissance offers a way out, getting there will be a contentious, expensive, and complex process. The viability of any energy strategy will directly depend on its alignment with climate change and need to reduce carbon footprints.

Technological Forces

The World Economic Forum meets annually in Davos, Switzerland, to discuss the great challenges of the world. The major topic at the Davos Forum in January 2016 was the fourth industrial revolution. The world's top business, political, scientific, and intellectual leaders expressed major concerns about humankind's ability to adapt to this technological juggernaut.

The fourth industrial revolution will generate a new set of challenges as the humanistic and technological worlds blur, demanding a rational accommodation between human and artificial intelligence in areas once the sole domain of human beings. It will accelerate the spread of smart technologies that alter the way we live, work, relax, and relate to one another. It will differ from the previous three industrial revolutions in terms of its size, scope, and speed and the complexity of change it will cause. In a crude sort of way, some see it as a form of outsourcing our brainpower and decision making to machines and, perhaps, desensitizing our relationship skills.

Building on the previous digital revolution, this one is sparked by sensor-laden smart technologies that fuse artificial and human intelligence. Quantum computing, artificial intelligence, 3-D printing, robotics, driverless vehicles, gene therapy, nano and biotechnologies, the Internet of Things, material sciences, voice-controlled tools, design software, and other gigantic advances are changing the way we do things. Machines will increasingly be used to conduct work done by humans at all levels. With billions of people interconnected with mobile devices, unprecedented processing power, instant information, and complex algorithms that automate and activate decision making, the whole ball game is rapidly changing before our very eyes.

Fears of robotizing or marginalizing humanity, creating more sedentary lifestyles, compromising interpersonal skills, and opening up complex new moral and ethical dilemmas are of great concern—or at least should be. It will change the workforce and skill sets needed and tax the ability of workers and employers to adapt, retrain, and reinvent themselves to meet future needs. In most cases, the task of reskilling workers to complement and align with the new technologies will take place at the worksite, and we can expect to live in a lifelong learning environment throughout our careers.

As these trends gain traction, a greater emphasis will be placed on human skills that machines can't replicate. The World Economic Forum issued *The Future of Jobs Report 2018,* which explains the changing dynamics of the workforce. There will be a growing emphasis on such skills as complex problem solving, critical thinking, creativity, people management, emotional intelligence, and cognitive flexibility.

This new world will exacerbate the inherent conflicts between national security, data needs, and personal privacy concerns and increasingly challenge our capacity to adapt to rapidly changing technologies in a timely manner. The opportunities are fantastic; the unintended consequences are disturbing. Technological wizardry, now almost a routine part of our lives, has an exponential growth curve that will vastly exceed our rate of absorption, and the disconnects will widen, intensify, and accelerate our collision with the perfect storm.

E-3: Environmental and Ecological Forces

Environmental Forces: Climate Change

A blip on the radar screen only twenty-five years ago, climate change is now a widely recognized, existential threat to the planet. While a dwindling number of skeptics dub it a hoax, the once-contested computer models used to predict it are no longer needed; we now have real-time, observable data that regularly confirms the growing threat

Wide-scale international efforts are underway to mitigate the rising level of GHGs. Sparked by rising global temperatures—the warmest years in recorded history—and dramatic ice melts, rising sea levels, and the increasing frequency of "once in a century" storms, droughts, floods, and fires, conditions are worsening, and so is our ability to respond effectively.

Still, the climate story of the decade has to be the collaborative international effort to address climate change and codify it through the 2015 Paris Agreement. It represents the culmination of twenty-five years of hard work, dating back to 1992, when 197 nations, including the United States, signed on to the UNFCCC and thus launched global efforts to address climate change. At COP-21 in

Paris, 195 nations sealed the deal, and the United States helped frame the final agreement. Pragmatically written to avoid the pitfalls of previous agreements, it featured a "bottom-up" rather than "top-down" mandated approach for setting goals and protocols, leaving nations the political wiggle room needed to implement policy within their own unique political circumstances.

Nations would submit an action pledge outlining voluntary emission reduction strategies and goals and then provide a mechanism for monitoring and reporting on their progress on a regular basis. The results were not binding, and nations were not told what they could or couldn't do. While recognizing that every nation had its own unique set of circumstances, the hope was to build a consensus and use peer pressure rather than mandates to limit global warming to an increase of two degrees centigrade or less from preindustrial levels by the end of the century. A call for progress, not perfection, it initiated a collective effort to save the planet from a threat hardly known two decades earlier, an extraordinary achievement and a testament to how strongly nations felt about the threat.

The world was stunned, therefore, when President Trump announced on June 1, 2017, that the United States would pull out of the agreement, a long and winding exit process that would take up to four years to complete. In addition, the Trump administration initiated steps to dismantle the efforts of the Clean Power Plan, limit the EPA's reach, and hobble other programs designed to promote clean energy, air, and water while regulating carbon emissions.

A major world polluter, the United States had been counted on to use its political and financial influence to give weight to the Paris Agreement. As a major force behind the accord, with an impressive track record of reducing our own carbon emissions, our decision to leave was hard for others to understand. Global outrage was immediate, and backlash was severe, as Fortune 500 companies, state and local governments, and a vast outpouring of grassroots organizations denounced the decision and proclaimed their commitment to the agreement despite the federal government's pullout.

The geopolitical implications and lost economic opportunities of this shortsighted decision will be fully discussed later. For now, the

United States has become an international pariah as the only nation not signing on to the Paris Agreement, a decision sure to haunt us in the coming years.

Ecological Forces

Throughout the decade, the struggle to provide the ecological necessities of life—air, food, and water—for an expanding global population continued to deteriorate. Air pollution in China, India, and elsewhere; the challenge of growing and distributing food to the undernourished and starving populations in developing countries; new health threats of Ebola and other epidemics; and the destruction of life-supporting ecosystems have all intensified. Perhaps the greatest—and most immediate—of all challenges is to provide accessible fresh water to a thirsty world.

The world's fresh-water crisis is worsening as a growing and thirstier population, with wasteful and pollutive water practices, competes for a finite supply. The uneven distribution of water, in which about 85 percent of the world's population lives in the driest half of the planet, compounds the problem. In this water-limited world, more than 660 million people live without easy access to safe drinking water close to home, and about one in four people use contaminated water. Major floods and droughts intensify the problem, and the projected 55 percent growth in the demand for fresh water from 2000 to 2050 is unsustainable under current conditions. We are consuming water far faster than it can be replenished and making up the deficit by drawing down on our aquifers. Our GRACE satellites show aquifer depletions throughout the world, and once the aquifer water is gone, it's gone. Then what?

The quality of our water supply is also under duress from the pollution generated by wastewater, sewage, farming, and industrial waste. Though solvable, it will require an enormous expenditure of monetary and political capital. Many of the poorer and most arid nations lack the resources and expertise to ensure their citizens have access to clean water. The stats are horrifying: at least a third of the world's people live with inadequate water sanitation and are exposed to cholera, typhoid fever, and other waterborne diseases. The Flint, Michigan, story is another sad example and proof that even prosperous, water-rich countries fall short of the mark.

Bottom line: whereas economies suffer when there is an inadequate supply of cheap energy, and the citizens' health is directly affected by polluted air, the inaccessibility of fresh water will affect the health and well-being of humanity more quickly and lethally than any other natural threat. Geopolitically, it is a threat multiplier that will continue to spark regional wars, famines, and a destabilizing mass migration of populations.

E-4: Expectations and Behavioral Forces

The promise of the American Dream has been scaled back by a number of challenging trends and events. The middle class, once a breeding ground for upward mobility, is shrinking as income inequalities widen. The availability of family-supporting jobs stagnated as inflation-adjusted wages failed to grow at a rate commensurate with the growth of GDP and escalating living costs. Even with two wage earners and a growing willingness to take on household debt, access to the American Dream has become less available to a growing number of households. The Great Recession of 2008 reinforced the trend as savings and retirement accounts were decimated, home values cratered, and millions of jobs disappeared in a fortnight. The results were devastating, and the ripple effects—and painful memories—are long.

Large numbers of shell-shocked Millennials graduated from college deep in debt, with diminished prospects of securing a solid career or well-paying job. By mid-decade it was estimated that as many as half of the college graduates were either underemployed or unemployed. Many opted to live at home—more by necessity than choice—and, like their parents, hope to resurrect their own personal balance sheets. As one measure of the hunkering-down effect, household debt declined for nineteen consecutive quarters from the height of the Great Recession before inching up again.

By 2017 the Millennials were the dominant generational cohort, and their actions and behaviors shaped the economy and society in many ways. Millennials are getting married later in life and raising smaller families. By living with family or renting, they influence the home-building industry. Aggregate student-loan debt—now over $1.3 trillion—hampers upward mobility, and loan-default rates are climbing. The thriving subprime auto market is likewise showing greater signs of defaults and late payments.

The return to a solid economy, however tepid, was steady through 2015. By 2017 the economy was once again hot. Unemployment hovered at about 4 percent—considered full employment by most economists—and the stock market was repeatedly reaching new record highs. Families were spending, and household debt exceeded the levels that prevailed shortly before the crash. The bull market neared its tenth straight year in 2019, and the global economy was relatively strong. Still, an uneasiness lingers. Despite impressive aggregated numbers on Wall Street and elsewhere, the euphoria has not been generally felt on Main Street, where the rank and file still struggle to get by. Perhaps memories of the dot-com bubble and Great Recession still prevail.

In polls taken on attitudes toward the American Dream, a dwindling number felt they would live better than their parents. In fact, an effort was made in 2016 to quantify the American Dream by looking at whether or not children made more money than their parents. Dubbed the American Dream Composite Index,[6] it determined that 92 percent of those born in 1940 made more than their parents. For those born in 1980, only 50 percent were likely to top their parents' earnings. It suggested that though the economy was growing, the gains in economic growth were not spread out evenly; a disproportionate amount was skewed toward a smaller group of people at the top.

To be sure, there are no shortcuts to achieving the American Dream. And, while it may not be as accessible to many as it once was, neither was it a given for the class of '61. It still required a lot of hard work and grit, and Art Jentsch reflects that determination.

Art Jentsch

By almost any measure, Art Jentsch has led an exemplary life, a personification of the American Dream and all the good qualities that go with it. A humble and unpretentious man with an easy-going manner, he personifies the spirit of the American Dream with his hard work, playing by the rules, entrepreneurially acting on new opportunities when they are presented, and upbeat persona that can find humor in almost any situation. He values the important things in life, like family, friends, and community, and his commitment to these relationships is reflected in the long-term connections he has maintained for so many years in so many ways with so many people; call it "staying power."

Married for fifty-four years to a wonderful lady by the name of Colleen Donahue (a North High classmate), with two children, Christine and Mike; eight grandchildren; and three great-grandchildren that he sees regularly, Art gradually built a four-acre compound on Rice Lake where he has lived since 1969. His house is a collector's dream, with coins, cards, antique toys, jewelry, and angels, and even a wall dedicated to Custer's Last Stand. It warmly reflects the hobbies and interests of the Jentsch family, which include boating, biking, walking, and the many international trips that he and Colleen have taken since he retired.

There was no free lunch. Art worked his way through school—with a family—and graduated from the University of Minnesota with a degree in Recreational and Park Administration. He started and ended his long career at the Brainerd State Hospital, where he worked his way up the ranks. He was identified as a "comer" early on in his career and was awarded a scholarship by the Joseph Kennedy Foundation to complete an intensive master's degree in education at the University of Minnesota. His employer supported the effort, and Art immersed himself in school.

Leaving Brainerd and going back to school with a family was not easy. Art, however, took a longer view of what it could mean for his career and family. He also worked and saved in this busy period to bankroll a new side career in the real estate and rental business. Through hard work and perseverance, he bought, fixed, and accumulated rental properties while still working at his regular career job, and the business began to grow.

Art officially retired at age fifty-five and shifted to his new career as owner of a robust real estate and property rental operation. A multitasker, he managed his business while he and Colleen traveled, pursued their hobbies and interests, and stayed active in a multitude of ways—with family always the most important thing.

Art is a living example of what it means to pursue and achieve the American Dream while staying grounded in the things that really matter. In an age of quick fixes, fleeting relationships, and lack of commitment, Art's staying power, sense of community, and the values that he and Colleen live by are rare qualities that are appreciated by all.

Looking ahead, there is little doubt it will take the same kind of work ethic Art Jentsch displayed to achieve the American Dream going forward. While all generations have had their own unique challenges, we are in the early stages of a new paradigm that will rock the world—and not all in a good way.

The fourth industrial revolution will widen the disconnects between the job skill sets needed and those available. Those with the prerequisite skills will do quite well, but a far higher number will be consigned to a dimmer future, another example of how the American Dream will become less available to a growing number of Americans.

As the name of this book implies, we have complicated their plight by leaving younger generations with a frightening stack of our IOUs. The unfunded entitlement liabilities, massive debt, and staggering costs of financing that debt will be an economic anchor that stifles future growth and opportunity. The warming planet, depleted physical resources, diminished access to fresh water, and pollution everywhere are all IOUs that we're passing on as a result of our behaviors.

The future challenges to our society, culture, and lifestyles are daunting. At the end of the day, the issue of achieving—let alone having access to—the American Dream may play second fiddle to the very act of survival. We will explore the challenges and strategies for coping in this new world in the next part of this book.

Mike Conley

I flunked retirement, and it doesn't bother me a bit. In fact, it is exhilarating.

My passion for addressing the perfect storm and the raw deal we were passing on to future generations had intensified, and I was energized by the idea of taking it all to a new level as we entered the new decade. Looking back, I'm amazed at how much my life had changed as a result of this aspiration.

It started with recollections from my college years of the books written by Ayn Rand and George Orwell. They used the art of storytelling to get their respective messages out—which they did with great effect—and it inspired me to do the same. I decided to write a novel that would show how the perfect storm could play out, and I titled the book *Lethal Trajectories*. Published in late 2011, it was a fast-paced techno-thriller, but I wanted it to be more than just a novel. Accordingly, the book contained thirty-five pages of endnotes to document the key concepts within it, and I also published a thirty-two-page how-to supplement, the *Weathering the Storm* guide. Many of the prognostications in the book have come true.

The book was a catalyst for several new initiatives. It opened the door for a host of speaking engagements on radio and TV, and Rotary Club and other presentations. While these efforts helped to sell books, my real goal was to introduce people to the issues that so concerned me. It also led to other opportunities.

I set up a new company, Weathering the Storm, LLC, and with it a website of the same name. The mission of my new company was simply "to awaken, engage, and help people to weather the storm." The storm, of course, is the perfect storm that looms in our path. This led to another initiative, a course called "The Perfect Storm" offered through the OLLI program at the University of Minnesota. I taught it for three years and was energized by the process and the great people I met.

As a result of these activities, and the feedback I received from students, the groups that I had spoken to, and subscribers to my website, I was encouraged to write the book that you are now reading. They were interested in the issues and what they could do about them.

I have no idea what will come of this book, but the process—the journey, if you will—was well worth the effort. Anything after that is pure gravy.

On the home front, things were equally gratifying. My daughter, Heather, a social worker and counselor, married a good man by the name of Matt Hoiland, a sustainability manager, in April 2014. My other daughter, Kristen; her husband, Todd; and their kids, Keri and Samuel, after living in Jakarta, Indonesia, for many years, moved back to the US in 2016. Now, instead of flying twelve thousand miles to visit them, we can do the same in about twelve minutes. Sharon and I are ever so thankful for the many family gatherings we often have; just call us happy campers.

Get-togethers with our grandkids are also special reminders of the fiduciary responsibilities we all have to leave those following us with a planet, environment, economy, and opportunities as good as those we received from our predecessors. Let's just call it maintaining access to the American Dream.

The coming years will be challenging, and the things we do today to be good stewards of all we have been given could profoundly impact the quality of life we leave behind for others. It's hard to know what could come from our efforts, but at a minimum, I want to be able to look back and at least be able to say, "I tried."

In the final analysis, that's about all any of us can do.

Summary of the 2010s

The long global economic recovery came at a price; the seas of red ink that sustained it will be a permanent drag on future growth. Climate change emerged as an existential threat, and the fourth industrial revolution came into its own. Geopolitically, the Trump administration shattered the status quo. We moved closer to the perfect storm as follows:

1. **The global economy recovered, but the price tag was disproportionately high.**

   - The massive new debt produced huge carrying charges that will stifle future growth.

- Borrowing our way into prosperity, as we have this decade, is not a sustainable solution.

- All bubbles burst; weakened, we are ill prepared for the next global meltdown.

2. **The geopolitical balance of power shifted, and the outcomes are uncertain.**

    - The US moved away from its traditional global role, creating a destabilizing power vacuum.

    - Nuclear proliferation and asymmetric threats—such as cyberwarfare—intensified.

    - China, with strong connections to Russia, emerged fully as a new superpower.

3. **Climate change became globally recognized as an existential threat.**

    - The 2015 Paris Agreement galvanized the world, but the United States exited the treaty two years later.

    - The impacts of climate change intensified and were deemed a threat multiplier by the US military.

    - Dire warnings abound, but world responses fell far short of the actions needed.

4. **The new energy renaissance offered a ray of hope, but energy shifts are daunting.**

    - Technologies exist, but transitioning away from fossil fuels will be risky and costly.

    - Clean energy became the hottest growth industry in the world.

- Strong opposition from oil-producing nations complicated the process.

5. **The cracks in the American Dream widened further.**

   - The shrinking middle class and wage gaps reduced opportunities for many in the United States.

   - Millennials replaced boomers as largest generational cohort.

   - The fourth industrial revolution gained traction and increased destabilization.

SNAPSHOT: *2010–2018*

	2000	2010	2018
Population in Millions			
World	6,145.0	6,958.2	7,632.8
USA	282.2	309.3	327.2
US Financials in Billions			
GDP	$10,117.5	$14,838.9	$20,235.9
Fed. Receipts	2,025.2	2,162.7	3,329.9
Fed. Outlays	1,789.0	3,457.1	4,109.0
Surplus / (Deficit)	236.2	(1,294.4)	(779.1)
Gross Fed. Debt	5,628.7	13,528.8	21,462.3
Interest on Debt	223.0	196.2	325.0
US Domestic Averages			
Wages	$40,343	$39,856	$46,464
Cost of new house	134,150	232,800	318,500
Cost of new car	24,750		

Points of Interest

- China and Russia connect; new cyber- and asymmetric warfare took center stage

- Paris Agreement united world on climate change, but the USA bailed out once again

- Debt exceeded GDP; interest on debt climbed over 65 percent

- Record bull market under Obama and Trump, but concerns mounted: how long will it last?

Snapshot Road Map: *The Snapshot compares key data points from the beginning of one decade to the beginning of the next. Sources are provided under Part II in the endnotes.*

PART III

Weathering the Storm

An optimist sees an opportunity in every calamity;
a pessimist sees calamity in every opportunity.

—Winston Churchill

Our journey into the future begins here in Part III. The prognostications will be disturbing for most, but visionaries will see solutions and new opportunities embedded in the challenges we will face.

Make no mistake: our journey through the perfect storm will be perilous, and our lack of preparation, to date, will complicate our arduous trek. That said, there is still time to mitigate some of the sharper edges of the storm and, in the process, use the crises as an opportunity to reenergize the American Dream and our respective futures. Hard, but not impossible.

To do this, we will need to throw out our old playbook and challenge the conventional wisdom and paradigms surrounding it. We can forget about panaceas and quick fixes to circumvent the storm because there is no way around it. As Einstein warned, "We cannot solve the world's problems with the same thinking that created them."

The forecasts provided in Part III developed from my scenario-planning methodology. While I make no claim to predict the precise time or exact nature of the events that will trigger the perfect storm, I have developed a range of the likeliest scenarios based on the trajectories developed in Part II and the latest data available. The scenarios are expressed in relational terms with respect to the sequencing, flow, and timing of events.

Chapter 15 opens with a look at the future scenarios and trajectories likely to occur in the 2020s. Using these projections as a baseline, chapter 16 paints a graphic fictional picture of the perfect storm and how it could play out from beginning to end, including the chain reaction igniting it and what it might be like to live through it. In chapter 17, I offer a plan, Reenergizing the American Dream, as a proactive response to the perfect storm and a catalyst for restoring our magnificent dream—all as part of a greater global effort. It will seem like a stretch until we recognize that we *will* reach a point at which the pain of *not* acting exceeds the pain of acting in ways we might never have imagined possible. The book concludes in chapter 18 with my conclusions, lessons learned, and personal reflections.

-15-

The 2020s: Predictions

*I know not with what weapons World War III will be fought,
but World War IV will be fought with sticks and stones.*

—Albert Einstein

ears from now, the surviving members of the class of '61 will
likely look on the roaring twenties of the new millennium as
pivotal years in history. We might also recall how our chronological age of seventy-six at the beginning of the decade did not
always comport with our self-image of being younger—that is, until
our creaking bodies debunked this disconnect with our brain to
remind us that we were, indeed, over three-quarters of a century
old and not getting any younger. It was one of many disconnects we
would experience on our long journey.

It was not hard to feel disconnected. The blurring rush of
changes seemed to surpass our rate of comprehension, leaving us
perennially behind the learning curve. Though we were moving
inexorably closer to the perfect storm, we failed to grasp the warn-

ings and connect the dots. Our inability to do so may be one of our greatest failures—ever.

In retrospect, the global power structures didn't change overnight, nor did climate change happen out of the blue. The crippling debt that would soon paralyze the global economy and constrain human opportunities was just a set of abstract numbers that policy wonks chewed on. The world's dwindling supply of fresh water, oil, and other finite resources—the result of more than a century of waste and depletion—shrank so gradually. The proliferation of nuclear weapons and asymmetric warfare seemed manageable at the time, and the decline of the American Dream, and the dysfunctional political system that helped foster it, was something we would all muddle through—or so we thought.

We will do a little crystal-balling in this chapter and forecast how the simmering storm forces previously covered will play out in the future. My methodology for doing so involves little more than extrapolating out current storm trajectories and scenarios to a point where they could erupt into the perfect storm, probably within a decade or so, but maybe earlier. I hope it will spark a wake-up call to act while there is still time

We will focus on five looming megathreats and the collateral forces propelling them. In doing so, we will stray somewhat from the perfect storm model because the all-pervasive nature of these threats crosses over all four of the E-Cells. The five great threats are as follows:

1. Global destabilization and the ticking time bombs

2. Climate change and the sustainability of life as we know it

3. Energy and technology in a race against time

4. An American implosion that could rock the world

5. Resilience and our capacity to persevere.

Global Destabilization and Ticking Time Bombs

The interconnected global systems of world trade and commerce, currency exchanges, banking and transactional protocols, international laws, military ties, dispute-resolution mechanisms, alliances, customs, and cultural connections have more or less worked to raise the overall prosperity levels of the world since the end of World War II. Unfortunately, these global institutions can, if misused, work against a sound world order. For example, the global financial meltdown in 2008 demonstrated how rapidly and contagiously a crisis can spread. With few firewalls to prevent the problems of one nation from spreading to others, an economic sneeze from either superpower can escalate into pneumonia in other countries.

In the best of times, there will always be routine conflicts between nations, but when critical global institutions are weakened or compromised—as they are now—those conflicts can quickly escalate into military conflicts, trade wars, or asymmetric actions designed to weaken a nation and destabilize the world order. When global challenges arise that transcend all nations, such as climate change, fresh-water shortages, pandemics, or the destruction of our key life support systems, any or all threats are greatly magnified. Global nuclear war is not the only existential threat humankind now faces.

The world is in an uncomfortable state of stress, sensing—but not appreciating—the epic forces at play below the waterline. Some pose a direct threat to humankind, while others amplify the threats. We will explore three destabilizers in particular: the global debt bubble and threats to our global institutions, the changing role of the United States and its destabilizing side effects, and the new cold war.

The Global Debt Bubble and Institutional Threats

Global debt increased by over 50 percent in the ten years following the Great Recession of 2008. Though enormous efforts were made by central banks and national governments to spend, borrow, devalue, and print their way back to a sustainable prosperity, it was an uphill battle. The results did not reflect the efforts as aggregated debt grew at rates far exceeding global GDP growth. Simply put, it took a disproportionately high amount of debt (input) to achieve a modest growth rate (output), a poor prescription for long-term, sustainable growth.

National fiscal policies were loaded with deficit spending, public-works programs, excessive leveraging, and underfunded welfare programs in a quest for growth at all costs. Debt was the vehicle of choice in this quest, and the central banks of the world, like our Federal Reserve, provided the monetary juice to make it happen. Their efforts to keep interest rates low, boost liquidity, and even devalue currencies to make their respective exports more competitive were noteworthy. Our Federal Reserve's creative use of QE programs to pump liquidity into the system, while successful, left the Fed with a balance sheet that quadrupled from 2008 to 2016 to $4.5 trillion, a balance the Fed is now struggling to decrease without cratering the economy.

By the end of the 2010s, governments, companies, and households were drowning in a sea of red ink. As debt has now exceeded GDP in many countries, including the United States, opportunities for achieving the growth rates needed to sustain highly leveraged economies will become increasingly rare.

As we enter the 2020s with global debt levels in the $240 trillion-plus range—well over 300 percent of the world's GDP—the cost of servicing that debt will put a major strain on both public and private budgets everywhere. For many nations, it will mean spending less, cutting expenses, raising taxes, or borrowing more. Those with the capacity to print money, like the United States, will do so. Countries will also game the system with a greater use of tariffs, currency manipulations, trade wars, and attempts to bolster their position as a world reserve currency at the expense of others.

The United States is particularly vulnerable if the dollar loses its status as the world's primary reserve currency. Many nations resent what they consider to be our aggressive fiscal and monetary policies, along with our growing tendency to weaponize the dollar and its attendant international mechanisms in the form of sanctions to achieve a geopolitical goal. A serious run at our reserve currency status or the petrodollar system could plunge the United States into a major depression.

The world's ability to weather the next economic crash has deteriorated. It poses a significant global economic threat, and the prognosis is not good. The international community cannot forever borrow its way into prosperity: in the end, all bubbles burst.

The Changing Role of the United States and Its Destabilizing Side Effects

In a world in which stability equals security and security equals stability, the United States—a key architect of the global systems now in play and a pillar of stability since the end of World War II—has abruptly become a destabilizer. The new "America First" policies have stunned the world and left friends and foes alike scrambling to recalibrate their policies in a world that has suddenly become highly unpredictable.

In a blink of the eye, the United States changed its worldview, making significant shifts in policies that had long anchored the geopolitical structures of the world. From globalism to nationalism—and often unilateralism, when we didn't get our way—our move away from the collaborative approaches that were once a hallmark of our foreign policy has been swift, and with little consultation with traditional allies. With a focus on quick fixes and opportunistic transactions, the reciprocity of the past has been overshadowed by the need to win at the expense of others. By discarding treaties, abusing alliances, and shortchanging diplomatic efforts that fell short of the new America First mantra, we have done irreparable harm to our nation.

In this milieu, we have painted ourselves as victims of a cruel world that has taken advantage of us because we were supposedly naive and didn't know how to make a deal. (Never mind that we were the architect of many global institutions that made deal making possible, with huge built-in advantages, like the petrodollar and our world reserve currency status). It manifested in our pulling out of treaties and alliances we deemed unfair, with threats that they would not be renegotiated if they weren't made fair. It triggered a my-way-or-the-highway hubris, with little thought given to the long-term consequences. Opponents of this strategy claimed it ran counter to our national values, with an odious side effect of weakening our domestic and global institutions. We created, in the process, geopolitical voids that China and others were more than willing to fill.

While it is hard to know how it will all play out, many of our new policies have ignored Newton's third law of motion, which says that where there is an action, there will be a reaction. While the impacts of our unilateral actions have not yet been fully felt—as stunned nations regroup and recalibrate their policies—we can see examples of the world working *around* us and not *with* us.

Our European allies, frazzled by our seeming lack of commitment to NATO, disliked learning about crucial international decisions through nocturnal tweets rather than previous consultations. Nor did allied leaders like being publicly ridiculed when they disagreed with our policies. For that matter, our southern neighbor, Mexico, didn't like being told it would build us a border wall at its own expense.

The stakes are high when treaties and agreements are unilaterally broken, or when new tariffs or trade wars are threatened as a way to restructure past agreements made in good faith. In our global economy, the mere threat of a trade war between giants like China and the United States—representing about 40 percent of the world's total GDP—sends shockwaves around the world. Likewise, when a global threat such as climate change—considered by all nations of the world to be a crisis that must be dealt with globally—is dismissed by the one global power most capable of making a huge impact, the United States, we have a major problem.

Breaking away from a multilateral treaty is an especially big deal when we consider the excruciatingly difficult dynamics involved in reaching an agreement. Nothing is perfect, and no one side gets everything they want; nations give a little to get a little. The giving part is particularly difficult and gets undue attention in comparison to the overall benefits of a treaty. National leaders put their careers on the line to convince their constituents that a treaty is in their best overall interest, and they often go down with a treaty if it fails. As such, every word and paragraph in a treaty is intensively vetted by all sides. Sadly, this hard work is often overlooked by pundits who cherry-pick the less attractive features in order to dub the entire treaty a failure.

A review of a few unilateral actions taken by the United States paints a disturbing picture. As the backlash from our actions sinks in, and as nations respond to them, the consequences could be severe. Consider the following actions taken by the United States, their destabilizing consequences, and counteractions that are likely to follow:

1. **The Trans-Pacific Partnership:** This Pacific Rim treaty, designed to facilitate trade and reduce barriers across the Pacific with eleven other countries—excluding China— was scratched by the United States. It will further isolate the United States, and the one real winner will probably be China.

2. **NAFTA:** The United States told Canada and Mexico to either change the treaty or suffer the consequences. A new treaty is now awaiting ratification, but if and when it is ratified, will the changes be worth the ill will it has generated? Probably not.

3. **The Paris Agreement:** The United States, a key architect of the climate accord, announced its withdrawl from the agreement in 2017. As the world's one notable exception, one might ask, what is to be gained by this, and will our new pariah status

not work against us in the future? Worse, can world actions succeed without our active participation?

4. **The Iran Nuclear Agreement:** The United States, one of the key players and signers of the agreement, unilaterally announced its decertification of the agreement and promptly reimposed sanctions on Iran that were detrimental to all of the signatory nations. It has brought Iran, Russia, and China closer together, and Iran has now reinstituted its uranium enrichment program. The real winners are the Iranian hardliners who opposed the treaty from the get-go.

5. **The Intermediate-Range Nuclear Forces Treaty:** Signed with the USSR in 1987, it limited the development and deployment of new intermediate-range missiles. The United States formally suspended the treaty in February 2019. With nuclear weaponry an existential threat, will any temporary gain from this offset the threats or costs of a new arms race?

6. **Trade Wars and Tariffs:** The United States has implemented new tariffs on China, our allies, and other nations deemed not to be "treating us fairly." This has rattled international markets. While not a full-fledged trade war at the time of this writing, it has disrupted markets and supply chains. Nations continue to retaliate, and history has shown that no nation really wins a trade war.

The list is longer, but it is difficult to see how a nation or leader burned by our unilateral actions would be eager to strike up a new agreement with us. Like the old adage says, "Fool me once, shame on you; fool me twice, shame on me." Our credibility and brand as a trustworthy nation have suffered, and the future will be murkier because of it. In our rapid transition from a stabilizer to a destabilizer, the toxic aftershocks will be enormous.

And so, as we face the future, the backlash from our actions has changed the geopolitical dynamic in ways we cannot yet comprehend, and it will be a daunting task for the United States to regain the trust and standing that it once had. In a changing world in which collaborative efforts are needed to fend off another global economic crisis, or deal with widespread cyberattacks, or slow the ravages of climate change—or all three at once—the United States will find itself more isolated. Nations will find ways to work around and not with us, and that is not a good place for a superpower to be.

The New Cold War

The new cold war is still evolving. Unlike the first cold war, with its strong ideological focus, clear-cut sides, well-defined operating parameters, and the ability of the lead nations—the United States and USSR—to maintain order within their respective coalitions, this one is still up for grabs. The new cold war has a different look. It was given a boost in 2017 and 2018 when China and the United States came to a crossroad and took opposite turns. The United States turned inward with its new America First policy, and China looked outward with its expansionist OBOR policy. America's abrupt shift away from traditional policies and historic alliances stunned partners and adversaries alike and left nations scrambling to recalibrate their respective foreign policies; a work still in progress.

As the dynamics of the new cold war evolve, the geopolitical arena will remain highly destabilized. The search for a new equilibrium will be complicated by an emergent Russia flexing its global muscles, an explosion of new asymmetric threats, the insidious impacts of climate change, competition for scarcer resources to supply a growing population, and newly constructed barriers to collaborative action.

The need for intelligence sharing, stable alliances, and collaborative cybersecurity efforts will intensify. It will require a shift toward soft-power initiatives that foster diplomacy, cultural and economic ties, and alliances of mutual interest to complement the hard levers of power associated with military and economic strength. This dualistic approach was recognized by General James N. Mattis when he informed Congress that if they cut back on soft-dollar support for the State Department, they had better increase his budget for ammo. Predictability, or at least the avoidance of surprises, is critical in dealing with complex interrelationships between nations; managing them strategically and not transactionally—as though the interconnections did not exist—is an art we have recently forgotten. Reestablishing our relationships in the 2020s will be a challenge.

In this tinderbox, we can expect a proliferation of flash points with a capacity to ignite a major conflagration. Rather than speculate on specific events, we will focus here on three of the likeliest platforms for conflicts: the Eurasian connection; asymmetric and existential threats; and accidental wars.

The Eurasian Connection:

China's emergence as a superpower and the reemergence of Russia are rapidly changing the geopolitical equation and power structures. A new Eurasian connection between them could become a powerful counterbalance to the United States and its traditional allies. Though China has adroitly maintained a lower global profile— preferring quieter economic overtures to muscular approaches—its growing stature as a superpower will make such "neutrality" more difficult and magnify the intensity of potential conflicts.

A Eurasian connection would include a powerful bloc of nations within a giant arc extending from Asia to Eastern Europe, with large parts of the Middle East in between. It is more than just an idea. In addition to the bond now growing between Russia and China, the two nations, as cofounders in 2001 of the SCO, have a platform that will rival NATO. The SCO has gained traction over the years, and with the recent addition of Pakistan and India as full members, and Iran waiting to upgrade its status to a full membership, its eight full members now account for half of the world's population, a quarter of its GDP, and about 80 percent of the Eurasian landmass.

Turkey, in particular, is a country of great strategic importance, given its gateway location, between Europe and Asia. If it were to leave the EU for a full SCO membership, the strategic ripples would be severe. While SCO members are not always in lockstep—and some are even adversaries, like India and Pakistan—it still represents a potent force.

In this Eurasian milieu, Russia has a huge market for its natural resources and high-tech weapons, such as its S-300 and S-400 surface-to-air missile systems, which have already been deployed in Iran, China, Syria, and Turkey (to the chagrin of the United States). With their veto powers in the UN Security Council, both Russia and China can block sanctions and actions against nations they support. If Russia opts for a more aggressive stance in Eastern Europe, or if China ramps up its presence in the China Seas, Vietnam, or elsewhere, each country will have the other's back, an alliance that will greatly complicate counteractions by the United States and whatever allies we have left.

Economically, both China and Russia will continue moving toward transacting trade in non-dollar currencies, such as the ruble or yuan, thus weakening the dollar's cherished position as the world's dominant reserve currency—a huge potential threat to the United States. Geopolitically, the United States is no longer the only game in town, and delusions about going it alone with unilateral actions, power plays, or sanctions not vetted with allies would be inadvisable. The global dynamics of yesteryear have changed, and so must we.

Asymmetric and Existential Threats

Asymmetric warfare is rapidly becoming the weapon of choice for nation-states or splinter groups. Recent Russian intrusions into elections in the United States and the weaponization of social media are portents of things to come. Cyberattacks on critical institutions and infrastructures will degrade the credibility of and public confidence in these cornerstones of our nation, and as our digital dependencies expand, the destructive potential of cyber-risks will increase exponentially.

Cyberwarfare has escalated far beyond the realm of nuisance hackers with mischievous intentions or digital burglars engaged in identity theft. It can now hold entire information systems hostage for a sizeable ransom, disrupt data and supply chains, pursue cyberespionage, and imperil electrical grid systems, air traffic control, critical infrastructure, and sensitive financial information sectors, to name a few. With the rapid explosion of internet-connected home devices, such as Amazon's Alexa, as well as digital operating systems in cars, planes, and even agricultural equipment, opportunities for cyberattacks have increased dramatically. Network-connected devices, which today may include your refrigerator or laundry machines as well as your computer and cell phone, are particularly vulnerable. As attacks shift from data theft to data manipulation, the threats become infinitely more insidious and toxic.

Over time, digital forensics will improve, but it will remain challenging to identify the perpetrators of cyberattacks in a timely manner. Even if attackers are identified, there are no clear-cut policies in place to determine appropriate responses. The threats will intensify, and nation-states will deploy increasing levels of resources toward cybersecurity and offensive capabilities. As the capacity for damage increases, cyberattacks could pose an existential threat to a nation under attack, and the risk of an "accidental" war will increase dramatically.

Space, the newest battlefield, poses a whole new set of challenges to national security. The armed forces of the United States are heavily reliant on satellite systems to exploit their high-tech military superiority in communications, reconnaissance, and precision-guided weaponry. The loss of satellites to enemy-directed attacks could sharply mitigate our military edge on land, sea, and air. Space warfare will escalate the threat levels and further destabilize the growing cold-war playing field.

The proliferation and expansion of nuclear weapons is a truly existential threat, and the nuclear club continues to grow. North Korea is unlikely to ever divest of its weapons, and Israel has a formidable nuclear arsenal and second-strike capability that will assure the complete destruction of any enemy. Pakistan and India have nuclear arsenals aimed at each other, and Russia, China, and the United States seem determined to beef up their arsenals as well in the coming years. An Iranian move toward nuclear capability will invite Saudi Arabia and other countries to follow suit.

Nuclear capability also gives asymmetric warfare exponential power. A dirty bomb developed by a well-financed terrorist group could deal deadly, long-term damage to a major port or city. Likewise, an EMP weapon would greatly leverage the destructive punch of nations with a limited nuclear arsenal. While a conventional atomic bomb could destroy a major city, an EMP-configured bomb of comparable size could instantaneously wipe out electrical infrastructure across a vast area. For a digitally connected nation such as the United States, an EMP attack would be catastrophic.

This is not *Star Wars* stuff. We have known about the EMP phenomenon since the early days of atomic weaponry, though we did not appreciate its significance until later years. While unconfirmed, it is likely that larger nuclear powers have some form of EMP weaponry, and North Korea may well be one of them.

Accidental Wars

In this complex age of connectivity, doomsday weaponry, and fierce competition for finite resources and markets, the potential for conflict is almost limitless. Regional clashes over fresh water, for instance, will become an international trip wire. As flash points erupt and response times are cut to the bone, opportunities for miscalculations and unintended consequences will intensify.

In the Cold War, the ground rules were understood, and high-tech weapons were available to only a few nations. The doctrine of mutually assured destruction[1] ensured that those weapons would never be used, and the two superpowers had hotline protocols and other mechanisms in place to defuse potential conflicts and reduce the chances for accidental wars. In this new cold war, with infinitely more moving parts and a proliferation of deadlier weapons, the chances of setting off an accidental war have escalated. With a rise in the speed and intensification of flash points and few effective mechanisms to defuse them, the trajectories are ominous. Looking ahead, any one of the following could be deadly:

- Maritime conflicts over EEZ territorial waters in the China Seas, Arctic, and elsewhere

- Escalating tensions in Eastern Europe as a renewed Russia seeks past glories

- Confrontations with North Korea, Iran, and future acquirers of nuclear weapons

- Regional conflicts over access to fresh water and other resources required to sustain life

- Asymmetric attacks conducted on a coordinated, global scale

- Discontinuance of petrodollar system and/or a new currency war

- Rise of nationalism and authoritarian regimes; growing levels of civil unrest

- Black Swan events—though rare—like a long duration pandemic could totally disrupt global order.

In closing, the economic and geopolitical storm clouds are gathering as we enter the new decade. The global debt bubble is an economic time bomb, with the United States drowning in red ink from sea to shining sea. When the bubble bursts, other global challenges, including climate change, trade wars, cyberwarfare, and asymmetric threats, will complicate dynamics. The world, stunned by the global retrenchment of the United States and China's new outreach, is struggling to adjust, and the tensions of the new cold war will intensify as a destabilized world seeks a new equilibrium.

Climate Change and the Sustainability of Life as We Know It

With the exception of an all-out nuclear war, climate change and sustainability challenges may pose the greatest threat to us. We have failed to capture the sense of urgency this onslaught truly deserves. Like a chronic disease ignored in its early stages, it may reach a tipping point beyond which it is irreversible, and our failure to respond aggressively while there was time will haunt us when conditions worsen.

Climate Change

In early October 2018, we were warned in the IPCC's Special Report on *Global Warming of 1.5 C* that we had about a dozen years to reverse a carbon emissions trajectory that, left unchecked, would lead to an irreversible global warming meltdown. Written to scientifically quantify the specifics of achieving the Paris Agreement's goals of limiting global warming to a 1.5°C increase by 2100, it painted a stark picture of what that new reality would look like and how much worse it would be if the increase reached 2°C (3.6°F) or more.

We are already experiencing the effects of the 1°C increase that has occurred since the industrial revolution, and we have only 0.5°C remaining of the target threshold. Every fraction of a degree more will have a noticeable impact and little margin for error. A half-degree increase in our household thermostat setting may seem minuscule, but heating the whole planet by that amount will dramatically impact planetary life. The IPCC report revealed we would have to slash GHG emissions by 45 percent in twelve years to get back on target for the 1.5°C goal. By contrast, the emission-reduction commitments made at Paris would put us on trajectory for a 3°C increase (5.4°F). It will take draconian measures to get back on track.

Efforts to date have been woefully inadequate, and we are losing ground. Using the baseline established by the IPCC and monitoring key checkpoints and trajectories along the line, the picture is frightening. After slow growth in the early stages, the trajectories progressively worsened from 1950 to 2000 and thereafter resembled a runaway freight train. The last five years, in particular, clearly reveal the daunting task ahead, especially along the following trajectories:

GHG Buildups: Atmospheric GHG levels may provide the best measure of our relative positioning on climate change. Expressed in terms of CO2 ppm, they equate almost directly to global temperature levels: the higher the ppm, the warmer the temperatures. To put it all in context, ppm levels fluctuated in the 200–300 ppm range for hundreds of thousands of years prior to the industrial revolution, but the threshold of 300 ppm was not breached until 1909. By early 2019, it had risen to 411 ppm, an astonishing increase of 37 percent, and it is now climbing at a more rapid rate. About a third of that increase occurred in this century alone. This is warp speed in geological terms and an almost irreversible shock to our environmental and ecological systems.

Global Temperatures: It's no surprise that global land temperatures also increased: eighteen of the first nineteen years in the twenty-first century were the warmest years in recorded history. Further, Arctic temperatures are increasing over twice as fast as the rest of the planet, changing weather patterns in the process. Shifts in the polar vortex and the violent storms it helps to produce are part of our new norm.

Oceanic Changes: Over 70 percent of Earth's surface is covered by oceans, which have absorbed about 90 percent of the heat added by climate change. This, in turn, has expanded the volume of water, jeopardized sea life, destroyed coral reef systems through acidification, and fast-tracked polar ice melts. Studies show that the temperature of the top 2,300 feet of ocean has increased more than 0.3°F since 1969, and scientists are concerned that it could eventually disrupt thermohaline circulation patterns, the oceanic conveyor belt that helps regulate climate. Reversing these disruptions could be the equivalent of trying to stop a tsunami with sandbags.

Ice Melts: The increased rate of sea-ice melts, Greenland glacial collapses, and thawing of Siberian and Canadian permafrost—a toxic time bomb that releases huge volumes of heat-retaining methane gases—is staggering. Arctic Sea ice cover has shrunk dramatically in recent years and in 2018 was about 8.5 percent lower than the average between 1981 and 2010. Arctic temperatures are rising at about twice the rate of other parts of the planet, and rapid sea-ice loss is intensifying the albedo effect (see chapter 2) and other feedback loops that will further accelerate the warming.

Rising Sea Levels: Melting ice sheets and the thermal expansion of warming waters are elevating sea levels. NASA's global mean sea level indicator reveals that in this new millennium, the rate of sea level change has increased at almost three times the rate observed in the previous century. The trend is ominous, considering that about two-thirds of the world's largest cities are located in low-lying coastal areas. Miami, New Orleans, and other cities will be increasingly vulnerable to coastal flooding and storm surges. Ticking time bombs in the form of abrupt ice-sheet melts in Greenland and West Antarctica could have catastrophic impacts across large sectors of the globe.

Collateral Damage: Collateral damage from climate change takes many forms. The severe weather patterns and "once in a lifetime" storms that now regularly occur will intensify, bringing increased damage and loss of lives. Floods, droughts, wildfires, and desertification—the loss of arable land—are growing in frequency and intensity, destroying or disrupting delicate ecological systems in the process.

Geopolitically, climate change is a threat multiplier that will spark regional conflicts over fresh-water and food supplies. The geopolitical backlash will be profound as nations compete for a dwindling piece of the global resource pie. The global population is projected to grow by almost 11 percent, from more than 7.7 billion people in 2019 to more than 8.5 billion in 2030. If per-capita consumption ratios stay the same, the stress on our planet and its finite base of natural resources will be severe.

The ecological carnage of our "play now, pay later" ways will also worsen. The loss of rainforests and coral reefs and the pollution of land, water, and air have reached dangerous levels. The plastic waste dumped in our oceans is of particular concern. Plants and animals are going extinct at increasing rates. The loss of any one part of our planet's ecosystem weakens and degrades the entire system and puts everyone and everything at greater risk.

Fresh-water shortages will continue to be our most immediate ecological threat, and the collateral effects on our food chains, health, and well-being are well documented. Water shortages pose an exponentially growing risk as an increasing population with greater consumptive patterns has used water at twice the rate of population growth over the past century. New technologies are often water-intensive; fracking a well, for instance, requires up to five million gallons of water or more for production purposes. Growth in demand for water has long exceeded the available supply, and we are rapidly depleting our aquifers: the resulting picture is not good. According to some projections, two-thirds of the world's population could be living under water-stress conditions by 2025, and water pollution will contribute heavily to the threat.

Water is only one of many examples of ecological destruction. As we approach irreversible tipping points in land, water, food, air, and other resources, the global shockwaves will intensify. Regional wars over the control of scarce resources will increase in size and frequency. And, as conditions worsen, the risk of epidemics or pandemics will grow as a highly mobile population encounters new disease strains not treatable with current antibiotics.

Our planet's capacity to sustain life as we know it today is at risk, and the future costs of climate change and ecological degradation—direct and indirect—will be staggering. The capital and resources needed to adapt, unfortunately, will be far costlier than the mitigation initiatives that should have been implemented earlier. Barring an abrupt change in direction, our lackadaisical responses will produce significant threats in the coming decade. Welcome to the future!

Energy and Technology in a Race against Time

Seismic shifts in the energy and technology sectors will open new opportunities but also unlock unknown consequences. The speed at which we can transition our energy systems to a cleaner renewable energy mix will be heavily influenced by economic and geopolitical drivers, as well as the immutable laws of geology. Meanwhile, the fourth industrial revolution is stretching human capacity to adapt to new technologies rather than being overwhelmed by them. The race against time is on.

Energy Renaissance

Until recently, the global economy was driven largely by a mix of fossil-fuel-powered energy systems. Our economies and infrastructures were built around these legacy energy systems, and it was taken for granted that they would always be there. Only recently have we recognized that the affordability and accessibility of energy were no longer givens.

With new technologies, competitive renewable energy prices, and global markets seeking cleaner energy systems, the changing conditions have all coalesced to inspire the new energy renaissance. With cleaner power systems, smart-grid infrastructures, greater storage capacities, a growing mix of hybrid and electric cars, and demand-reduction activities that are lowering energy intensity levels (the amount of energy needed to produce a unit of GDP), the new renaissance is underway.

The renaissance was given additional traction by the several nations' commitment, after the Paris Agreement, to ban the production of gasoline- and diesel-powered vehicles by 2040. The message is clear: migrate to cleaner energy or suffer the consequences. Moving away from fossil fuels will require massive changes to power infrastructure, grids, transportation systems, and other components of our new power systems.

There will be winners and losers in this renaissance, and resistance from vested interests will be intense. The costs of transition will be high, and the risk of energy and economic disruptions significant. And, like changing a tire on a moving car, it will all have to be done under a growing demand for energy and an imperative to decarbonize our energy systems.

Future energy and climate threats mean different things to different stakeholders. Energy wonks know that the finite supply of fossil fuels—particularly oil—cannot meet the growing demand indefinitely. Climate scientists know that we cannot effectively address climate change without curtailing our carbon emissions. Economists understand that higher oil prices stifle a struggling global economy, and financial experts understand the staggering capital needed to build new legacy energy systems. Consumers remember 2008's gasoline prices and their impact on household budgets, and the military has felt the pain of protecting oil supply lines in the Middle East.

The global transition to a decarbonized economy running increasingly on renewably sourced electricity will be volatile. Energy disruptions, economic downturns, and geopolitical upheavals will be triggered by changing energy patterns. OPEC and other oil-exporting nations will feel threatened, and even the petrodollar system could be at risk. We can also expect energy systems to be prime targets for terrorist and cyber-attacks . And, lest we forget, the demand for oil will be heavy for a long time while peak production is still a threat. The easily accessible oil is gone, and new oil will be harder and costlier to find and extract. The surge in shale oil will buy some time, but its sky-high depletion rates give it limited shelf life.

The coming global energy transition will be promising, challenging, and destabilizing. Some of its key elements are as follows:

- The Crunch: Demand for energy will increase as climate change worsens and efforts to decarbonize take hold. Supply and demand will be problematic.

- Renewable Energy: As the major source of new energy and the baseload fuel for electrical production, expect sharp growth as pricing drops and infrastructures expand.

- Electrification: The trend toward clean-electricity energy systems will intensify, with accompanying shifts in power infrastructure and transportation systems.

- Energy Intensity: Expect improvements as renewables, demand reduction, conservation, and energy efficiencies improve and the level of energy needed to produce a unit of GDP drops.

- Oil: Still a crucial part of the energy mix—particularly in transportation—oil will see supply and demand disconnects in the early 2020s, but the pace of demand will slow. Shale oil, with its rapid depletion rates, will provide a cushion before peaking in the late 2020s.

- Natural Gas: Expect steady growth, with heavy liquid natural gas exports to continue. It will be a significant bridging fuel to our cleaner-energy future.

- Nuclear: While its energy share will drop in many countries, it will be a significant source of electrical power in China, India, and other countries in the 2020s.

- Coal: The pace of its demise will accelerate, but it will not be completely replaced as a legacy fuel.

Access to clean and affordable energy will be a driving force in the coming decade. The technologies and momentum of the new energy renaissance will provide great opportunities, but the task of transitioning from old to new legacy energy systems—without major disruptions—is formidable. We don't have much time to get it right.

The Fourth Industrial Revolution

Another great transition will pit our ability to absorb and assimilate new technologies faster than ever before. Technology can be a blessing and a curse. The latter is usually apparent after the new technology is rolled out and the euphoria that accompanied it has passed. As we have seen again and again in this book, once launched, tech advances can no more be reversed than toothpaste can be returned to its tube.

We have been programmed to believe that new technologies are always good, mostly benign, and panaceas for whatever ails us. While few would dispute that technology has been a boon to humankind, the potential side effects were often overlooked. Given the enormity of the fourth industrial revolution and blurring of lines between the physical, digital, and biological spheres, the outcomes are far from clear. Regardless, the technological leapfrogging to come will surpass our capacity for a rational integration into our normal routines by a wide margin. Klaus Schwab, founder of the prestigious Davos World Economic Forum, has suggested that humankind's single most important challenge today is to understand and shape this new revolution. It will bring positive outcomes, but we can also expect to see disruptive side effects.

The changes will be abrupt, pervasive, and in excess of the speed at which our production, management, and governance systems can assimilate them. It will create—at least initially—inequalities, worker displacement, unemployment, and glaring gaps in the skill sets needed in the workplace versus those that will be available. To stay abreast, educational and training systems will evolve into a lifelong learning process. The advent of faster, fifth-generation (5G) wireless technologies will change the job market further; one commonly quoted estimate suggests that 65 percent of children entering primary school today will end up working in jobs not in existence today. For better or worse, our educational systems are unlikely to respond to these rapid-fire changes in a timely manner without significant change.

We already see the changes in business and commerce. Amazon has transformed the market with a digital shopping model that has become our new norm. The modes of marketing, manufacturing, distributing, and buying products and services changed overnight, and big-box chains with household names collapse monthly, if not faster. The common denominator is using technology in a breakthrough manner, and business models must change fast to survive. Finding the capital and skilled workers to make it happen poses a new set of challenges.

Technologies of the fourth industrial revolution will render jobs obsolete faster than they create new jobs, and the trajectories will steepen as these technologies get better, faster, and smarter. Jobs that involve predictable, repetitious, transactional, and even knowledge-based functions will be vulnerable. Driverless vehicles and drones will replace drivers and operators, and white-collar claims adjusters, bank tellers, medical professionals, accountants, and Wall Street analysts will be replaceable by quantum computing, artificial intelligence, and self-learning systems with access to gigantic databases, growing ever more efficient, accurate, and versatile. Advanced robotics will increasingly replace drillers, miners, and construction workers.

The economic disruptions will be severe in the early stages, and it could take years to reach a new equilibrium. One study suggested that smart automation will displace as many as seventy-three *million* American workers by 2030. This is not a knock-on technology but rather a warning that its integration will not be a walk in the park.

China, with its 2025 plan[2] to be the world's greatest technology player, will compete with other eager nations for technological superiority, and quantum leaps will be made without thought for the consequences. The Internet of Things will connect platforms and systems, with embedded smart sensors in our appliances and the applications using them. As noted above, the digitally connected infrastructure of the United States and other developed nations will become highly vulnerable to cyberattacks, and the data and complex infrastructures that turn the wheels of our society will be at greater risk.

Without doubt, the technological cornucopia of the fourth industrial revolution will increase productivity and efficiency and make our lives easier in many respects, but it will come at a heavy and disruptive cost in terms of jobs and lifestyles in a society ill prepared to deal with it. The challenges of governing and regulating the darker sides, and educating people about and protecting society from them, will be formidable.

An American Implosion That Could Rock the World

It is almost impossible for Americans to imagine a United States that isn't the world's premier superpower and home of the perpetual American Dream. Citizens of the great empires of the past probably felt the same way. Great empires, after all, do not collapse overnight; the decline is usually a long process fueled by hubris, complacency, and unwise policies and practices that are unsustainable in the face of powerful new challengers.

While not in immediate danger of collapse, the United States fits this description well. Deep in the red and borrowing heavily to sustain our growth, we are racking up debt that can never be paid off. Like a giant Ponzi scheme, it will reach a point at which it can no longer be sustained and eventually implode under its own weight. The debt—both public and private—is pervasive across all levels of government, the private sector, and households throughout the country. We are swimming in red ink from sea to shining sea, and the headwinds are getting stronger.

While our accrued debt to date has been manageable—though not desirable—the situation is rapidly deteriorating. A confluence of four major forces is making it more problematic: aggregated debt levels now exceed our GDP, the interest paid to service that debt consumes an ever-larger part of our budget, rising interest rates and global pressures are picking up, and our underfunded entitlement promises of yesteryear, coupled with unfavorable demographics, are now coming due without the reserves to pay for them. As interest rates on government securities climb, so too will rates on cars, mortgages, and other consumer goods. In an economy that is 70 percent consumer driven, this is not a prescription for good health. A deeper look at these factors is revealing.

Debts and Deficits

Despite a booming economy sparked by recent tax reductions, the deficit in fiscal year 2019 will be close to a trillion dollars, with future deficits projected to be somewhat in that range. About 65 percent of our total budget is committed to mandatory entitlement programs, and only 35 percent to our total discretionary budget—which includes national defense—so there is little margin for significant budget cuts without entitlement reform. The latter is a hot potato that our politicians won't touch—at least for now.

The 35 percent of the budget that is somewhat eligible for a budget cut is further reduced when military cuts are taken off the table. Even if we chopped all other discretionary spending to the bone, it would not make that much of a difference in the total budget. Accordingly, the annual deficits will continue to climb until they can climb no more.

Amid these glaring realities, the tax reductions of 2018 were about the last thing we needed. It was an egregious additional mortgage taken on the American Dream to make things better today while sticking future generations with the debt. There was simply no need for it, other than playing well with many voters. As we look at the deficits and then consider the growth in subprime auto and student-loan debt, as well as a return to many of the egregious practices preceding the 2008 recession, the outlook for the coming decade is not rosy.

State and local governments are also strapped with underfunded retiree health and pension benefits, and our infrastructure is falling apart. Corporate America has gorged itself in debt sparked by the low-interest-rate environment, and households and consumers are now at debt levels that preceded the great crash. With this kind of mounting debt, there is little margin for error.

Debt-Servicing Charges

There is a charge for the debt we are carrying, and it will continue to grow as we pay a higher interest rate on a larger block of debt in the future. Though interest rates—and thus debt-servicing charges—in this present decade have been low due to the Fed's aggressive monetary policies, the debt-servicing charges are expected to accelerate dramatically. As one measure of the growing charges, the Congressional Budget Office has estimated that the interest paid on our debt will exceed the following budgetary categories within the following time frames:

- By 2020, the interest paid will about equal the Medicaid payments made.

- By 2023, the interest paid will exceed the total defense budget.

- By 2025, the interest paid will exceed the total non-defense discretionary budget.

- By 2028, the interest paid will exceed one trillion dollars.

Rising Interest Rates and Global Markets

Debt will continue to be our vehicle of choice for financing our deficits, but as our balance sheets deteriorate, the cost of capital—reflected in the interest rates needed to attract foreign and domestic investors—will climb. Even a slight uptick in interest rates of only a few basis points will make a huge difference, and an explosion of several hundred points—as occurred in the late 1970s—could send our debt-servicing charges into an unsustainable orbit.

The pressures on the Federal Reserve to keep interest rates artificially low at all costs will not work forever. When the balancing act fails, the impact on our financial structures will be chilling.

Entitlement Benefits

With ten thousand baby boomers now retiring daily and living longer, the potential payouts for Social Security, Medicare, and other mandated benefits are staggering. Worse, the surpluses intended to fund these benefits that were initially placed in trust funds were long ago transferred to the general operating budget and spent, replaced with government IOUs.

We are now nearing an inflection point on Social Security and the Social Security Disability insurance plan where the inflow from the Federal Insurance Contributions Act (FICA) taxes is no longer sufficient to cover the benefits paid out, a condition that will also affect Medicare in the not-too-distant future. When the government dips into the trust funds for payments, it will pull out a handful of IOUs from yesteryear. FICA contributions can be increased to some extent, but with fewer active workers paying for more retirees, the potential is limited. With an imputed entitlement liability that is three to five times greater than our GDP, the economic impact will be monumental.

As conditions deteriorate, the government will increasingly seek other means to fund its obligations, such as raising general taxes to supplement FICA increases, cutting benefits, borrowing more, and/or printing more money. It will likely come in some combination of reductions, freezes, and deferring eligibility for Medicare and Social Security benefits. The quest for revenue will intensify, and the cost of capital will climb precipitously. At this point, we are in real trouble; the great Ponzi scheme is nearing collapse.

With a debt that now exceeds our GDP by well over 100 percent, we are heading toward an irreversible tipping point. This is not a surprise; our political leaders have known about this festering Armageddon for years, and they have also known that it won't get resolved with cosmetic fixes and tax cuts projected to stimulate revenues. It is difficult to see how we will get through even the first half of the coming decade without a major economic upheaval.

If we fail to act, and if the world's largest economy goes into default, the global shockwaves will ignite the mother of all global depressions—and perhaps even the perfect storm.

Resiliency and Our Capacity to Persevere

The storm is gathering, but we still don't seem to grasp its implications. As it breaks, the disconnects between our expectations and behaviors will widen as we pass into a new reality. Our vulnerability will increase, and our resiliency will be tested to the bone. Our challenge will be compounded by an intergenerational changing of the guard, new demographic minefields, and the toxic baggage of previous generations.

In this shift of power, the class of '61 and large numbers of baby boomers will be long gone from the workforce and drawing on entitlement benefits. Millennials will comprise the largest segment of the workforce in the 2020s and will, by sheer weight of numbers, reshape our economy. The aging Gen Xers, though smaller in numbers, will hold key leadership positions, and Gen Zers—born in the new millennium—will be the fastest-growing cohort in the workforce.

So, what does it all mean? First, surveys have shown that about half of Millennials no longer believe in the American Dream. More distrusting of the government and key institutions than those preceding them, they have been clobbered by student-loan debt, a lack of meaningful career opportunities, and the market meltdown of 2008 that so dampened their optimism for the future. The Gen Xers are similar in many respects: both generations married later, had smaller families, and lived longer at home with their parents than those before. The Gen Zers, born and raised in a hyperconnected digital dreamland, show signs of being more pragmatic and, perhaps, more politically engaged at an earlier age than previous generations. Political parties will ignore these tectonic shifts at their own risk.

Generations X, Y, and Z will pay a stiff price for the indiscretions of their predecessors. They will directly experience the escalation of climate change, ecological destruction, and resource shortages of all kinds. They will drown in red ink from our crushing national debt and unfunded entitlement obligations. Saddled with this baggage, as well as rising healthcare costs, they will be on the front lines of the fourth industrial revolution.

Though more digitally connected than previous generations, the new breed of tech-savvy workers will find the 2020s highly disruptive, and workers not trained to compete in the new technological wonderland will fare even worse. Like a tsunami, it will render business models obsolete almost overnight and trigger job eliminations at rates far exceeding replenishment until a new equilibrium sets in.

Many middle-class jobs will vanish as driverless cars and trucks replace drivers and digital distribution systems replace traditional retail operations. It will hasten contraction of postal, transactional, and data-collection jobs as well as professional jobs in the healthcare, accounting, newscasting, publishing, and print media sectors, to name a few. Even the digitally gifted will scramble to stay ahead of the curve, while many more will be caught unaware, unprepared, and soon unemployed. Only Gen Z will have a leg up. Raised in an era of smartphones, drones, and instant communications, the fourth industrial revolution will be an extension of what they were born into. With DNA suited to this world, they may have the resiliency to quickly acclimate; others, not so much.

As smart connectivity improves almost exponentially, it is a given that cybersecurity will lag a few steps behind the most determined hackers and digital criminals. Privacy will be an ongoing issue, and social media will remain a mecca for personal-data miners, who will not have our best interests at heart.

The trajectories outlined in this chapter are a sobering extrapolation of current trends, and we are already well into many of them. Potential flash points are everywhere, and it is not hard to see how these powerful forces could collide in the coming decade. It might be more surprising if they don't.

To complete the picture, we will look at how the perfect storm could play out in the next chapter. We will then look at preemptive strategies to mitigate the damage in chapter 17 and launch an exciting new initiative to reenergize the American Dream.

Mike Conley

Try as I may, it is difficult to be overly optimistic about the future. There are simply too many adverse forces on a collision course that we aren't addressing. Our inability to respond forcefully to climate change, a world drowning in debt, and other ticking time bombs during the thin window of opportunity to do something about it is alarming.

Does this mean we should throw in our cards and call it a day? Quite the contrary: it means we should double down and do everything in our power to address the looming threats while there is still a scintilla of hope. Technology is not a panacea, and denial is not a strategy; the window of opportunity is rapidly closing.

Some might think I'm a doomsayer, but I see it differently. I truly believe in our resilience and grit, but they are hard to activate when we fail to even recognize the looming problem. It is for this very reason that I started my company and website, Weathering the Storm, and I will continue to speak out on these issues as long as the Good Lord will let me. I am gratified to see that the younger generations are getting it and making themselves heard, and I truly hope that older generations will join in on the effort.

Summary of the 2020s: Predictions

Extrapolating from the trajectories of previous decades, inputting the latest data, and plotting out trendlines and likely scenarios for the future, we can see the five greatest threats that will lead to the perfect storm, barring draconian actions to address them.

1. **Global destabilization will worsen and trigger a number of ticking time bombs.**

   - The global debt bubble is unsustainable, making us more susceptible to major meltdowns.

   - The United States' shift from a global stabilizer to a destabilizer has weakened a fragile global order.

   - The new cold war will get uglier; beware of a powerful new Eurasian counterforce.

   - Nuclear proliferation could lead to Armageddon, rendering all other threats moot.

2. **Climate change, resource depletion, and ecological destruction pose an existential threat.**

   - The rates of change are exceeding projections in vital areas: we are running out of time.

   - Climate change will progressively worsen, with costly impacts.

   - Climate change, as a threat multiplier, will exacerbate a wide range of global risks.

   - Epidemics and pandemics could accelerate as air, water, and land polution conditions worsen.

   - Earth will draw closer to its maximum carrying capacity.

3. **Energy and technology will likely be an Achilles' heel for an ill-prepared society.**

   - The energy renaissance is hopeful, but fraught with transitional challenges.

   - Weaning ourselves off of fossil fuels will be costly, disruptive, and menacing to stakeholders.

   - The technologies of the fourth industrial revolution will greatly exceed our rate of adaptation to them.

4. **An American financial implosion will rock the world, and a soft landing may not be possible.**

   - Our gross national debt cannot be indefinitely sustained at current rates of growth.

   - Unfunded entitlements, rising interest rates, and more red ink will lead to a tipping point.

   - Borrowing our way into prosperity will no longer be an option; a crash will be inevitable.

   - The economic tsunami of the crash will spark a global meltdown.

5. **Our ability to weather the storm is tenuous, and the longer we wait, the harder survival becomes.**

   - We are operating in uncharted waters, racing toward a future we don't understand.

   - We may not awaken to the threat in a timely manner or act while there is still time.

   - Our continuous mortgage on the American Dream will only aggravate the problem.

   - The window of opportunity is closing; will we have the resiliency and courage to act?

-16-

The Perfect Storm

It wasn't raining when Noah built the ark.

—Howard Ruff

Imagine, if you will:

Imagine that you have pushed your clocks ahead to the year 2030, and the decade-by-decade chronology you are about to read is an account of what transpired in the 2020s, when the perfect storm exploded with a fury that rocked the world.

Remember that the perfect storm could erupt in a variety of ways, and I am sharing just one possibility with you. My futuristic account is designed to describe the turmoil leading to the storm, the triggering mechanisms that ignited it, and the catastrophic chain of events that followed.

This fictional chronicle may seem far-fetched, but it is based on our current paradigms. Remember also that when all major systems and institutions break down, anything can happen. This projection extrapolates from current trajectories and assumes that we took almost no action, while there was still time, to change the outcomes.

1. A Chronicle of the Perfect Storm

The year is 2030, and the world is in shambles. No one can say with any certainty how it will all turn out. We don't even know if we're at the end of the beginning or beginning of the end. The institutions we once valued are in tatters, our economy is bankrupt, and the sense of security we once had is gone.

2020s: Early Stages

In retrospect, the early warning signs were there, but we didn't see them. Our overstimulated global economy underperformed relative to the liquidity we injected into it. The escalating trade war, tariffs, and global unrest were taking a toll that we didn't seem to appreciate. The North Korea, Iran, and Middle East quagmires seemed to never end, and the world was still struggling to adjust to our new America First policies.

The markets were nervous as global debt continued to climb. The United States led the way with annual deficits of around a trillion dollars that seemed to be the new norm. The Fed and its counterparts around the world lowered interest rates to create liquidity—at all costs, or so it seemed. The purchasing power of the US dollar fluctuated, and stock market performance charts looked like the EKG of a sick patient, with erratic swings into bear territory and back. Despite low unemployment rates, lower taxes, and relatively cheap energy, the financial markets—fearful of the fact that all bubbles eventually burst—were increasingly nervous.

By the early 2020s, the cumulative US debt and debt-servicing charges began to affect our material well-being. We were no longer the financial safe haven we once were, where foreign governments and others could park their surpluses; it was becoming harder for the Treasury Department to auction off securities. As interest rates on government securities began to climb in order to attract and retain foreign and domestic investments in the United States, China was not only selling off its holdings in our country but also attracting more of the global dollars once invested in our government securities.

As our debt mounted and interest rates climbed, we saw a marked drop in the purchasing power of our dollar. Between that and the increased impact of the higher tariffs we were paying on imports, households were feeling the pinch. It cost more just to live, and that meant cutting back on our vacation travel, trips to restaurants, and all other discretionary spending.

The rising interest rate on long-term loans began to affect the housing industry and the durable-goods purchases that went with it. We had lived in a low-interest environment for so long that we had forgotten what it cost to pay the rates of 7–10 percent that were around the corner. Businesses were not making the capital purchases they needed, and Millennials, still strapped for cash, could not afford houses at the higher rates. Car dealers were feeling the pinch as auto loans suddenly got far more expensive. They also noticed that default rates on the subprime loans they had made were rapidly climbing. Automakers had no choice but to reduce new-car production.

While we didn't recognize it at the time, the economy was slipping into the throes of a recession that would quickly worsen. As some of the subprime bubbles began to burst and small or undercapitalized businesses struggled, the financial realities could not be denied.

On Wall Street, the markets were dipping into bear territory as economic growth stagnated. Further, the love affair with artificial intelligence and the new productivity gains it was to provide in many sectors began to tarnish as large workforce reductions followed. Rising unemployment rates all but wiped out the productivity gains. What it did create, however, was a sharp decline in the consumer confidence indexes and a weary global economy that was ready to pull in its horns and hunker down.

America's former allies, still smarting from our disengagement from existing treaties and alliances in the 2010s, were unsympathetic to our plight so long as their direct interests were not at stake. Besides, they were having major problems of their own. Over the latter part of the past decade, they had gradually recalibrated their strategies to work around the United States, relying less on their former partner.

In doing so, they opened up new trading opportunities with China and Russia. Still, the deterioration of our enormous economy created fallout in their economies. Strapped for cash and watching the value of their investments in our government securities decline— along with the purchasing power of our devalued dollar—they reduced their holdings in US government securities. If our government needed more money, it would have to pay a far higher rate for it or roll out the presses and print more money.

On the geopolitical front, the Eurasian connection continued to grow. Anchored by China and Russia, the loose-knit alliance was bolstered by growing ties with India, Pakistan, Turkey, and Iran. With China's international capital commitments through its OBOR policy holding their own, and the high-tech military equipment Russia exported to its Eurasian partners, the powerful position once held by the United States and its fragmenting European coalition no longer looked as formidable. The prolific growth of cyberwarfare, space strategy, and other asymmetric threats had further weakened America's relative position; there were simply too many hot spots and flash points for the United States—with its overstretched military and debt-ridden balance sheets—to defend, contain, or cover.

On the energy front, we were encouraged by the new energy renaissance and the robust new job opportunities it opened up. Some of us even thought we could use it to lever ourselves out of our pressing economic issues. We tried to capture a share of the global market for renewable energy and collateral development efforts, but the tariff and trade wars we had sparked earlier, and our dissociation from the Paris Agreement, left China with an overwhelming lead that was difficult be overcome. At home, the boost was not sufficient to pick up the drag from so many other slumping sectors. Our nuclear arms race with Russia and China was also adding greatly to our debt. But I digress.

We were excited about booming production of shale oil in the United States but failed to grasp one of its insidious side effects: it cut deeply into OPEC revenues and complicated our relationship with Saudi Arabia. China, in the meantime, bought every barrel of oil the Saudis were willing to sell, and more. In deference to its largest customer, the Saudis allowed China to make oil purchases in yuan, outside the petrodollar system. The Saudis were also warming to China's growing military power and the leverage it seemed to have over its prime adversary, Iran. The alarm bells were ringing, but no one was listening.

The damaging effects of climate change—far exceeding previous estimates—were horrifyingly noticeable. Though the United States reentered the Paris Agreement as a full member in early 2021 and took dramatic steps to increase its efforts to fight climate change after that, we never regained the leadership position we had ceded to China when we pulled out of the accord in 2017. Worse, our absence in those crucial earlier years had slowed progress.

As "once in a century" storms intensified and sea levels rose, disaster-relief costs in the United States alone approached a half-trillion dollars or more annually, and it was only a start. To put that number in perspective, that same amount of money would have financed a full ride at a good college for well over four million kids. But that train left the station when we did not curb greenhouse gas emissions at the thresholds required by the Paris Agreement. Arctic warming and dramatic ice-sheet melts added to rising sea levels, and the methane gas released from the thawing tundra wiped out carbon reduction gains made elsewhere.

In the meantime, with a growing world population ravaged by storms and heat, fresh-water shortages reached a crisis point. Our planet's capacity to sustain a growing population with voracious appetites for anything and everything that was grown, mined, fished, built, or yet to be extracted was now stretched beyond its sustainable limits, despite the best technologies available to us. The growing gaps between the "haves" and "have-nots" fueled civil unrest, and Arab Spring–type uprisings erupted around the world on a regular basis.

Our planet was straining to maintain life as we knew it. Finite resources were becoming scarcer and costlier; food and water supplies were insufficient in all too many developing countries, and our institutions and governmental services were creaking at the seams. The world was ready to implode under its own weight, but that could never happen—or so we thought. Global power structures were also changing, and not in our favor, but no one wanted to believe it. How could it happen? Things like that just don't happen to us—or so we thought.

2020s: Middle Stages

By now, the financial policies of the United States were a global concern. Our deficit spending was out of control, and we were now borrowing over forty cents on every dollar we spent. Most baby boomers were collecting heavily on their Social Security and Medicare benefits, and both programs were now paying out more than they were taking in despite a few cosmetic reforms in benefit design and funding.

With only intergovernmental IOUs to draw on and nothing in the general operating budget to cover it, the government sold off assets, borrowed, and printed new money at a dangerous pace. Hemorrhaging red ink at unsustainable rates, we knew that something had to give, but no one moved on it. Too risky, I guess, for politicians to take bleeding-edge positions.

US government securities had lost their luster. We had already experienced several rating downgrades, and the cost of capital on the money our government borrowed was becoming acutely expensive. Our government's debt-servicing charges alone exceeded the entire military budget and more. The economy seemed to be in a semi-permanent state of stagnation and recession, and our rising entitlement-benefit payouts and exploding debt costs—supercharged by higher interest rates—left almost nothing for all other government programs. The notion of borrowing our way into prosperity was now DOA, but what else could we do? It just wasn't working.

To foreign governments struggling with their own rising debt loads and crumbling balance sheets, the United States had become a major part of their problem and not a solution. Crippled by the costs of the 2008 meltdown and earlier recessions we had barely staved off, there was precious little left in reserves that the world, as a whole, could use to fight off financial calamity. International institutions, such as banking, currency, and past trade alliances, were simply not functioning as they once had. The deterioration of these key institutions tracked closely with our disengagement from the international scene a few years back, when we were busy "making America great again."

Though warned by the IMF, World Trade Organization (WTO), and other countries and organizations to clean up our balance sheets, we did little to get our house in order; it was a political hot potato and not amenable to solutions because of the political gridlock and partisan politics that still ruled the day. In the meantime, the EU was struggling, the Middle East remained a powder keg, and the Pacific Rim nations looked increasingly to China for leadership.

Climate change worsened, and it was apparent to all nations that earlier actions to address it had been too little and too late. Major ice melts in Greenland, the Antarctic, and the Arctic continued, and the Himalayan melts and spotty water runoffs that once supplied large Asian populations with fresh water shrank to crisis proportions. Rising sea levels, costly weather patterns, and major losses in coral reefs and sea life arrived, as projected. The feedback loops were more aggressive than expected, and their toxic effects were nightmarish. A growing number of climate scientists felt we had reached an irreversible tipping point.

In the last quarter of the decade, the balance of power shifted noticeably. China's blue-water navy, capable of projecting power beyond its shorelines, rapidly grew. While still not at parity with the US Navy, China challenged American sea power with new bases in the Indian Ocean, China Seas, Gulf region, and South America. The Seventh Fleet in the China Seas, under the threat of China's growing anti-ship missile capability, was now at greater risk. On other fronts, warnings by a weakened NATO alliance to Eurasian-bloc countries to back off from their aggressive actions fell on deaf ears. The balance of power was rapidly shifting, and the United States no longer had the assets to plug all the holes.

China's courting of the Saudi government was also paying off. The Saudis began to look at China as not only their largest paying customer for oil but also as a military power that could protect their interests and even coerce Iran as the United States could no longer do. They began to openly wonder, who needs the United States? It was only a matter of time before the petrodollar transactional system and, almost by default, the US dollar's cherished position as the world's premier reserve currency began to shift toward something more favorable to China. China's draconian efforts to make its renminbi an acceptable world reserve currency were paying off.

When the Saudis, with full backing from all OPEC and several non-OPEC nations, decided to pull the plug on the petrodollar transactional arrangement, the stage was set for the explosive international economic crisis that would soon erupt. Under this new arrangement, the petrodollar system would be replaced by a weighted basket of currencies with the following weightings: China's renminbi at 35 percent, the US dollar at 25 percent, the euro at 20 percent, and 10 percent each for the yen and ruble. In simple mathematical terms, the central banks of the world no longer needed to hold a massive amount of dollars in reserve currency.

Though it was to be phased in over a period of five years, the new system triggered an immediate seismic shift in the world's reserve currency structure—once so heavily dominated by the US dollar—away from the United States and toward China. The results were immediate and catastrophic for the United States, and they directly contributed to the perfect storm that was about to follow; our worst nightmares were about to come true.

2020s: Late Stages—The Perfect Storm Erupts

It all happened so fast, and it left us stunned and reeling. The economic collapse ignited a chain reaction that unraveled and then overwhelmed the house of cards once called the global economy. It rapidly escalated into a free fall that toppled mighty banks, companies, and entire economies. Like the 2008 recession, triggered by the subprime mortgage fiasco in the United States, this one was also activated by America's woes. But this quickly became the greatest global economic catastrophe ever. The train wreck was in process, and no power on Earth could stop it.

With the new currency arrangements pointing toward a new global currency, central banks began dumping the huge surpluses of dollars once held to cover world trading transactions. The dollar, a fiat currency backed only by the so-called good faith and credit of the US government and not a precious metal, fell victim to the immutable laws of supply and demand. The vast glut of dumped dollars had no buyers, and its value—and thus its purchasing power—plummeted like a rock.

Frantic, the US Treasury Department doubled and then tripled interest rates credited on government securities to at least retain current investors, but to no avail. The rapid loss of foreign and domestic investments leaving the United States had become irreversible. The stock market lost over 61 percent of its value in a span of four trading days, with no limits on its downside, and went on to collapse almost entirely. Nations, institutional investors, pension funds, and others sold off their equity portfolios, but it was too late. Overleveraged hedge funds folded, and the mighty banking institutions deemed "too big to fail" were again failing. The Federal Reserve and its central bank counterparts around the world no longer had the capacity to stop—or even stem—the financial devastation that would soon follow. The deleveraging and readjustment processes erupted with a painful fury. Massive fortunes and national economies collapsed almost overnight.

The mighty tremors of the Wall Street collapse spread quickly to Main Streets all over the world. Like falling dominoes, one sector after another collapsed, leaving economic carnage in their wake. The airline travel and hospitality sectors felt it almost immediately. Corporations in survival mode made an all-out effort to preserve capital and cash flows, and all travel budgets were abruptly slashed to the bone. Business trips were canceled, and the planes and taxis that carried business travelers, as well as the restaurants and hotels that fed and housed them, lost their most crucial revenue streams. The crisis was amplified by the households that canceled family vacations. Destination locations soon emptied out and closed.

Corporate purchasing stopped almost overnight. Companies were left with large inventories collecting dust while debt and fixed costs drained their dwindling cash flows. Payments were deferred, and overdue accounts receivable soared. Large-scale corporate layoffs began in earnest, and the dramatic rise in monthly unemployment rates dwarfed even the worst days of the recession in 2008. Corporate liquidity dried up as banks pulled credit lines and called for payment on outstanding credit lines and other debt. Old-line legacy companies closed their doors for the last time, and with every closure, the long list of suppliers to those companies permanently lost a major revenue stream. This chain of events was playing out all over the world. The global meltdown had become unstoppable.

The spillover to state and local governments and private industry was swift. Federal grant money quickly dried up, and federal reimbursements for Medicaid and other mandated programs stalled. Massive governmental layoffs followed, and public-works programs ground to a halt from lack of funds—often with the bridges, roadways, and other infrastructure under repair left unfinished. Even government pensions and health plans were at risk. Riots, civil disorder, and new breadlines—reminiscent of the Great Depression—appeared everywhere.

The plight of the average working person and household was, perhaps, the most frightening of all. This was ground zero, and far too many people had no safety net or reserves to call on. Living through this nightmare was an absolute hell. It never occurred to us that this could happen. We lost almost everything we had in the bat of any eye, and many of us were too old to learn new survival skills.

Within six months of the market's collapse, the official unemployment rate had jumped to almost 46 percent—several points higher than the 25 percent rate reached during the worst days of the Great Depression, and it was still climbing. There was even talk about trimming back Social Security payouts, and retirees were terrified. With the purchasing power of the dollar almost 75 percent lower since this all started, a loaf of bread cost almost five times as much as it had six months earlier. They called it hyperinflation, but for anyone living on a fixed pension or Social Security, it was simply a devastating blow. Not surprisingly, suicide rates among the elderly skyrocketed, and other age groups throughout the world saw similar increases. We were now living in survival mode, and pity the person who needed expensive medicine or medical care. The ability to manage chronic diseases like hypertension or diabetes was no longer a given. Given the choice of paying for shelter, food, and medicine, the latter often came in a poor third.

Colleges and universities either closed their doors or curtailed their programs as enrollment plummeted and alumni dollars dried up along with state aid. Even schools with large endowments were in danger as the value of their investment portfolios dropped by well over a half; they were now using endowment dollars to support their general operations. Public schools were in dire straits, and in many poorer areas, schools simply closed their doors, putting a lot of angry young people out on the street. Law enforcement had become a nightmare, and unpaid government workers were not in a good mood.

In looking back on these initial stages, I see one big miserable blur. For most Americans, the news stories we heard shortly before the crash, about petrodollars and interest rates, were all a bunch of mumbo-jumbo jargon. The average retiree felt that with their Social Security checks and just a decent return on what little money they saved, they would be okay. Many working Americans clung to a sense of security in their 401(k) nest eggs—unwarranted, as it turned out. When we lost over half the value of our 401(k) plans in a span of a week, real panic set in. Suddenly, that house that we paid too much for—often on an adjustable-rate mortgage that seemed to climb to the stars—dropped in value, and the rising interest rates on our credit-card debt looked insurmountable. For adult children living with their parents, working mediocre jobs that paid too little to pay off their student-loan debts, the future was dismal. For students who had no job or school to go to—after it closed—it seemed hopeless.

Even the universal health plan they had enrolled in, with its heavy government subsidies, was becoming unaffordable. Families and households were all in desperate straits.

Housing foreclosures ran rampant, and would-be buyers were scarce. Rental-property prices soared, and the escalating monthly rents were beyond the range of many. It was not unusual to find two families living under the same roof and others living in their cars.

The massive layoffs following the crash corroborated the fact that many American families were only a paycheck away from the poorhouse. Panic set in, and all spending was curtailed. Limited driving and meatless diets were common moves in the new survival game. As credit cards were tapped out and with no real sources of income coming in, medical and dental care were postponed, and prescriptions not absolutely needed for survival went unfilled. Churches were filling up with frightened people, and morgues were overflowing with suicides and casualties of preventable health problems.

Mortgage and rent payments were chronically late or skipped altogether, and the housing market collapsed under the weight of delinquent payments, foreclosures, and excess housing inventory. Furniture and appliance manufacturers went under, as the new homes they would typically equip were no longer being built. The new-car market died, while family cars were nursed along with tender, loving care and little money. Used-bike sales and car repair were among the few areas of the economy holding their own.

Governmental safety nets were strained and increasingly unable to meet the minimum needs of the people. Desperate people do desperate things, and civil disorder broke out in several major cities. Rioters were burning and looting whatever stores were still open, and an activated National Guard became almost a permanent fixture in many cities as martial law was declared and rigidly enforced.

Then two things that no one could ever have imagined happened.

First, the United States government, for the first time, defaulted on its debt. The interest due on trillions of dollars of debt held by foreign governments and institutional investors in our government securities went unpaid. Though a scaled-back payment was made, the damage was done. Other nations followed suit, and what remained of the global economy shattered; the paper currency systems were in tatters. Gold and other precious metals became the new currency of the realm, and global trade all but ground to a halt.

Second, government entitlement programs were scaled back for those already receiving benefits. Social Security benefit reductions—based on income—were a crushing blow for tens of millions of retired Americans. Medicare and Medicaid programs also scaled back coverages and reimbursements, and it quickly put medical providers, pharmaceutical firms, doctors, and other personnel in a precarious position, unable to meet the ballooning needs of a stressed-out population.

Sadly, similar events played out all over the world. With the World Bank, sovereign wealth funds, IMF, and treasuries of developed nations tapped out, there were no longer any outside resources to bail out troubled nations; each country had to fend for itself. In developed nations, governmental safety nets were wearing down under the strain; in underdeveloped nations, entire infrastructures, including water, sewage, and waste-removal services, were left in various states of disrepair or collapse. Local and regional wars broke out, with fresh water and food usually the major drivers. With medical supplies and sanitation in short supply, cholera, Ebola, and other contagious diseases broke out in epidemic proportions.

As institutions collapsed and basic security became a matter of survival, societies reshaped as best they could. As in a country devastated by war, with no visible means of external support from which to rebuild, local militias, collective farms, communes, church support groups, cooperatives, and other pseudo-governmental structures began to emerge. The long-term prognosis was almost as bleak as the short term. There was simply no end in sight, and we could now feel, deep in our gut, exactly what the perfect storm was all about—and it was very, very painful.

The first definitive proposal was provided by the newly elected president of the United States in her inaugural address in 2029. She gave what many historians likened to Winston Churchill's "blood, sweat, and tears" speech from the darkest days of World War II. She was not only the first woman to be elected as US president but also the first elected under the banner of the New Independent Party forged by a citizenry exasperated and burned out by a dysfunctional two-party system that was totally incapable of governing. Emboldened, she told the people not what they wanted to hear but rather what they needed to hear.

Her long-term prognosis for the post–perfect storm world was chilling: a grim warning of what we could expect in the coming decade—or at least during her presidency. Among her many themes, the following three were particularly noteworthy:

1. The American economy—and that of the rest of the world—would have to be rebuilt from the ground up. Currency systems, tax codes, fiscal and monetary policies, the institutional roles of the Federal Reserve, Treasury, Wall Street, and the national banking and financial systems, to name a few, would have to be radically revamped. This process would require draconian measures and untold hardships in the years it would take to complete.

2. A global currency system for all international transactions would be needed to replace the current fragmented systems. Further, it would require some form of precious metal backing to replace the fiat currency system backed only by the good faith and credit of the sponsoring government.

3. The days of "smoke and mirrors" government budgeting would have to end. Government budgets would have to balance: no gimmicks or pie-in-the-sky projections, no more kicking the can down the road, and no more hiding behind a system devoid of accountability. This would apply at all levels of government and to all entitlement systems operated by them. We knew we wouldn't get there overnight, but our politicians were all on a short leash.

The ramifications would be profound in the decade to come. Addressing the perfect storm and reengineering a system that had been in decay for several decades would be a long and brutal battle, and we all knew it.

- We hunkered down with no expectation of a government bailout, since the money and resources simply were not there.

- Entitlement benefits for current and future retirees were reduced by 15–22 percent or more for an indefinite period of time. With the economy in a free fall, FICA and Medicare revenues were insufficient to fund current benefit levels. The plight of fixed income pensioners was indescribable. Having to choose between food and medicine, many succumbed to sicknesses or malnutrition.

- Wage and price freezes were imposed, and interest rates would remain in the double-digit range for the foreseeable future. A new rationing system was imposed to prevent hoarding and ensure that limited resources could be more widely dispersed. It reminded the eldest among us of World War II.

In the months and years that followed, the urgency of day-to-day survival began to ease, replaced by a grim realization that many of the changes underway were likely to be permanent. Like so many other generations that had lived through horrible times, we developed a stoic attitude; our expectations were whittled down to the bone. The things that were once givens, such as twenty-four-hour electricity, access to fresh water on demand, sewage systems that worked, grocery stores that were stocked to the brim, medical help whenever needed, and a rich assortment of government safety-net services, were no longer sure things. The frills of yesteryear were replaced with a focus on the bare essentials.

One of the most noticeable societal changes was a recognition that virtually all levels of government lacked the capacity to take care of us, and we were on our own. We looked more to our neighbors, communities, churches, and other local organizations for support. In some respects, it resembled what the United States might have looked like for many in the nineteenth or early twentieth centuries. Our survival skills, long dormant, were once again rekindled by necessity. Vegetable gardens expanded everywhere, and we became better at fixing and reusing things we would have thrown away only a few years before. We ramped up our efforts to conserve water, energy, and any other resource of potential value, for everything was in short supply.

Globalization as we knew it was dead. We purchased more and more products and services that were made locally rather than shipped in from distant locations. Our lifestyles shifted from a luxury-craving, throwaway culture to making do with basics, for we simply had no choice in the matter.

Complexity was out; simplicity was in. Thanks to a lack of money, resources, and spare parts, we automated fewer things and returned to manual effort. Our mobility was also severely limited. Air travel—what little there was of it—was a luxury reserved for the well-off, as it had been a century earlier. Some economies, now more regionally and locally focused, thrived, but many more floundered and failed.

The idea of growth for growth's sake was also a thing of the past. Businesses and households were looking for ways to downsize or, as we liked to say, "right size." Smaller was better. Our living standards had declined dramatically from the pre-storm era, but people were resilient. Some even liked the simpler lifestyle.

At this stage of the game, none of us really knew how it would end. Matter of fact, we still don't; it's an evolving thing. One advantage, if you could call it that, was that the dramatic shutdown of economic activity meant we were using far less energy, and our carbon footprint shrank immeasurably. Unfortunately, it was still too little and too late. The rising sea levels, monstrous hurricanes, floods, droughts, and wildfires continued, but we didn't have the resources for repair or replacement. Our nation's infrastructure deteriorated badly, and we heard it was far worse in many other countries.

We were fortunate that, despite all the regional wars, there were no nuclear confrontations. That, at least, gave us a little hope.

The overall damage to human life, health, property, and society was incalculable, and we know there is still more to come. Whether we will ever fully recover is questionable. For those of us still left from the class of '61, it most certainly won't happen in our lifetime.

Well, that's the story, and it's not a pretty one. I only hope that younger people will learn from this and not repeat our mistakes. If there's one thing I've learned, it is this: there's a price to be paid for everything. Sometimes it is paid on the spot, but at others it's less obvious. The true price might be paid years later, in ways we never imagined, and it is a wise person who can ferret through it all and see things for what they really are.

Historic Storm Forces

This chilling account may seem far-fetched, but is it? Historically, most of the things portrayed in this fictional account have happened in one form or another—particularly the hardships of a devastating war—but never has a catastrophic global meltdown of this magnitude happened as a result of pent-up forces on widely varied fronts erupting at about the same time. Webster's definition of a perfect storm, "a critical or disastrous situation created by a powerful concurrence of factors," would certainly seem to apply here. That said, let us look at examples of historic storm forces and then imagine all of them happening at about the same time.

During World War II, significant parts of Europe and several Pacific Rim nations were decimated, leaving tens of millions of homeless refugees without food, water, power, security, social structures, governance, and all the institutions and infrastructures that make up a society for a period of time. While the United States came through it unscathed, the Greatest Generation endured hardships of another kind in the Great Depression. With unemployment rates of 25 percent and no safety nets in the form of Social Security, Medicare, or other government programs, folks were on their own. Fortunes were lost overnight in the stock market crash of 1929; banks closed, assets were frozen, and the indelible picture of "Okie" caravans leaving the dust bowl and their foreclosed farms for better opportunities out west personified the times.

The horror of hyperinflation and dramatic loss of purchasing power in a defunct currency has also happened before. The Weimar Republic[1] of post–World War I Germany fell to it, and it happened in Venezuela more recently. The United States had a taste of inflation back in the 1970s, when the misery index reflected a combination of inflation and an unemployment rate of close to 20 percent.

The loss of infrastructure, fresh-water access, and sanitation, combined with disease epidemics, happens with great regularity in developing countries. Water shortages are already an international source of tension. Egypt has been at odds for decades with Ethiopia, one of its neighbors upstream on the Nile, and drought is a stress factor in Syria's ongoing civil war. In 2019, hundreds of civilians were killed, and fifty thousand displaced by conflict over water and land resources in Mali.

While the United States has been relatively immune, such hardships happen worldwide with greater frequency than we might like to admit. With the protection of two mighty oceans and a powerful navy to safeguard our homeland from invasion, and with a rich abundance of natural resources, cheap energy, productive farmland, space to grow, and viable institutions and security, we have had an incomparable opportunity to develop and grow. The American Dream we have so dearly held for generations personifies our exuberance, energy, and advantages. Ironically, it also makes it that much harder for us to imagine the hard times depicted above. But it can happen here.

When the basic institutions and infrastructures of a society are weakened to the point of collapse, and when hubris, greed, a sense of entitlement, and loss of integrity take over, bad things happen. A central goal of this book has been to illustrate how our society has changed over time in ways that have weakened us. Our quest to sustain our unsustainable lifestyles by passing on our IOUs to those following us and drawing down on their allotment of resources to support our habits—in effect, mortgaging their access to the American Dream—comes with a heavy price tag. We are now being presented with those IOUs, and they will only worsen.

In this fictional account of the perfect storm, I have tried to show how quickly the good life can disintegrate when major institutions start to fail us. Our challenges are systemic and interrelated, and when multiple sets of forces collide with others—as in the perfect storm—nasty eruptions will follow. So, if it all sounds too far-fetched to be real, just ask where we would be as a society if the entire nation went bankrupt, major institutions collapsed, entitlement programs were inoperable, and the purchasing power of the dollar dropped like a rock—all at the same time. Indeed, this is what the perfect storm is all about.

That's the bad news. The good news is that, though it's late in the game, there are still many things we can do to mitigate the coming storm—assuming that we awaken to the catastrophic threat it poses. A comprehensive response is presented in the following chapter. Keep the faith; there is still much we can do.

Mike Conley

This fictitious picture of the perfect storm is not a pretty one, and it could certainly unfold in a variety of other ways. It is hard to believe a catastrophe of this magnitude could happen, but it is precisely this disbelief that demotivates us from addressing the oncoming storm with everything we have. Unlike a nuclear Armageddon, which would wipe us out immediately, the perfect storm leaves, at least, a little space in which to maneuver. Let's not waste it.

The old saying that we should "plan for the worst and hope for the best" makes perfect sense in this situation, and I hope folks will give it a good deal of thought. If not for ourselves, then for our grandkids and the future we are leaving them.

Summary of the Perfect Storm

The fictitious chronicle in chapter 16 extrapolates what the perfect storm might look like, how it could develop, and what it might be like living through it. The potential triggering mechanisms and outcomes are endless, so this is but one example. Written in 2030, it describes the upheaval of the 2020s that led to the storm and calls to attention the following points:

1. The triggering mechanism could be a single event or a confluence of factors that eventually overwhelm the system and erupt. In this case, it was the latter.

2. In our scenario, a chain reaction of forces and events ignited and intensified the storm and then created aftershocks that passed into other areas. The cycle of destruction continued to repeat itself over and over again.

3. Our ability to withstand the storm's forces, or at least mitigate its effects, was lessened by the weakened conditions of our major institutions, infrastructure, fiscal and monetary systems, governance, and more. The weaker we are as a society; the greater and more lasting the storm's impact will be.

4. In our "play now, pay later" culture, we have compromised our future by unrestrained debt, overuse of scarce resources, waste, overindulgence, and shortsightedness, and we have severely damaged our future health in the process. This is what mortgaging the American Dream is all about. Our diminished capacity stacks up poorly against a storm of enormous destructive power.

5. The shocking story of the perfect storm may seem impossible, but is it? Many of the events mentioned in our story have already happened—just not at the same time. The

perfect storm represents a new paradigm, and that makes it more difficult to imagine how bad things could be. Our best bet will be to plan for the worst and hope for the best.

Note: Though nuclear war is quite possible, I did not factor it into the equation. As a doomsday scenario, it would render the entire perfect storm construct a moot point, as civilization would revert back to a Stone Age, or worse.

·17·

Weathering the Storm

*You cannot solve the world's problems
with the same thinking that created them.*

—Albert Einstein

In a sharp turn from the gloom and doom of the previous chapter, I now offer a message of hope. It doesn't have to be this way. Instead, like the mythical phoenix, we can rise from the ashes and use the fires of the looming storm as a catalyst for rejuvenation. The good news is that we are not starting from scratch; a number of efforts suggested are already underway.

As you review the transformational plan that follows, though, please keep this thought in mind: while the plan would be difficult to implement in our current dysfunctional political system, all things are possible when conditions deteriorate—as they will—to a point where the pain of major change is exceeded by the pain of doing nothing. Half measures will avail us nothing, and the sooner we realize the immensity of the effort and mindset shift required to address the perfect storm, the better off we will be. I hope we will come to this realization sooner rather than later.

The perfect storm is a global challenge and requires global solutions; piecemeal efforts will not suffice. It will require an integrated and mutually supportive framework across all levels of society, from global to grassroots, that all humanity can rally around and leverage to maximum advantage. I present such a framework here in multiple layers of global, national, and grassroots strategies that will align with and support efforts at all levels. *It might be modeled along the lines of the Paris Agreement, with nations signing on to work toward a set of international goals within a framework that allows them to develop their own unique strategies.*

With this in mind, the following plan, called Reenergizing the American Dream (RAD), represents an American version of how such a plan might look. The RAD plan is designed to address the perfect storm and shore up the sagging American Dream. It builds on our American strengths, values, and aspirations and provides opportunities to collaborate with other nations.

While the American Dream is not dead, but rather in dire need of a transfusion, the RAD plan uses global crises as a catalyst for repositioning America for the perfect storm and a better future. The plan is developed around a principles-based framework that other nations should find easy to embrace, and it calls for all key players to align in a common effort.

Reenergizing the American Dream

Objectives

1. Get positioned for the perfect storm and use it as a catalyst to reengineer the sagging American Dream.

2. Address the world's five great existential threats, as outlined in chapter 15.

3. Develop new opportunities for sustainable growth while addressing the perfect storm.

Guiding Principles

RAD adheres to five guiding principles for framing and coordinating solutions at all levels, foreign and domestic. The effectiveness of our collective efforts will be directly related to how closely the five principles are followed.

SWOT Analysis

Chart 17.1 provides a schematic starting point for our RAD repositioning effort. It illustrates the strengths, weaknesses, opportunities, and threats confronting the United States as we start our great journey of reengineering the American Dream.

Strategic Overview

RAD focuses on an American effort to do the following:

1. Reset our worldview to better leverage our collaborative global efforts.

2. Recalibrate and realign domestic paradigms and support structures.

3. Rebuild our financial foundations and reposition them for the future.

4. Revitalize our infrastructure with an emphasis on sustainable growth.

5. Reinforce total efforts with robust grassroots support tied to a national effort.

WEATHERING THE STORM · **323**

Chart 17.1: American SWOT Factors

S Strengths

Military, economic, and technological powerhouse

Human, natural, and physical resources; abundant water, food, and space

Historical hold on global power levers; global reserve currency, petrodollar systems, and alliances

Strong American brand for innovation and finance and track record of success

W Weaknesses

Debt, deficits, denial, and a creaking infrastructure ill-prepared for the future

Dysfunctional political system and deterioration of institutional trust and integrity

Shrinking middle class and growing educational and economic disparities

Erosion of American "brand," global distrust, and diminished access to the American Dream

O Opportunities

To use the energy renaissance as a springboard for reenergizing the American Dream

To reestablish global position as a leader in climate change and global affairs

To institute a major technological effort to thrive in fourth industrial revolution

To build a new, sustainable infrastructure, upgrade balance sheets, and restore institutional integrity

T Threats

Shifts in global power structures, a new cold war, hubris, and failure to adapt to new realities

Global economic meltdown: loss of dollar's reserve currency and petrodollar status

Asymmetric, cyberwarfare, terrorism, nuclear proliferation

A drift away from traditional American values toward nationalism and unilateralism.

Linear responses to exponential threats

Five Guiding Principles

As a framework for a globally organized effort to address the perfect storm, we need a set of operating principles around which all nations and their domestic and grassroots stakeholders can rally and plan. Assuming a global consensus can be reached, RAD will be framed around the following five guiding principles:

1) Systemic Thinking: The world is a complex collection of interconnected and moving parts; move one piece, and several others are affected. In order to connect the dots, create leverage, and develop effective responses, systemic solutions should be sought and considered in their totality, with an understanding of the cause-and-effect relationships between parts. It requires a credible process for a rational integration of the moving parts and recognizes the disconnects and unintended consequences that can be caused by misalignments. Systemic thinking requires that we do the following:

- Cast a Wide Net: Recalibrate and expand our worldview beyond the framework of local and national boundaries, to one embracing the planet and people as one interconnected system.

- Factor in Time: Recognize that time is working against us. Powerful feedback loops are hastening the degradation of our life-support systems, diminishing Earth's capacity to sustain growth at current rates. The bias to act must be urgent and powerful.

- Connect the Dots: Understand the interconnections between anthropogenic behaviors and their effects on our planet, support systems, lifestyles, and well-being. Denial and procrastination are no longer options.

2) Intellectual Integrity and Rational Processes: Critical thinking and an ability to face reality as it is—not as we want it to be—are crucial imperatives for change. Solutions should be grounded in science, measurable performance, solid metrics, collaborative processes, and accountability at all levels. Such efforts require that we do the following:

- Build Bridges and Not Walls: Provide platforms, tools, and incentives that conjoin all concerned parties and facilitate a dialogue of common understanding and interests.

- Jettison Zero-Sum-Game Thinking: Seek collaborative, win-win solutions. Though challenging, they offer the best hope of long-term progress; to get a little, we give a little.

- Trust but Verify: Know that collaborative solutions may tempt participants to game the system and weaken the overall result. Be clear on expectations and accountability as well as the rewards and consequences for actual endgame results.

3) Intergenerational Accountability: A lack of intergenerational stewardship has hampered access to the American Dream and its future promise for many. A misguided culture of denial, procrastination, and instant gratification has created a ticking time bomb for future generations. Solutions should be crafted with future impacts in mind and an understanding of the behavioral changes needed to achieve desired results:

- Proactivity: Embrace a willingness to aggressively act now on the festering threats of the future, always mindful to do no harm in the process.

- Perspective: Adopt a long-term outlook with impact reviews that weigh the costs to future generations of programs implemented today, with safeguards against abuses.

- Engagement: Encourage engagement at all levels and foster a greater sense of personal ownership, responsibility, and accountability for our actions.

4) Robust Resiliency: The perfect storm's challenges are formidable and will require behavioral changes geared to doing more with less. It calls for an engaged, resilient, and motivated citizenry with a political will to resolutely address our challenges. A strong sense of common purpose—global and domestic—is needed to overcome the barriers of resistance, nationalism, and national borders. Specific steps will include the following:

- Strengthen Our Global Institutions: Bolster the platforms, tools, systems, access to capital, and incentives that conjoin nations, facilitate collaborative progress, and eradicate barriers that exacerbate global threats.

- Enhance Living Standards: Close the gaps between developed and developing nations through inclusivity, resource sharing, foreign aid, and expanded opportunities. Reverse the contraction of the middle class in the United States and elsewhere, and recognize that a sea change in elevated living standards can be beneficial to all.

- Encourage Participation: Seek governance models in which an engaged citizenry feels ownership in the process, awareness of the issues, and willingness to hold leaders accountable. Avoid actions that disenfranchise voters, discourage grassroots efforts, contaminate the media, and restrict the free flow of information.

5) Opportunities and Best Practices: Just as the race to the moon in the 1960s was a powerful catalyst for basic research, new technologies, educational breakthroughs, quality improvements, and an explosion of new cottage industries to support the NASA space programs, a galvanized effort to address the perfect storm and restore the American Dream could reap similar benefits. The opportunities for pursuing low-hanging fruit and harvesting best practices for replication elsewhere are enormous. Steps to fast-track these new engines of growth include the following:

- Partnerships: Join the public, private, and educational sectors in a common effort, with a willingness to share resources and information in a collaborative global effort.

- Incentives: Encourage innovation through tax incentives, basic research funding, and removal of bureaucratic barriers to success, creating educational opportunities directed toward a continuous learning environment geared to new fourth-generation technologies.

- Innovation: Institutionalize a process for identifying and replicating best practices, and offer public/private funding opportunities for the most promising ventures.

Conclusions

A consistent theme throughout is that solutions to complex threats require collaborative efforts at all levels. The sense of urgency, political will, and processes needed to develop collaborative responses are currently insufficient. The RAD plan is based not on what is politically possible today—with which very little would ever get done—but rather on what will be needed to survive at some reasonable level. As conditions worsen, the world will need to decide whether to, as Benjamin Franklin said, "hang together or hang separately," and that, in itself, may be the greatest challenge of our time.

With the above principles in mind, we move on to the five strategic initiatives of the RAD plan that address our challenges at a global, national, and grassroots level. We will start by resetting our worldview and how we work with other nations for a better result.

1. Reset America's Worldview to Leverage Global Efforts

Our status as the world's premier superpower has been a part of our national DNA for so long that it is hard to imagine it being any other way, but the world is rapidly changing, and the United States must change with it or lose ground. Stuck in neutral and outmaneuvered in subtle but important ways, we need a reality check on our role in a changing world.

We are now stretched thin and overextended. With seismic shifts in the global power structures and a domestic economy that resembles a giant Ponzi scheme ready to bust, time is running out. Simply put, we have little choice but to get repositioned for the twenty-first century, and that means looking at the world through a different set of lenses.

The global challenges we face—such as climate change, trade wars, cyberwarfare, nuclear proliferation, resource shortages, global pandemics, and more—cannot be solved unilaterally. As they interconnect and converge at a rapid pace, effective solutions will require nothing less than a systemically organized global effort.

Sadly, with the growth of nationalism, terrorism, and unilateralism, the world is moving away from a worldview that embraces the planet and its inhabitants as one codependent megasystem . The United States has of late abdicated its traditional role as a constant in a world of change—precisely the wrong time to go AWOL— and we will need to reengage with the world if we are to make any headway in addressing our global challenges.

This doesn't mean relinquishing our national identity for a higher order, but it calls for recognition that we have a common atmosphere and ecological systems, finite resources, and shared constraints on Earth's capacity to support life as we know it. Our days of unilaterally calling the shots, levying sanctions, breaking treaties, and thumbing our nose at global efforts to address climate change and other challenges are numbered.

Though we currently spend as much on the military as the next seven largest national military budgets combined, it is only one aspect of global leadership. Our worldview is in need of recalibration. From a global perspective, a policy inventory reveals our overreliance on muscular military power, under reliance on collaborative soft-power diplomacy,[1] and overindulgence in the hubris of unilateralism: not a prescription for success.

Assuming we can find the collective will to address the global threats that transcend national boundaries, we might respond to the world's five great existential threats—outlined in chapter 15—as follows:

1. **Global Destabilization and Ticking Time Bombs:** The United States must reengage with and vigorously support the global institutions that deal with world governance, trade, economics, treaties, alliances, and diplomatic protocols and take up the global persona we were once so instrumental in creating. It will require a greater sharing of wealth and resources; a collaborative approach toward dealing with cyber, nuclear, pandemics, and other global challenges; and a de-escalation of new cold-war tensions.

2. **Climate Change and Sustainability of Life as We Know It:** The United States should immediately rejoin and aggressively participate in the Paris Agreement, with financial, technological, and leadership support, walking the talk with a powerful domestic response that addresses climate change and showcases the exciting new economic opportunities such actions avail.

3. **Energy and Technology in a Race against Time:** The race to decarbonize legacy energy systems and fast-track the new energy renaissance without disrupting the global economy is a challenge made to order for a determined America ready to use its core competencies and resources to mobilize a world effort, but it will require a reset in our global viewpoint.

4. **An American Implosion That Could Rock the World:** The economic dominance of the United States carries the potential to derail the entire global economy if it craters. With more at stake than just our citizenry, a reset of our fiduciary thinking

and commitment to strengthening our economic foundations is both a domestic and global necessity.

5. **Resilience and Capacity to Persevere:** The ability to address global challenges in their totality, work together toward common solutions, share resources, and enjoy the leverage of working collaboratively is crucial. Awakening to and acting on these global threats with global responses could make or break humankind.

Make no mistake: turning it around will not be easy. It will likely take a global catastrophe to spark the transformation, or, if we are lucky, it could bubble up at a grassroots level among younger generations dissatisfied with the status quo. Whatever the catalyst, our lenses will need to be recalibrated in at least three critical ways:

- Sharing Leadership: Our best results will come from leveraging our efforts with others. It will mean shifting from the zero-sum-game approaches of yesteryear to soft-power approaches that can produce win-win scenarios. It will require a greater willingness to give something in order to get something by building bridges and not walls.

- Humility, Not Hubris: It will require a greater willingness to participate as part of the whole and not as the core that every nation is supposed to orbit. It will require greater openness, free trade, and a spirit of collaboration as opposed to an overreliance on walls, trade barriers, tariffs, sanctions, or military threats. It will mean abandoning protectionist and unilateral policies that just don't work.

- Moral Leadership: It will mean refocusing on the world as a whole, taking the high road with respect to addressing climate change, arms controls, trade, world development efforts, immigration policies, and sharing American resources and know-how to address the global challenges with which we are all a part. The world once looked to the

United States for leadership and, as a trustworthy partner, we delivered: it is a practice worth restoring.

Conclusions

If this collaborative approach fails to resonate, consider the alternatives: China will fill any leadership voids we leave; we will be increasingly marginalized by traditional allies and others fed up with our policies. The institutional levers of power—such as the reserve currency and petrodollar system—will deteriorate, and many nations will look for ways to work around rather than with us. It is hard to see how we will not be the ultimate losers in this new world order if we don't reset our worldviews and change our ways.

2. Recalibrate Our Domestic Paradigms and Support Structures

The United States' persona as the land of opportunity and home of the American Dream has captured the spirit of our nation more than anything else. Indoctrinated from childhood, we believed in our institutions, the rule of law, opportunities for all, and democracy.

But something happened along the way: we developed an addiction to debt, overconsumption, and instant gratification. Self-indulgent, we drifted from values we had inherited from the Greatest Generation, and in the process, we began to distrust our institutions and political processes.

Though we have drifted, it is still correctable. Our task will be to build on our strengths and recalibrate domestic paradigms to once again align with our values, beliefs, strengths, and better angels. In this effort, we will need to revisit and reform our political systems; restore integrity in our laws, institutions, and processes; and rebuild on our strengths.

Revisit and Reform Our Political Systems

As grade-school kids, we learned about our democracy and its three coequal branches of government, but little was said about the darker undersides, such as political polarization, monied self-interest, powerful lobbies, uncompromising ideologues, and more. Structurally, the levers of power found in our gerrymandered congressional districts, campaign financing—which influences candidate selection, platforms, policy choices, and access to power for those who can pay to play—and built-in mechanisms that favor incumbents are all part of the political system. In this toxic environment, advocacy journalism and charismatic talk-show hosts have fostered a new partisan agenda in which *compromise* has become a dirty word and reaching across the aisle a career breaker for newer politicians.

The deck is stacked, and reforms may only come via a grass-roots juggernaut of disenchanted voters demanding reform. While congressional term limits and reforms in the electoral college system require constitutional changes, a number of reforms can be taken outside of this process with respect to structures, practices, and participation:

- Structural Changes: Replace the current gerrymandered congressional districts with redistricting that equitably represents all constituents, institute campaign finance reforms to curtail spending limits, require greater transparency and full disclosure controls, and consider term limits and electoral college reforms.

- Practices: Reform governmental practices that obscure transparency and accountability; mandate that Congress live under the same programs it legislates for its constituencies; and curtail lobbying activities, funding, and private industry sweetheart deals in which former government officials and high-ranking military officers are allowed to work for former vendors.

- Participation: Encourage greater voter involvement by removing impediments to voter participation, foster a political environment that generates greater voter turnout, and secure the voting process to make it less vulnerable to manipulation by hostile governments.

Restore Integrity in Our Laws, Institutions, and Processes

Our faith and trust in traditional American institutions is gradually eroding. It is happening in all sectors of the country, in public, private, religious, media, military, and educational institutions. Indeed, the very values we stand for are under duress. As societal stabilizers, they sustain us through the good times and bad, and their steady erosion will not end well for us.

Its progress is insidious. For example, it happens when the EPA subverts its mission of protecting human health and the environment by looking the other way on climate change, clean air, water, and energy. It happens when elite colleges fudge admissions standards for students with an ability to game the system and buy their way in. It happens when churches pay out more for litigation and punitive damages than they do for charitable work. It happens when banks "too big to fail" get a free pass (moral hazard) if things go bad for them, and when laws are unequally applied and favor a system based on getting the best "justice" money can buy. It happens when our leaders forget that we are a nation of laws rather than of individuals.

It can take decades to build institutional credibility—and one egregious event to destroy it. There are no easy answers, but we need to restore the integrity of our laws and institutions. The following actions will help restore credibility and integrity in our institutions and minimize catastrophes before they occur:

- Mission Creep: Our institutions get in trouble when they go beyond their defined purposes and enter areas they should never be in. In the process, they dilute their core mission and compromise their legitimacy as an entity their stakeholders can trust.

- Transparency: Institutions of all forms—governmental, nonprofits, judicial, law enforcement, and others—should be held to a high level of transparency, accountability, compliance, and oversight, with zero tolerance for cheating and a bias toward continuous improvements in their performance.

- Enforcement and Oversight: The apparatus for effectively measuring and monitoring performance should be an integral component in all institutional entities. The compliance and oversight mechanisms—public, private, nonprofit, and voluntary—should fit the entity they represent. The public deserves nothing less.

Rebuild on Our Strengths

America is rich in physical, natural, and human resources and has shown its innovativeness and resilience time and again—perhaps never more so than our response to the Soviet Union's stunning launch of Sputnik in 1957. The National Defense Education Act, enacted shortly thereafter, authorized a comprehensive educational effort at all levels, with a heavy emphasis on math and science, and NASA was also created. A dozen years later, we put men on the moon.

The United States is once again facing a significant technological challenge, the fourth industrial revolution, and our major competitor will be China. The manner in which we work, play, process information, and compete in the world markets will change dramatically. This revolution will disrupt our workforce, educational systems, and technological developments, and we will need to rapidly retrofit our educational, training, and R&D efforts to remain viable—all traits that play well to our core competencies as a nation.

China has already invested heavily in gaining the upper hand, and it will take a space-race-level response on our part. A few key initiatives in this area should include the following:

- R&D Efforts: Ramped-up federal programs to fund basic research—including long-term research and pilot programs—with joint public/private efforts that will fast-track promising initiatives in crucial areas, such as digital and artificial intelligence, clean energy, and water conservation.

- Education and Training: In a new world of lifelong learning, continuous learning opportunities will be vital to our economy, workforce, and national interests. Development of the supporting apparatus should be a top public and private effort.

- Financing: Access to and affordability of education at all levels is problematic. Current efforts are fragmented, and results mixed. The cost of higher education and the student-loan debt crisis is debilitating, and substantive subsidies and loan relief are vital. At an aggregated level of $1.5 trillion, student-loan debt is now the second-largest debt category—after home mortgages—in the United States, and default rates are climbing. Like our entitlement programs, the crisis will worsen without immediate attention. It might be wise to revisit the GI Bill as a good first start.

Conclusions

At present we have a dysfunctional political system and a growing distrust in our institutions. Does anyone think we can go on like this? It will most certainly take a massive grassroots movement to turn the tide.

3. Rebuild Our Financial Foundations and Reposition for the Future

The US balance sheets are in shambles, with annual deficits in the trillion-dollar range, gross government debt exceeding our GDP, staggering interest payments on that debt, and underfunded entitlement programs that will soon pay out more than is taken in. State and local governments are also in dire straits, with underfunded medical and pension obligations, and household and corporate balance sheets are mired in red ink.

Through labyrinthine accounting practices, creative new ways to monetize debt, fiscal and monetary policies on steroids, and a lavish use of the Treasury's credit to fund wars and other crises, we are drowning. As a nation, we have mortgaged our future to finance a lifestyle we can no longer afford.

A day of reckoning will surely come when the big three—entitlement programs, interest on debt, and defense spending, which now consume over 65 percent of the total budget—reach a tipping point. Broke, and with little left to fund other programs, the government will tax, borrow, slash benefits, sell off assets, and print more money, but like all Ponzi schemes, it will collapse under its own weight and trigger a catastrophic meltdown of epic proportions. The longer we put it off, the worse it will get.

The treatment will be harsh, but we will soon have no alternatives other than radical surgery. That said, and with no illusions about the daunting political difficulties involved, the approach we require is aggressive incrementalism. This means pushing ahead as hard and fast as possible with corrective measures without killing the patient, our economy. We must directly address the three greatest cost drivers in our system by reducing debt and deficits, restructuring entitlement programs, and redesigning our healthcare system

Reduce Debt and Deficits

Left unchecked, our runaway debt will crater the economy, bankrupt our nation, and all but destroy our way of life. While it is late in the game, we can still take several proactive strategies to mitigate the greatest risks:

- Establish the Imperative: Every citizen should be expected to participate in the process of rebuilding our financial foundations. As in World War II, the notion of shared sacrifice in service of a cause greater than ourselves is an imperative.

- Debt Recalibration: Our massive debt will never be paid off, but we can make it more manageable. It should start with a mandated plan to incrementally reduce debt and the debt-to-GDP ratio. Budget deficits should decrease as a percentage of GDP on a sliding scale per annum until revenues and outlays reach an acceptable level. The mandate will challenge our leaders to make the tough choices that they were elected to make while reducing our aggregated debt-to-GDP ratio in an intentional fashion. The mandate will also give our politicians the air cover they require—a political must.

- Budget Transparency: The Gong Show of our current budgetary process obfuscates accountability and perpetuates deficits as a routine practice, and it has to stop. It will require a third-party referee that functions independent of Congress and the White House—or even a more powerful and independent Congressional Budget Office—to certify the budget and audit results. It would outsource to a private entity the task of ferreting out waste, fraud, and abuse; compensation would be a percentage of dollars saved. Congress should also be required to pass an annual budget without the use of continuing resolutions that merely defer tough decisions. All new programs should require an identifiable source of revenue and/or provide commensurate cuts elsewhere to fund new programs without identifiable revenue sources.

- Intergenerational Impacts: A protocol to measure the long-term cost impact on future generations—devoid of the bogus ten-year congressional pro forma illustrations now used—should be instituted. Programs that backload costs to future generations without equivalent value to them should be rejected. Protection of institutions deemed "too big to fail" and use of taxpayer dollars to bail out moral hazard risks—an insidious form of privatizing profits and socializing risks that allows entities to make risky decisions in which the consequences of their decisions can be passed off to others—must end.

- Structural Reforms: The list is long, but two in particular are important: eliminate the dual mandate (see chapter 3) imposed on the Federal Reserve to oversee monetary policy and the banking system and assume oversight responsibility for a viable economy and low unemployment rates (goals that are often contradictory), and end the practice of allowing Congress to shift the costs of unfunded mandates to state and local governments.

Restructure Our Entitlement Programs

Social Security, Medicare, Medicaid, and other programs are under severe stress. Now exceeding 60 percent of the federal budget and rising, they must be addressed if this country is to remain financially solvent. Through mission creep, benign neglect, and political leaders' paranoid fear of angering voters, it is reaching a crisis point. With vast surpluses of the FICA-generated revenues from yesteryear spent long ago to finance general operations and little left to fund the coming explosion of entitlement obligations, the imputed liabilities are staggering and well in excess of our future capacity to fund them.

There are no good options for making it solvent, but we can take concrete—though draconian—steps to shore up our entitlement programs. The solutions will require a blend of the following policies:

- Revenue Enhancements: Increase the breadth and depth of FICA payroll taxes—recognizing it will hurt the economy—and find new revenue sources to bolster the financial integrity of our entitlement programs.

- Benefit Reductions: Reduce benefits, limit cost-of-living adjustment increases, tighten eligibility periods, and adopt robust means-testing protocols with benefit reductions for those better able to pay. Grandfather in benefits for existing recipients and reduce future payments to well-to-do recipients.

- Policy Practices: The list is long and includes disallowing the use of excess FICA funds for general operations and establishing a "lock-box" to protect funds; avoiding mission creep and the addition of new unfunded benefits; privatizing efforts to reduce waste, fraud, and abuse; and using the massive leverage of Medicare and Medicaid to promote healthier living, tort reform, pharmaceutical cost reductions, and other healthcare reforms listed in the next section.

Redesign Our Healthcare System

With healthcare costs in the United States approaching 18 percent of GDP and climbing, the access and affordability of healthcare for all is a chronic and costly problem. A huge drag on government, corporate, and family budgets, it affects both the economic health of our nation and our competitive posture abroad.

The system is not working for too many people, and cosmetic reforms are only of marginal value. The stakes are high, and the vested interests powerful. Meaningful reform will only come with bipartisan support and a general recognition by all stakeholders that it can't go on like it is. Key features of a new approach to be thoughtfully implemented over an extended period of time should include the following:

- Public/Private Plans: Migrate toward a hybrid national health plan in which the public and private sectors function in a coordinated manner for optimal results. The private, employer-based health market—covering over 150 million Americans—should remain intact where possible, with a national health plan made available to those without access to a quality plan. As the ultimate bearer of risk for the national plan, the government should use its leverage to negotiate pharmaceutical and other discounts for all plans—private and public—and to standardize systems, simplify state insurance codes, institute tort reform and the costly practices of "defensive" medicine that go with it, and provide favorable incentives for healthier living. Meanwhile, the private insurance industry would administer the delivery of all benefits in both the public and private sectors and engage in provider network development, managed care services, cost-containment initiatives, wellness programs, advocacy services, supplemental plans, health savings accounts, home services, geriatric care, and other specialized care as needed. Working together, a portability of coverage that precludes "job-lock" and assures a continuity of insurance coverages with no coverage gaps between jobs would be provided.

- Structural Reforms: Fast-track FDA approval processes and importation of proven drugs; reform and digitalize cumbersome back-office administrative processes; weed out costly state mandates; reduce barriers to the accessibility and affordability of care; and encourage online medical caregiving. Mandate that providers publish the costs of their services and subsidize medical tuition for doctors and medical personnel willing to serve in needier areas. Ramp up mental health and addiction treatment programs, focusing on demand reduction—versus interdiction—as the most effective way to fight the opioid crisis.

- Personal Accountability: We will all need to be more accountable for our lifestyles and personal habits and take ownership in this process by making ourselves better and wiser users of our healthcare services. Create incentives for engaging in healthier living practices with financial rewards and tax breaks.

4. Revitalize Infrastructure with an Emphasis on Sustainability

America's aging infrastructure is a growing drag on the economy, environment, and our competitive global posture, but it could also revitalize our economy with new engines of growth and sustainable, enduring foundations. Building a revitalization plan around a theme of sustainability is a difficult challenge, but it is attainable, and the positive impact on future generations would be huge.

Resources are tight, and the plan itself must conform to an overarching goal of building a competitive twenty-first-century economy. The proposed initiatives fall into three succinct categories: energy and environment, sustainability and demand reduction, and the circular economy.

Energy and Environment

Energy and environmental goals are integrally linked and must be thought of as a package deal. Simply put, cleaner energy leaves a smaller carbon footprint, which in turn supports the battle against climate change. Coupled with new technologies and a changing marketplace, the energy renaissance now underway could wean us off the almost total dominance of fossil fuels. Coupled with robust demand-reduction efforts and an eventual migration toward an even more sustainable circular economy—covered later—the outcomes could be truly transformative.

In our energy-intensive economy, the transition away from fossil fuels must be well orchestrated, with an understanding that fossil fuels will continue to play a crucial role in our energy mix until renewable power and other energy alternatives are available at sufficient scale to meet our growing energy needs.

Strategically, an economy powered by electricity produced by the cleanest fuel systems available offers a *scalable* alternative to an energy system reliant on fossil fuels. Of at least equal importance, it provides the best opportunity for meeting the multiple energy needs of the future and the aggressive decarbonization efforts that will lead to a cleaner environment. A transition to this energy mix will require several major shifts:

1. **Carbon Tax:** Tax carbon emissions to incentivize the market and use carbon tax revenues to offset the cost of the energy renaissance transition.

2. **Cleaner Energy:** Build or retrofit power plants, grid systems, and related infrastructure, with constant efforts to upgrade facilities to the cleanest fuels available for generating electrical power. Phase out coal-burning plants as rapidly as possible— particularly those lacking "cleaner" fuel options, such as carbon capture and sequestration (CCS)[2] capabilities. Natural gas and nuclear power will continue to provide a long-term bridging fuel as a growing mix of new renewable energy power gradually comes online.

3. **Renewable Energy:** The opportunities are unlimited. As the price points for renewable energy continue to drop,

the cheaper, cleaner, and safer nature of renewable fuels will continue to gain traction with utilities, policymakers, and consumers. As a high-growth industry, technologies supporting energy storage, improved intermittency, and utility should be subsidized. Over time, public support for cleaner energy; the dramatic creation of new job opportunities (even now, new job creation in the clean-energy arena exceeds that of the fossil-fuel sector by a ratio of at least five to one); and innovative new ways to decouple utility company incentives for "producing" to incentives based on saving energy will make renewables even more attractive.

4. **Grid Modernization:** A critical part of the energy renaissance will be construction of a national electrical highway system equivalent in scope to the transcontinental highway system built by the Eisenhower Administration in the 1950s. This smart system would be loaded with sensors; upgraded long-distance power lines; "hardened" transformers and power distribution sites that are less susceptible to electromagnetic, terrorist, or cyberattacks; and a capacity to better integrate distributed-power systems, microgrids, and high-quality electrical power on an as-needed basis.

5. **Electrified Transportation Systems:** The migration toward an electrified transportation system featuring high-speed railways, electric and/or hybrid cars, and electrified mass transit systems is now underway. The market has already moved in that direction, with several countries mandating the discontinuance of new gasoline and diesel-powered cars on or before 2040.[3]

The challenge of transitioning current transportation systems from fossil fuels to electricity will be formidable. With shale oil projected to peak—much as crude oil peaked in recent years—by the end of the decade, demand for oil could easily exceed supply *before* the new transportation systems are fully in place—a threat of great concern and all the more reason to hasten the energy transition in this race against time.

Sustainability and Demand Reduction

In our struggle to address our future energy and environmental challenges, nothing is more promising—or cost effective—than adopting robust demand-reduction programs across all levels of society. Demand reduction, in its simplest form, is about finding new ways to do more with less and reduce our carbon footprint in the process. It can take many forms, such as initiatives for energy efficiency; energy conservation (reducing waste through recycling, repairing, reusing, and repurposing); and behavioral modifications, in which we consciously seek more sustainable and cost-effective ways to live our lives and conduct our business.

Target-rich areas for demand reduction are everywhere and include our transportation systems, new LEED-certifiable[4] commercial building and retrofits of existing structures, agricultural practices and water conservation, energy production and transmission structures, residential dwellings and appliances, and waste management and pollution control. A regulatory apparatus that rewarded conservation and penalized waste would aid these initiatives. The ultimate goal would be a circular economy, as described later. Sample initiatives might include the following:

- The "Negawatt" Concept: Introduced by Amory Lovins of the Rocky Mountain Institute, the negawatt represents a theoretical unit of energy (measured in watts) that can be directly and quantifiably saved by an energy-conservation or efficiency action and redeployed elsewhere. In this manner, we can do more with the same amount of energy, perhaps precluding the need to build a new power plant by virtue of the energy saved. The equivalent carbon savings could also be sold or traded as an emissions credit once the carbon marketplace is more fully developed.

- Buildings and Residences: Improved technologies and efficiencies in the areas of heating, cooling, lighting, water conservation, and localized—distributed—energy provided on-site will reduce costs and improve ROI. Real-time practices have quantified the savings, and LEED certification already increases the value and market attractiveness of new construction.

- Agricultural Practices: More planful soil use, crop rotation, and other conservation practices will lead to greater sustainability. With over 70 percent of our nation's water supply used for farming, opportunities to produce more while using less water through drip irrigation, crop selection, and other proven conservation practices will reduce the rate of aquifer depletion while making more water available for other uses. Dietary changes, especially a reduction in water-intensive meat products, will immeasurably help the equation.

- Conservation and Waste Management: Efforts to recycle, reuse, and repurpose waste, water, and industrial debris will, over time, reduce costs, pollution, and our environmental footprint. On a larger scale, a move toward a circular economy could leverage all efforts in an exponential manner.

The Circular Economy

Traditional linear economies—our prevailing economic models—follow a take-make-dispose cycle. As resources become tighter, waste and emission threats intensify, and a growing population with heftier consumptive patterns pushes the supply-side boundaries to the limit, it will become harder to maintain. The circular economy (CE) model takes a longer and broader look at how we use our finite resources. It replaces the throwaway culture of the linear economy with a regenerative model that expands and extends the life cycle of basic materials used in a manufactured product through recycling, repurposing, and reusing materials, but it is more than recycling alone—much more.

It places great emphasis on the front-end design of products, processes, and the types of material they use. It fosters a regenerative cycle by designing out waste, pollution, and toxic elements that would preclude the recycling and reuse of materials. It builds resiliency into the system by extending the life cycle of materials, repurposing and then reusing materials that would have been discarded in new products, and repeating the process time and again.

Several companies have introduced the CE into their tighter product loops with good results, but it has yet to be extended across a broader scope of our economy to maximize its true potential value. While the opportunities for a better bottom line, conservation of resources, and a cleaner planet would be immense, the challenges of expanding the CE processes across multiple chains of the economy are formidable. It will take a number of public and private enablers to make it work:

- Standards: The establishment of cross-industry standards and guidelines to ensure interchangeability of materials and moving parts

- Alignment: An alignment of incentives, cross-chain processes, skill sets, and collaborative mechanisms to foster the repurposing process of transferring "expended" resources from one product to the next—especially challenging in cross-industry participation

- Access: An open access to collaborative financing, risk-management tools, and cross-chain training opportunities to foster the CE culture, value chains, and systemic efficiencies

- Value Chains: An expansion of the tight circular controls of singular CE entities to a broader, cross-chain arena with robust oversight mechanisms that incorporate the above components

5. Grassroots Initiatives

With the completion of the previous two legs of our strategic triad—global and national initiatives—we now move to the third leg: grassroots and personal initiatives. The mere mention of topics like global warming and the national debt seem so overwhelming that we are often discouraged from doing anything about it—so why try? When we feel like this, it is inspiring to recall the words of Peter Marshall, who said, "Small deeds done are better than great deeds planned."

For example, we caught a glimpse of the explosive power of grassroots actions following President Trump's declaration that the United States would pull out of the Paris Agreement. The outcry from our citizens, local governments, and corporate America galvanized into the We Are Still In movement. National polls now identify climate change as a major voter concern, Millennials and Gen Z—the generations that will pay the severest price for our neglect—are actively engaging around this issue.

Grassroots efforts do not happen overnight, nor do individual households readily respond to national challenges unless pressed to the wall. As of late, we may be close to tipping points on many fronts, such as our growing deficits, student loans, gun control, and immigration, but we will stick with climate change here for modeling purposes. The shift from apathy to advocacy is an interesting dynamic and usually happens in phases, as illustrated in Chart 17.2: Continuum of Engagement.

Chart 17.2: Continuum of Engagement

1 Awakening	2 Discovery	3 Leverage	4 Advocacy
An event triggers an interest in an issue and heightens level of awareness.	It sparks an interest in learning more in an intensified process of discovery.	In joining, learning, and working with like-minded groups, ability to make change increases.	Willingness to give time, talent, and treasury and commit to a more activist role increases.

It is encouraging to see a growing level of engagement within the younger generations, which now outnumber the baby boomers and Silent Generation. With an opportunity to change our country's course, they will be highly motivated as they increasingly feel the pinch of the IOUs passed on to them by previous generations. Older people concerned with the plight of their kids and grandkids could also increase their engagement. Some, however, will resist, mired in denial, ignorance, or apathy.

Our journeys will vary, but the engagement process will remain constant. Rather than attempting to lay out a step-by-step process for increased engagement, I will instead share my own personal journey—using the Continuum of Engagement as a model—in the hope that it will help others in their own personal journeys of discovery.

My Awakening

I related in chapter 13 how I first became interested in the perfect storm and its intergenerational impacts. In my earlier research on the correlation between the burning of fossil fuels and climate change, I was flabbergasted to discover that one gallon of gasoline produced twenty pounds of carbon dioxide. The science behind it helped me truly appreciate the interrelatedness of energy, environment, economics, and my own personal expectations. (Look ahead to chart 17.3, at the end of this chapter, for that data.) This realization was a game-changer for me.

At the time, I owned a Piper Archer III airplane and flew it about 150 hours a year, on average. My plane burned about 10 gallons of high-octane aviation fuel per hour, or 1,500 gallons per year. Using the carbon footprint formula in chart 17.3, I was horrified to discover that I emitted about 15 *tons* of new CO_2 into the atmosphere every year. With a shelf life of a hundred or more years, my emissions would remain in the atmosphere throughout the lifetimes of my kids, my grandchildren, and their grandchildren. Not much of a legacy for a grandfather to leave, is it? I sold my plane and no longer fly privately. In doing so, I could not only save energy but also reduce my carbon footprint, save money, and leave a better world for my grandkids. What's not to like about a deal like that? I applied this thinking to the types of vehicles I drove, going from a Jaguar to a Prius, and to my other energy uses, and with every new step I learned more.

My Discovery Process

This transportation "aha" moment inspired me to learn more, and the more I learned, the more I wanted to learn. One of life's lessons for me has been that if you really want to learn more about something, try writing about it, teaching it, or selling it. I did all three. I had to start from scratch, and this meant a commitment to doing the research, attending conferences, talking to people involved in these areas, and building a base of knowledge.

In the process of discovery, I developed a personal plan for addressing the challenges of the perfect storm. A dynamic process that keeps me on my toes, it revolves around the 4-E Forces discussed throughout this book. I set the following overall goals, and the longer I've pursued them, the less active effort it has taken to plan for and pursue them:

- **Energy:** Rightsizing my energy habits to do more with less

- **Environment**: Reducing my carbon footprint as climate change intensifies

- **Economics:** Positioning my finances for the shakier economic landscape ahead

- **Expectations:** Changing my behaviors to conform to new realities

With these goals in mind, I worked on an action plan in preparation for the coming storm. To establish an energy baseline, I did an audit of my energy use at all levels—from cars to lawn mowers—and analyzed my energy bills and consumption practices. It's amazing how a close look at the data can lead to new goals and more effective energy monitoring. I then evaluated my household carbon footprint using one of the free carbon-emission calculators available on the internet. With very little paperwork, it provided a baseline from which to measure and monitor my carbon behaviors on a regular basis.

With this information in hand, I crafted a plan with specific goals. I found many targets of opportunity for saving energy, costs, and emissions, and a good many of them I could do at a modest cost. Examples include insulating our attic with a higher R-value (more heat-resistant) product, fine-tuning our furnace, weatherizing our house, using Energy Star–rated products where possible, tinting our sun-porch windows for greater cooling and heating savings, replacing lighting with LED bulbs, changing behaviors in little ways (such as resetting thermostats to more efficient levels), and reusing, repairing, and recycling where possible. These are only a few of the small, but important, steps I took, and on the internet, you can find a large range of additional, practical steps that can be adapted to anyone's needs. In doing these things, it is important to establish metrics, monitor performance, and make adjustments as necessary—something I should do more frequently.

On the financial front, circumstances vary by individual, so no one approach is right for everyone. However, as the storm approaches, the global economy and world markets will become increasingly volatile, and once it erupts, it will be too late. (See chart 3.1 for a summary of the risks.) The best general advice I can offer is to work through your circumstances with a trusted financial advisor. However, I found the following steps helpful in my financial planning process:

- Use a long-term planning horizon with a focus on the underlying forces that drive the market and economy. Consider carefully the early warning signals they can provide.

- Recognize that today's government safety nets and entitlement benefits may not be as readily available tomorrow. Look for alternative assets to supplement them.

- Consider that food, water, power, security, medical care, and other life staples may not always be as readily available as they now are. Learn to be more self-sufficient (a work in progress for me).

- Understand that improving cash flow, liquidity, and asset reserves as well as rightsizing and reducing expenses now will better prepare us for tomorrow's uncertainties. Start now; don't wait. Save now; let the power of compounding work for you.

- Appreciate that future reductions of the dollar's purchasing power should be a factor in considering any long-term, fixed-rate investments, which could lock in capital at below-market rates in the future for years to come. Beware of long-term financial entanglements.

- Be aware that the fiat paper currencies of today could be at risk tomorrow. Adding precious metals and hard assets to the investment mix will help hedge against this threat.

- Acknowledge that bubbles always burst, and the herd mentality that precedes them may be an early warning to pull back. If it looks too good to be true, it probably is.

- Connect the dots by making a periodic review of the financial threats that could unfold, as well as current ability to deal with them. Consider any investment portfolio gaps that exist and what it would take to close them. Remember that financial conditions often change; stay up to date, flexible, and ready to adjust accordingly.

Like finances, expectations and behaviors are also highly personal. I made several simple changes that, on the aggregate, made a difference, such as biking more, eating less red meat, getting more engaged, and staying current on new trends and developments in these areas of interest. The sooner we learn that a fulfilling and sustainable life doesn't mean living in a cave or going without electricity, the better off we will be. We lived in California in a situation where water was rationed at 190 gallons of water per day per household. A hardship at first, we later found it fun to figure out better ways to do more with less.

My Leveraging Process

The more I researched the perfect storm, the more I learned about the terrific organizations out there—mostly in the nonprofit and educational arenas—that can be of tremendous help. The meetings, seminars, literature, and networking opportunities they provide are of incalculable value. These organizations also promote engagement in public policy by identifying key issues, working with affinity groups to leverage our efforts, and supplying guidance. This leverage leads to the last initiative.

My Advocacy Efforts

Once I had discovered this new knowledge and connected with groups and people that allowed me to leverage it, I wanted to take the message to others—to become an activist. This step probably has more to do with one's passion for the issues than anything else. I wrote articles and posted them on my website, taught OLLI courses on the perfect storm through the University of Minnesota, and participated on several boards and advisory groups in matters related to these efforts. I most certainly get back more from these efforts than I give.

The big picture can seem overwhelming and beyond our reach; it's tempting to throw up our hands in complete surrender. That's called being human. Still, we should never underestimate the power of motivated people working together in a common cause for a greater good. Margaret Mead said it better than anyone when she observed that "a small group of thoughtful people could change the world. Indeed, it's the only thing that ever has."

And so, my friends, I call on you to get involved, learn more about the threats we face, leverage your efforts with others, and know that you can make a difference—if not for yourself, then for your loved ones.

Chart 17.3: Our Carbon Footprint - One Person Makes a Difference

How can a gallon of gasoline create 20 pounds of carbon dioxide?

- It seems impossible that a 6.3-pound gallon of gasoline could produce 20 pounds of carbon dioxide (CO_2) when burned. However, most of the weight of the CO_2 comes from the oxygen in the air rather than the gasoline.

- When gasoline burns, the carbon and hydrogen separate. The hydrogen combines with oxygen to form water (H_2O), and carbon combines with oxygen to form carbon dioxide (CO_2).

- CO_2 molecule with one carbon atom (atomic weight 12) and two oxygen atoms (atomic weight of 16 each)

- A carbon atom has a weight of 12, and each oxygen atom has a weight of 16, giving each single molecule of CO_2 an atomic weight of 44 (12 from carbon and 32 from oxygen).

- Therefore, to calculate the amount of CO_2 produced from a gallon of gasoline, the weight of the carbon in the gasoline is multiplied by 44/12 or 3.7.

- Since gasoline is about 87% carbon and 13% hydrogen by weight, the carbon in a gallon of gasoline weighs 5.5 pounds (6.3 lbs. x .87).

- We can then multiply the weight of the carbon (5.5 pounds) by 3.7, which equals approximately 20 pounds of CO_2!

Data Sources: Physical and chemical properties of gasoline: Department of Energy (DOE), Alternative Fuels Data Center (AFDC), Properties of Fuels.

C=12

O=16   O=16

CO_2

12+(16x2)=44

Source: https://www.fueleconomy.gov/feg/climate.shtml

CO_2 Factoids

- CO_2 is a greenhouse gas.

- It comes from many carbon sources, eg., gasoline and coal.

- It stays in the atmosphere for 1–2 centuries.

- Future genertions are the recipients of our CO_2 emissions.

- Do the math: Everyone counts

- The 20:1 emissions ratio is for real!

Summary of Weathering the Storm

Designed to mitigate the sharper edges of the perfect storm, the Reenergizing the American Dream (RAD) plan recognizes that global challenges require collaborative global solutions. RAD disregards the conventional political wisdom that helped create the mess we are in today and not only responds to the storm threat but uses it as a catalyst for restoring access to the American Dream. If the RAD plan sounds far-fetched, keep in mind that desperate people do desperate things. The five major elements of RAD are:

1. **Reset our worldview to think and act in collaborative global terms.**

    - Replace unilateralism and zero-sum-game solutions with new win-win approaches.

    - Build bridges and not walls; replace hubris with humility, for we are in this together.

    - Restore our brand as a nation; moral leadership is not dead.

2. **Recalibrate and realign our domestic paradigms in accordance with RAD principles.**

    - Enact intensive political reforms at all levels of government, recognizing that the status quo is not working.

    - Restore institutional integrity and trust through transparency, accountability, and compliance.

    - Build on our core strengths, diversity, and technological prowess.

3. **Rebuild our economic foundations, financial security, and balance sheets.**

   - Institute debt-reduction programs at all levels as a top national priority.

   - Restructure entitlement programs, funding mechanisms, and trust-fund security.

   - Redesign the healthcare system with both public and private skin in the game.

4. **Revitalize infrastructure around a heavy focus on sustainability.**

   - Fast-track the energy renaissance and the transition away from fossil fuels.

   - Implement aggressive sustainability management and demand-reduction initiatives.

   - Create vast new economic engines of growth through the above initiatives.

   - Expand opportunities to create new circular economies on a broader scale.

5. **Reinforce grassroots initiatives for broader participation at all levels of society.**

   - Seek broader participation and engagement through education and grassroots efforts.

   - Strengthen the middle class through tax incentives and other public/private programs.

   - Prepare and train the workforce for the fourth industrial revolution.

-18-

Closing Reflections

*Cherish your yesterdays, dream your tomorrows,
and live your todays.*

—Unknown

T here are similarities in making a movie and writing a book. Both are made up of segments, and each scene or chapter takes on an all-consuming life of its own while the work is in progress. Some parts require several takes or rewrites to meet the director or author's expectations, and closure is often a challenge because there always seems to be just one more tweak needed to make it better. Throughout this laborious process—which does not always occur sequentially—it is hard to grasp what the end product will look like after all the parts are assembled.

As such, there is joy in completing the final manuscript but also concern for consistency of the message in the whole—not to mention the gnawing anxieties about how it will be received. Still, while the heavy lifting is done, one begins to reflect on the project as a whole, the research that went into it, the writing process, and the lessons learned. I would like to close the book by sharing a few of these reflections while they are still fresh in my mind.

For openers, I knew from day one that this would not be an easy book to write. It was an ongoing challenge to pare back content and focus only on the essentials. Almost eight decades of world history, fourteen presidential administrations, and a number of disciplines—history, geopolitics, economics, energy, environmental, behavioral science, and more—had to be somewhat explained to complete the story. The personal stories and reflections of those living through these times prompted me to think of this book as a multidisciplinary textbook with a personality.

I found it fascinating to research these game-changing trends and milestone events and then track their aftershocks over the span of several decades. As I did so, a few themes emerged that seemed almost embedded in the DNA of these milestones.

The first has to do with the difficulty we have in identifying and appreciating milestone events at the time of their occurrence. Some, such as the moon landing or JFK's assassination, are obvious, but most play out over a course of time and are less easy to spot. We might see an initial blast of news coverage, but interest soon fades as other news stories crop up and divert our attention. Thus, a good many milestones are recognized only later, in the rearview mirror of history.

The second is our tendency to apply linear thinking to exponentially growing threats. We are hardwired to think in linear terms, but many of our most serious threats are multisystemic and advancing at a far more rapid pace—often exponential—than we recognize. This myopia often leads to responses that are too little, too late or even prevent us from acting with the urgency the threat demands. Our escalating debt and climate change are two prime examples of this tendency.

The third theme is a blind faith in technological panaceas. The speed of advances in technology often surpasses our rate of absorption, and we are left to deal with the unintended consequences. Little thought was given, for example, to data security in the earlier days of the internet, and cyberwarfare is now one of our greatest global threats. The impact of the fourth industrial revolution will make everything else pale in comparison. Beware!

The last theme, pardon the cliché, is that there is no free lunch. There is a price to be paid for everything. We either pay now or pay later, and the repayment often comes in forms that we had never imagined. Sadly, we often choose the latter, as we have with the IOUs we are leaving for future generations to pay. Our gain, their pain. Really, we are better than that.

Writing this book also reinforced things I had known and opened the doors to things I had not fully comprehended or even imagined. It gave me a panoramic perspective of my life, from its beginning to present times—and maybe even a little into the future. By revisiting the milestones of past decades and then my own recollections of and experiences during those timeframes, I connected the dots and appreciated things that had previously eluded me. In this detached manner, I was able to revisit the times, events, and experiences that had so shaped and reshaped my worldview, values, and priorities, and it was a fascinating adventure.

In this journey of discovery, for instance, my concept of time seemed to shift, and it was a deeply moving experience. An old-timer once said that "life is like a roll of toilet paper; the closer you get to the end, the faster it goes." It's crude, but it makes perfect sense. Looking back over the decades, I was struck by a nostalgic blend of memories, past challenges, and remembrances of dear friends and family now gone but never forgotten. It was beginning to sink in at a gut level: this thing called life has an expiration date, and there are no do-overs.

At a class of '61 get-together in August 2019, our best guess was that 153 out of our 600 or so classmates had passed away, or roughly one in four. Many were good friends who, in my mind, would be forever young. Indeed, two of my best friends, Brad St. Mane and Bud Schaitberger, who had so graciously contributed their reflections to my book, passed away within months of each other in 2017. There's hardly a day I don't think about them in some way or another.

I now see time in finite terms and not as the infinite resource it seemed to be when I was younger. With the clock winding down, I appreciate, more than ever, its precious value and consciously try to savor those moments once taken for granted. Time is also a priority changer. The things I treasure now—family, a strong faith, good health, deep friendships, and being true to my values—were overshadowed in the past by cosmetic things like getting ahead, making a sale, having a good time, and the like. As a young man, I was often too busy with life to appreciate it.

One of the joys of writing this book was reconnecting with former classmates for the Reflections & Profiles interviews and getting updated on their lives. In retrospect, my high school years, from 1958 to 1961, had a larger impact on me than I had imagined, and I could say the same about my hitch in the navy. My classmates, like me, all grew up in modest circumstances and, as their reflections revealed, achieved their piece of the American Dream by virtue of their own efforts and not inheritance. They had no sense of entitlement and seemed universally grateful for what they had— particularly their health and families. I feel richly blessed that all of them are a part of my life.

In looking back, I am also amazed at the lasting significance of a few serendipitous experiences. The circuitous set of circumstances that led me to Sharon, my bride and best friend of over fifty-two married years, and even the haphazard manner in which I took a job with a truly great company where I would start and end my career are examples. Life has to be about more than being at the right place at the right time.

Likewise, I am struck by how adversities that once seemed insurmountable would become pivotal turning points in life. I developed an arthritic back shortly after retiring, and I remember bemoaning the lost chance to get my golf game in reasonable shape or run a marathon. It led me, however, to long-distance biking, something I truly enjoy doing to this day. It helped me realize that doors may close, but windows will open.

Perhaps my most serious adversity was a twenty-one-year off-and-on battle with alcoholism. It started at age sixteen and ended at age thirty-seven. It led me from the dark abyss to a twelve-step recovery program, in August 1980, and I have never looked back, other than with a deep sense of gratitude. It opened the door to a new life and a far better way to live and enjoy it.

I give full credit to the twelve-step program and the Higher Power that inspired it for introducing me to a quality of life I could never have imagined. It taught me that though we can't control the direction of the wind, we can adjust our sails. I also learned that it is hard to be envious, angry, and resentful when we are grateful for all that we have. Working with others in recovery is like working in the miracle business. The best part was and is the spiritual awakening it triggered in me.

The twelve-step program acknowledges our need to connect with a higher power but does not define who or what that might be; it is up to each of us to decide that for ourselves. For me, it is the God of the Bible and my Lord and Savior, Jesus Christ. Others in the program may see it differently, but the common denominator seems to be the power we get from the meetings we attend and the program we work. For me, the group is a perfect example of the Grace of God working His miracles through others at a boots-on-ground level.

If this book has taught me anything, it is the fragile nature of life, and that there are no sure things in it. We have little control over anything in life, and our inability to accept this fact can lead to destructive behaviors and bitter disappointments. I believe there is something deep within us that yearns to connect with something greater than ourselves, and our inability to find it can lead us to search for gratification in all the wrong places: power, money, status, sex, possessions, or whatever may briefly sate the appetite but never satisfy it. Life is full of uncertainties, and I find it ironic—and yet wonderful—that the only thing we can truly count on in this life is that which we can't see: faith and the Grace of God.

We are in for some deeply troubling times, and I don't know whether we have the vision, determination, and resilience to weather the storm. It is most certainly within our grasp, but I have deep concerns about whether we will awaken in time to respond in an aggressive manner that will permit some kind of soft landing.

My guess is that there will be one or two lesser storms before the big one—the perfect storm—clobbers us with a force we are incapable of even imagining. I would be surprised if it doesn't occur late in the 2020s. If the lesser storms shake us out of our lethargy and we respond as we are capable of responding, there may still be time to mitigate the worst of its effects. We will see.

In closing, some may wonder why a guy my age would feel so passionate about the topics covered in this book—let alone write two books about them—and the answer goes something like this: I was blessed with access to the American Dream and the opportunities it afforded me. I am now deeply concerned that these same opportunities will not be as readily available for my kids and grandkids—Keri and Sammy—because of the intergenerational time bombs we have passed on to them and their peers. I have no illusions that my book will make much of a dent, but if it moves the needle even a minuscule amount in the right direction, it will be well worth the effort. The alternative is simply too painful to consider.

—Mike Conley

Endnotes

Part I

Chapter 1

1. The expression *perfect storm*, dating back at least three centuries, did not gain national prominence until it was used by Sebastian Junger, in his book of that name, published in 1997. Junger's book was based on the Halloween nor'easter of 1991, in which a confluence of unusual weather forces came together at the same time to produce a massive storm of considerable energy.

Chapter 2

1. GRACE satellites: Launched by NASA and the German Aerospace Center in a joint mission in March 2002, the Gravity Recovery and Climate Experiment satellites measure gravity anomalies and movement of water through the oceans, land, and atmosphere. A GRACE-FO (Follow On) satelite was launched on May 22, 2018 to continue the work of the first GRACE satelite—now decommissioned.

Chapter 3

1. International Monetary Fund (IMF): The IMF was established at the Bretton Woods Conference in 1944. A world organization designed to foster global monetary cooperation, financial stability, high employment, and sustainable economic growth; it depends primarily on the World Bank for its resources. Parenthetically, the World Bank was established, among other things, to provide loans to lower-income countries.

2. Special Drawing Rights (SDRs): SDRs are units of accounts within the IMF and not a currency, but they represent a claim to currency held by IMF member countries. The value of the SDR is weighted and determined by a basket of currencies that includes the dollar, euro, yuan, yen, and pound sterling. Inclusion in this club is a sign of global economic clout.

3. OPEC: The Organization of the Petroleum Exporting Countries was founded in 1960 to coordinate global petroleum policies and leverage the activities of all OPEC producers with respect to energy and other collateral interests. Now thirteen nations strong, its impact on global oil markets has been significant.

4. Quantitative Easing (QE): QE is an unconventional monetary tool that was used by the US Federal Reserve to pump an enormous amount of monetary liquidity into the economy in short order by purchasing government bonds and other financial assets. It was conducted in three phases from November 2008 to October 2014, and it pumped up the Fed's balance sheets by about $3.6 trillion in purchases. At this writing, it is in the process of *tapering* off—that is, selling back—these assets, and it will be a long and challenging process.

5. Marshall Plan: Named after Secretary of State George Marshall, it was officially called the European Recovery Program. To prop up war-torn Western European economies, the United States pumped over $12 billion (well over $100 billion in today's dollars) into the plan, which was widely heralded as a major factor in rebuilding the shattered European economy.

Chapter 5

1. Climate scientists' statement: In a statement hotly debated by climate deniers, lead author John Cook and the Consensus Project (theconsensusproject.com) state clearly in their literature that "97 percent of climate papers stating a position on human-caused global warming agree; global warming is happening and we are the cause." In a peer-reviewed study, near unanimity is a powerful observation.

2. Photosynthesis: This amazing life process used by plants, trees, and other organisms converts energy from sunlight into chemical energy and requires carbon dioxide and water to complete the process. In doing so, it releases oxygen and absorbs CO_2. Hence, the continuing devastation of the rainforests could have a catastrophic impact on Earth's atmospheric system.

Part II

The Snapshot of statistical information at the end of each chapter in Part II provides a tool for measuring changes from decade to decade. For greater consistency, a limited number of data sources were used to avoid the large variances that can occur when data is extracted from a large multiple of sources. The three major categories of population, US financials, and US domestics are sourced from the following unless otherwise noted:

Classification	Data Sources
1) Population:	Source: US Census Bureau
World Pop.	US Census Bureau: (Note: The world population for 1940 is a UN estimate).
USA Pop.	US Census Bureau.
2) USA Financials:	Source: OMB: Office of management and Budget: President's Budget: FY 2020 Historical Tables: (All tables illustrated for years 1940–2024)

Classification	Data Sources
GDP:	Table 10.1—Gross Domestic Product and Deflators used in Historical Tables: 1940–2024
Fed Receipts:	Table 1.3—Summary of Receipts, Outlays, and Surpluses or Deficits (–) in Current Dollars, Constant (FY 2012) Dollars, and as Percentages of GDP: 1940–2024
Fed Outlays:	Table 1.3
Surplus/Deficits:	Table 1.3
Gross Fed Debt:	Table 7.1—Federal Debt at the End of Year: 1940–2024
3) USA: Domestics: Source: The People History: Comparison of Prices Over 70 Years (thepeoplehistory.com) 1940–2013 (2017 not available)	

Note: For ease of comparison, decade data are compiled between years ending in zero. For example, the decade of the 1960s is presented in a timeframe of 1960–1970 and not 1960–1969.

Chapter 7

1. The Cold War: The long conflict between the United States, with its Western allies, and the Soviet Union, with its Eastern Bloc, started after World War II and ended with the fall of the USSR in 1991. In this forty-five-year conflict over ideology, geopolitics, and military and economic power, there were many conflicts, proxy wars, and crisis points but no large-scale direct fighting between the two superpowers. While bitterly contested, it acknowledged unwritten "rules," spheres of influence, and the knowledge that there would be no winners in an all-out nuclear war, which helped to provide an uneasy stability.

2. The GI Bill: The Servicemen's Readjustment Act of 1944, or GI Bill, provided a range of benefits for veterans, including low-interest loans, tuition reimbursement, and living expenses for school. An unqualified success for returning World War II vets, the program has continued ever since, with several improvements made over the years.

Chapter 8

1. Interstate Highway System: The Federal-Aid Highway Act of 1956 was enacted on June 29, 1956. Designed to construct 41,000 miles of new interstate highways, it was the largest public-works program ever undertaken up to that time. It was to be funded on a 90/10 percent basis of federal and state money. In practice, it is funded by taxes on gasoline and diesel fuels placed in a Highway Trust Fund. Through mission creep and failure to adjust for inflation, it has been chronically underfunded for years and always a point of budgetary contention. Still, it was a monumental infrastructure boon to the country.

2. National Defense Education Act (NDEA): The enactment of the NDEA on September 2, 1958, was heavily influenced by the launch of the Sputnik satellite by the USSR. Fearing that the USSR was getting ahead in education and the

sciences, the US government made this massive effort to create new opportunities for students with loans, scholarships, and funding for research, sciences, foreign language studies, and mathematics. It also established the Science Information Institute and Science Information Council, as well as other programs to stimulate training and education.

Chapter 9

1. Six-Day War: Amid growing tensions between the Arab world and Israel, the United Arab Republic (Egypt) blockaded Israel's access to the Red Sea, and Israel reacted. In a war lasting six days, (June 5–10, 1967, Israel won a smashing victory. It captured and occupied the Gaza Strip and Sanai Peninsula from Egypt, the West Bank and East Jerusalem from Jordan, and the Golan Heights from Syria. Tensions in the area would remain high for decades to come.

2. Unified budget practice: Under this arrangement, the receipts and outlays from federal funds and the Social Security trust funds were consolidated. Under the Johnson administration, in 1968, Social Security surpluses were counted as revenue against the budget, which made the deficits look smaller. It was changed by the Budget Enforcement Act of 1990, which excluded the Social Security trust funds and postal services from the budget. It did not, however, stop government borrowing from the trust funds to help finance general operations.

Chapter 10

1. Misery index and stagflation: These two concepts dovetailed in the second half of the 1970s. The misery index, as it was used in the 1970s, added the seasonally adjusted unemployment rate to the annual inflation rate. In 1980, President Carter's last year in office, the misery index had peaked above 21 percent before falling. Stagflation refers to a situation in which inflation is high, economic growth slows, and the unemployment level remains steadily high.

2. Paris Peace Accords: The agreement signed on January 27, 1973, between North Vietnam, South Vietnam, the Vietcong's Provisional Revolutionary Government, and the United States effectively ended the active involvement of the United States in the Vietnam War. In reality, American military operations were already winding down before the agreement. Though the war continued, it did not go well for South Vietnam after the US withdrawal, and in April 1975, Saigon fell, and the war ended.

3. Iran hostage crisis: Following the forced departure of the shah on January 16, 1979, Ayatollah Khomeini returned from exile on February 1, 1979. A hardline Iranian government assumed control, and on November 4, 1979, the US embassy was taken over by demonstrators. Ninety people were taken hostage, sixty-six of them Americans. The crisis consumed the Carter administration, and the hostages' release was not secured until minutes before Ronald Reagan was sworn in as president on January 20, 1981. In return for the American hostages, $8 billion in frozen Iranian assets were released.

4. Watergate: On June 17, 1972, the Democratic National Committee headquarters at the Watergate office complex in Washington, DC, was burglarized. The burglars were caught, and their efforts traced back to the White House. The Nixon administration was charged with obstruction of justice, which led to impeachment hearings. President Nixon resigned on August 9, 1974, before the hearings were

complete, and on September 8, 1974, he was granted a full pardon by President Gerald Ford. Watergate thereafter became synonymous with political corruption, and the suffix *gate* is often affixed to the scandal of the day to emphasize severity.

5. Yom Kippur War: Following a surprise attack on Israeli positions by a coalition of Arab forces in the Golan Heights and Sinai, the Israelis regrouped and promptly trounced Syria and penetrated the Suez Canal area in a march into Egypt. The war ended on October 25, 1979, just nineteen days after its start on October 6. It brought the two superpowers into a near confrontation, because they supported opposite sides, and it ended with new territorial gains for Israel. Ultimately it led to the Camp David Accords, in 1978, to normalize relations between Egypt and Israel.

Chapter 11

1. The S&L crisis: The savings and loan crisis resulted in the failure of over one thousand S&Ls between 1986 and 1995, along with other related failures. Caused by a combination of factors, including stagflation, slow growth, the deregulation of the industry, and relaxed regulatory oversight environment and fraud, it cost US taxpayers about $132 billion.

2. Hezbollah: Labeled a terrorist organization by the United States, Hezbollah was founded in 1985 and is headquartered in Beirut, Lebanon. A Shia-centered organization, it is a powerful proxy for Iran in its ongoing conflict with Israel. Described as a "state within a state," Hezbollah has institutionalized its presence with seats in the Lebanese government, a radio and TV satellite operation, and provision of social services, all in addition to its military capabilities.

Chapter 12

1. Association of Southeast Asian Nations (ASEAN): ASEAN is a regional intergovernmental coalition formed to promote economic cooperation, trade, social progress, and other regional programs. Formed in 1967, with ten current permanent members, ASEAN hosts an annual "Plus Three" meeting with China, the Republic of Korea, and Japan, and a "Plus Six" meeting adding Australia, India, and New Zealand to the mix. An East Asia summit meeting includes the ASEAN Plus Six, the United States, and Russia. The Pacific Rim nations are certainly well covered.

2. Japan's "Lost Decade": A period of severe economic stagnation befell Japan from 1991 to 2010; in reality, it could be dubbed the "lost twenty years." Triggered by a bursting asset/price bubble prompted by the collapse of subprime loans and a Japanese stock market crash, Japan's GDP fell from $5.33 trillion in 1995 to $4.36 trillion in nominal terms in 2007. Real wages also fell, and prices stagnated. Though the crisis eased in the 2010s, Japan continues to grapple with the consequences.

Chapter 13

1. The Shanghai Cooperative Organization (SCO): The SCO was launched on September 19, 2003, as a Eurasian political, economic, and security alliance. Led by China and Russia, it also included Kazakhstan, Kyrgyzstan, and Tajikistan. It continued to expand, adding India and Pakistan as full members in June 2017. There are lesser classes of membership, with several nations now applying for an upgraded status. By 2017 the eight full members of the SCO represented about

a half of the world's population, a quarter of its GDP, and about 80 percent of Eurasia's landmass.

2. Exotic financial instruments: These instruments and practices included a toxic mix of credit default swaps, collateralized debt obligations, and egregious use of derivatives—with a combined notional value of nearly $300 trillion—tied together through a hodgepodge of counterparties, "shadow banks," and hedge funds and sprinkled with synthetic derivatives to sweeten the pot. Hedging, leveraging, and defaults were all part of the game, and it all worked until it didn't. The task of unraveling these instruments and determining the counterparty risks and obligations was no easy matter following the crash.

Chapter 14

1. GDP purchasing power: A nation's GDP is usually measured in its currency, and we often use that currency in relation to the US dollar to generate a comparative GDP. The United States comes out on top using this formula, but exchange rates and cost of services can skew the results. An alternative method is to use a purchasing power parity (PPP) adjustment for comparing what a basket of comparable goods and services (similar to the Big Mac Index) would cost by nation. Using the PPP adjustment ratio to compare GDPs, China has already surpassed the United States as the world's largest economy in terms of its purchasing power.

2. Russian surface-to-air missile systems: Russia's S-400 surface-to-air missile is one of the best, if not the best, air-defense systems in the world. Capable of knocking out most non-stealth attacking aircraft at any altitude or speed, with a growing ability to intercept ICBMs, it is a potent system that can negate the penetrating power of most air strikes. Iran, a purchaser of the S-300 system, could make an airstrike by Israeli forces a costly operation. China has purchased the system, and Turkey is in the process of doing so.

3. China's One Belt, One Road (OBOR) policy: Borrowing from the Silk Road strategy of old, the OBOR policy rolled out by China in 2013 represents a major effort to reach out to other nations with offers of capital and resource support for infrastructure development programs. As an initiative to build economic ties with other countries, it plays well against the void left by new America First policies. In some respects, it echoes the Marshall Plan's goal of rebuilding economies, and it reflects China's growing economic power and prowess on a global scale.

4. Exclusive Economic Zones (EEZs): The United Nations established EEZs to define a nation's control of underseas mineral, gas, oil, and other resources and extend them to a distance of two hundred nautical miles from coastal baselines. However, many EEZs overlap and cause conflicts over ownership. Such conflicts happen regularly in the China Seas, and they will occur in the polar regions as well as warming temperatures melt the ice and make underseas minerals more accessible.

5. The Asian Infrastructure Investment Bank (AIIB): The AIIB, inspired by China, was launched in 2016 as a multilateral development bank to support infrastructure-building projects in Asia and the Pacific Rim. As a potential rival to the World Bank and IMF, the AIIB has 102 member nations representing 78 percent of the world's population and 63 percent of global GDP.

6. American Dream Composite Index: Researchers at Xavier University's Williams College of Business developed this statistically validated model and measures to quantify the American Dream and introduced it in 2011. With a growing database, they are fine-tuning the model with findings that reinforce the multidimensional nature of the American Dream.

Part III

Chapter 15

1. Doctrine of mutually assured destruction: The doctrine of mutually assured destruction recognized that both superpowers at the time—the United States and the USSR—had the capability to completely annihilate each other in a nuclear war, even if one side launched a preemptive strike against the other. This no-win scenario was, in effect, a deterrence against nuclear attack. The doctrine worked throughout the Cold War, though the Cuban missile crisis, in October 1962, tested the doctrine with a display of brinkmanship.

2. China's 2025 Plan: China unveiled its breathtaking Made in China 2025 plan in May 2015. The plan is to transform its economy from being the factory of the world to being a producer and leader in the production of high-tech, high-value goods. The blueprint calls for an upscaled position as a leader in information technology (such as artificial intelligence, the Internet of Things, and smart systems); robotics; green energy and vehicles; aerospace; medicines and pharmaceuticals; and other high-end sectors. The Chinese government has poured fortunes into this effort, and it is a significant threat to the long-standing leadership of the United States in these arenas. The threats of industrial espionage, theft of intellectual properties, and patent abuses were no small factors in the trade war now brewing between China and the United States.

Chapter 16

1. Weimar Republic: Following the loss of World War I, Germany was strapped with debt from the war it had financed by borrowing. Between 1921 and 1923, the Weimar Republic experienced inflation and then hyperinflation through its indiscriminate printing of marks, staggering reparation payments, and other associated problems. As a measure of the impact of hyperinflation, the cost-of-living index increased fifteenfold between June and December of 1922.

Chapter 17

1. Soft diplomacy: Hard power is muscular with strong coercive elements, particularly in the military and economic arenas. Soft power is noncoercive and based more on relationships, cultural ties, shared political values, foreign aid, diplomacy, solid alliances, good communications, mutual trust, and integrity. It calls for active and collaborative participation, and it requires a robust state department with a strong emphasis on a track record of predictability and reliability. Disengagement, unilateralism, and zero-sum-game approaches are the antithesis of this effort.

2. Carbon capture and sequestration (CCS): In this process, carbon dioxide waste from a large, localized source is captured and deposited in a storage site—usually

with favorable geological characteristics—that will help keep the CO2 out of the atmosphere. While not yet brought to a global scale, there were seventeen operating CCS projects in operation in the world as of 2019. As climate change intensifies and coal-based energy and other carbon-intensive products are still produced, this process offers a way to mitigate at least a portion of the carbon footprint.

3. Combustible car mandates 2040: The Paris Agreement and the quest to reduce carbon emissions were huge catalysts for a growing global movement to ban new gasoline- and diesel-powered cars. China, India, France, Norway, the United Kingdom, and several other nations have called for such bans by dates ranging from 2025 to 2040. The writing is on the wall, and automakers are responding. At this writing, the US government and the State of California are locked in a jurisdictional battle over setting emission standards for automobiles, a legal donnybrook that will be closely watched by all stakeholders.

4. Leadership in Energy and Environmental Design (LEED) certification: LEED is a green building certification program used worldwide. Developed by the US Green Building Council, it promotes a rating system and protocols for the design, construction, operation, and maintenance of green buildings, homes, and even neighborhoods. While developing a LEED-certified building is costlier up front, the return over time in energy and environment-related cost savings is significant. Response to the certification to date is robust, and it will grow as climate change and rising energy costs add to its attractiveness.

Index